EVIDENCE AND ITS FUNCTION
ACCORDING TO
JOHN DUNS SCOTUS

Franciscan Institute Publications

PHILOSOPHY SERIES NO. 7

EVIDENCE AND ITS FUNCTION ACCORDING TO JOHN DUNS SCOTUS

By

PETER C. VIER, O. F. M.

Published by
THE FRANCISCAN INSTITUTE
ST. BONAVENTURE, N. Y.
1951

Cum permissu superiorum

TABLE OF CONTENTS

PART ONE
EVIDENCE IS THE FOUNDATION
OF CERTITUDE

PART TWO
EVIDENCE OF PRINCIPLES AND CONCLUSIONS

INTRODUCTION

The problem of evidence as the ultimate criterion of truth and motive of certitude has claimed the attention of most neo-scholastics. Yet there have been few attempts at retracing the concept of evidence to the old Masters. The reason for this is simple enough, since the greater number of modern scholastics have been reared in the Thomistic school of thought. The concept of evidence as an epistemological factor, however, is as yet unknown to St. Thomas. As Geyser[1] observes, the term *evidentia*, as employed by Aquinas, does not have the technical sense of the ultimate source of certitude. Although this connotation is already known to St. Bonaventure,[2] it is with Scotus that it first finds any extensive application.

Scotus' keen interest in the history of thought brings him face to face with the scepticism of the Academicians on the one hand, and with the illuminationism of the Augustinians on the other. Both of these schools agree in denying that man is able to obtain true knowledge with his natural faculties only. While the former despair altogether of arriving at any truth, the latter try to safeguard true knowledge by an appeal to some sort of illumination from on high. Scotus' teaching on evidence as a natural and absolutely secure criterion of truth represents a reaction against both of these extreme positions.

According to Scotus evidence covers the whole range of human knowledge, from the first principles down to sense knowledge. While recognizing the eminent character of the self-evidence proper to first principles, he in no wise limits evidence to them. Contingent knowledge, too, is regulated by evidence. And where the internal or external senses are insufficient to convey certainty, the Franciscan Doctor contrives to save true knowledge by complementing the imperfections of sense knowledge through the superior evidence of the first principles.

1. "Zur Einfuehrung in das Problem der Evidenz in der Scholastik" in *Beitraege zur Geschichte der Philosophie des Mittelalters*, Supplementband (Muenster, 1923), pp. 174 ff.
2. *In 1. Sent.* dist. 8, p. 1, art. 1, quaest. 2; *Opera Omnia* (Quaracchi, 1882-1902), I, p. 155a.

It is the purpose of this dissertation to present an analysis of Scotus' concept of evidence and a description of its principal applications in the various kinds of knowledge. Many of the particular topics we are to examine have already been treated with more or less detail by other writers. Our modest enterprise, however, seems to be sufficiently justified by the fact that Scotus' doctrine as a whole has never been treated *ex professo* under the specific aspect of evidence.

We do not pretend to give an exhaustive treatment of this important subject. There are a number of interesting problems more or less closely related to our subject which we cannot deal with for lack of space. Thus we must omit the significant question of the function of virtual evidence in Scotus' theory of demonstration, the problem of evidence *in moralibus,* etc.

In an effort to obtain the best possible texts, we have had recourse to several manuscripts. Our quotations from the *Oxford Commentary* are taken in the main from the Assisi manuscript. cod. 137.[3] Occasionally, however, we prefer to quote from the Vivès version[4] in view of certain obscurities and omissions in the mentioned manuscript. In either case the more important variants will be indicated in the form of footnotes. As for the prologue and first book of the Parisian lectures, our basic texts will be taken from the so-called *Reportatio Examinata,* cod. Vienn. 1453, which contains the unedited text authenticated by Scotus himself.[5] The corresponding passages of the Vivès edition will be referred to in all our quotations from both the *Oxoniense* and the *Reportatio,* except when the text is found in the manuscript only. For instance, this reference: *Oxon.* I, d. 3, q. 4, fol. 31r, b; n. 5, IX, 168a stands for *Opus Oxoniense,* book

3. Concerning the value of this manuscript cf. C. Balić. O.F.M., *Annua Relatio Commissionis Scotisticae,* II (Rome, 1939-1940), p. 51, note 1: "Codicem A, vel potius patrem ejus, "Librum" quem Duns Scotus scripserat et dictaverat prae oculis habuisse, ex non paucis notis criticis quas affert, iure meritoque concluditur. Ipse enim centies alias redactiones, "libros alios" crisi subjicit, pristinum textum, prout in "Libro Joannis" prostabat, indicando."

4. *Joannis Duns Scoti Opera Omnia,* (Paris, 1891-1895).

5. Cf. A. Pelzer, "La grande Réportation examinée avec Jean Duns Scot" in *Annales de l'Institut Supérieur de Philosophie* V (Louvain 1923), p. 461: "La souscription du copiste, d'après laquelle la grande reportation a été examinée avec Duns Scot, mérite toute créance, à cause de l'âge de l'exemplaire."

I, distinction 3, question 4, *Assisi Ms.*, folium 31 recto, right column; Vivès edition, marginal number 5, volume IX, page 168, left column.

For our translations of the texts from Book I, distinction 3, question 4 of the *Oxoniense* we are indebted to Richard McKeon's *Selections from Medieval Philosophers*, II, *Roger Bacon to William of Ockham* (Charles Scribner's Sons, New York, 1930), pp. 313-350.

PART ONE
EVIDENCE IS THE FOUNDATION
OF CERTITUDE

CHAPTER I
HISTORICAL SURVEY OF THE PROBLEM

In this historical survey, be it noted, our attention will be focused almost exclusively on the so-called Augustinian current of thought. This is done in view of the fact that it is this trend of thought with which Scotus most frequently comes to grips when treating the problem of evidence and certitude. The background of his most detailed treatment of this problem is the interpretation given by his illustrious contemporary, Henry of Ghent, to the Augustinian theory of the *rationes aeternae*. [1] This theory, in turn, cannot be grasped in its full significance except in connection with the Platonic doctrine of the Essences. Scotus' own solution to the problem of infallible knowledge of truth, as will be seen, represents a reaction to the opinions of the aforementioned school of thought. Aristotle's views, insofar as they influence Scotus' doctrine, will best be treated in connection with the particular topics where the Franciscan Doctor makes reference to them. We shall therefore set out with Plato's original doctrine of the Essences or Ideas. In the following sections of this chapter we shall consider the Christian version this Platonic theory has been given by St. Augustine and his followers, particularly Henry of Ghent.

A. PLATO'S SOLUTION OF THE PROBLEM OF TRUE KNOWLEDGE

The search for a criterion of truth has always harassed the human mind. Man, in his inquiry for knowledge, finds no rest until he arrives at a secure criterion by which to measure the value of his knowledge. There have been many attempts to solve this fundamental problem of philosophy. Many of the earlier philosophers, especially Heraclitus and his disciples, despaired altogether of

---

1. *Oxon.* I, d. 3, q. 4; IX, 162a-207b.

obtaining true knowledge. The mutability of all sensible things, on which they so strongly insisted, led them to attach a merely relative value to all human knowledge. [2]

These sceptical views have exercised a permanent influence on the Academy, whose scepticism was so radical and uncompromising that "Academician" and "Sceptic" have become synonymous terms in the history of philosophy. All the Academicians admit is a probable knowledge of truth. [3] However, not all the ancient thinkers deny the possibility of arriving at a certain and infallible knowledge of truth. One of the most ingenious attempts at saving the value of knowledge is that of Plato.

As Geyser puts it, [4] Plato was the first to reach the deep conviction that all thinking and knowing is determined by absolute Essences which exist of themselves. Plato speaks of mathematical, ethical, aesthetical, and ontological Essences, such as Unity and Multiplicity, Straightness and Curvedness, Justice and Wisdom, Beauty and Truth, which are said to be eternal, immutable, and unique, each in its own order. No one can arbitrarily formulate the concepts of these Essences. On the contrary, they regulate the knowledge, not only of man, but even of God Himself. They cannot, therefore, be conceived by anyone, unless by being contacted and intuited by the knowing mind. Thus the Essences appeared to Plato as existing of themselves, and consequently he attributed to them the qualities of eternity, immutability, and uniqueness. Furthermore, it is to the image of these Essences that the divine Demiurgos shapes all sensible things. Since they are the only realities which truly deserve the name of reality, and are for this reason the first cause of all other realities, the Essences must also be considered to be the last and unshakeable basis of knowledge in the proper and strict sense of the word, i.e., of that knowledge which is valid at all times, in all places, and for all men. Plato distinguishes this

2. Cf. E. Zeller, *Outlines of the History of Greek Philosophy*, 13th ed., transl. by L. R. Palmer (London 1948), p. 48.

3. Cf. St. Augustine, *De vita beata*, c. 2, n. 14; *Florilegium Patristicum*, Fasc. XXVII (Bonn, 1931), p. 12.

4. L. Geyser, "Zur Einfuehrung in das Problem der Evidenz in der Scholastik," in *Beitraege zur Geschichte der Philosophie des Mittelalters*, Supplementband (Muenster 1923), pp. 161-182.

perfect kind of knowledge (Episteme) from that inferior knowledge which produces mere opinion (Doxa). [5]

How do we arrive at this knowledge according to Plato? Is it through abstraction from empirical data? Such an attempt seemed inadequate and absurd to Plato. For the properties of Essences are diametrically opposed to those of the world of experience. First of all they are independent of time, unique, and perfect, whereas empirical data are temporal, manifold, and imperfect. Moreover, things are named according to Essences, precisely because they participate, to a certain degree, in the perfection of Essences. Now it is impossible to know the perfect through the imperfect. But, on the other hand, he who is able to know the perfect can also determine the grade in which it is realized and reproduced in things. For instance, how would I be able to judge beauty or justice in man, unless I knew in advance in what beauty and justice consist? We must be capable, then, of knowing pure and absolute Beauty and Justice as they exist in themselves. Our knowledge of the Essences cannot proceed from the external experience of the senses, or from the internal experience of the activities of our soul. It is had through an immediate and spiritual intuition of the Essences on the part of the mind (*Nous*). This immediate contemplation of the Essences is analogical to that of the act of sensible seeing. The eye, in a sense, apprehends its object immediately with the help of sensible light; hence the analogy. The first condition for sensible seeing is the sun, and this in a threefold aspect. First, the sun gives objects origin, growth, and visibility; secondly, the sun gives the eye, in shaping it, the faculty of seeing; thirdly, the sun gives actual sight to the faculty, by filling the eye with light.

Similarly, there is a supreme fountain of light for intellectual or spiritual knowledge. This is the Idea of Goodness, which for Plato is probably identical with God. Goodness performs a threefold task. First, it gives visibility to the Essences; secondly, the *nous* or human mind receives from it the faculty of intuiting Essences, because of the mind's likeness to Goodness; thirdly, it illumines

---

5. Geyser, *loc. cit.* Cf. E. Zeller, *Die Philosophie der Griechen* (Tuebingen, 1859), Zweiter Teil, p. 412 ff.

the mind, enabling it to contemplate the Essences in which Goodness reflects itself. Hence, for Plato, the grasping of the ultimate foundation of knowledge assumes the form of a spiritual intuition of eternal Essences and their relations, through the intervention of a spiritual light which infuses[6] these supra-empirical objects into the soul.

How is certitude of this knowledge to be acquired? Such a question would have appeared ridiculous to Plato. Indeed, what could be clearer or more certain to the mind than what it contemplates in the spiritual light of the Original Sun? No one doubts the existence of an object which is seen in the full light of the material sun. Likewise the described spiritual knowledge of Essences admits of no serious doubts. "Here, then," concludes Geyser,[7] "we have the Platonic concept of evidence. Evidence means for Plato a knowledge which is immediately certain of its truth by reason of the infusion of the eternal Essences into the *nous*."[8]

One of the weak points of Plato's theory is the relation of the Essences to God. Plato's Ideas do not proceed from God, nor do they exist in God. On the other hand, God contemplates them and shapes things according to them. This, however, implies dependence in God, and is therefore, incompatible with a true concept of God. The Neo-Platonists have attempted to correct this weakness of their master's system. Plato himself had shown the way by placing the Idea of Goodness above Being. Plotinus tried to remove God still further from other concepts, in order to safeguard His absolute independence of all things outside of Himself. Hence Plotinus thought it necessary to transfer consciousness and knowledge from the First Being into its immediate derivative, or *Nous*.[9] It is in this *Nous* that Plotinus places the eternal Essences. The derivative of

6. This seems to be the best rendering of Geyser's term "einstrahlen."

7. *Loc. cit.*, p. 166.

8. The above description of Plato's concept of knowledge, as well as the critical remarks that follow, are based mainly on the cited paper of Geyser. Geyser refers expressly only to the *De Republica.* For detailed references to this and other pertinent *Dialogues* vide Zeller, *Die Phil. der Griechen*, pp. 412-457.

9. Plotinus uses the term *Nous*, or thought, to designate the highest of the beings produced by the First Being, while Plato applied the term to the principle of thought in man, i.e., to his soul. Cf. Zeller, *Outlines of the History of Greek Philosophy*, pp. 294f.

the *Nous* is the soul, which intuits the Ideas in its original principle or *Nous*.

More than Plato, Plotinus insists on making *light* the center and origin of all knowledge. The Original or First Light irradiates first the *Nous*, then the soul, then the sun, and finally matter which has no radiation proper to itself. Accordingly Plotinus describes the intuition of eternal Essences by the soul as an effect of the radiation of the Essences (in virtue of their own spiritual light) into the soul.

Plotinus' own theory, however, as is obvious, presents no satisfactory solution to the problems left unsolved by Plato. Essences for him continue to subsist, in a sense, outside of God. It was reserved to the genius of St. Augustine to develop this theory to its highest perfection, and furthermore, to make it compatible with Christian dogma and a true concept of God. [10]

B. TRUE AND CERTAIN KNOWLEDGE ACCORDING TO ST. AUGUSTINE

St. Augustine has dedicated considerable thought and effort to the problem of knowledge and certitude. While rejecting the absolute scepticism of the Academicians, he agrees with them in refusing to make sense-perception the ultimate criterion of true knowledge. He does not reject the value of sense knowledge as such; he even defends it against the Sceptics. [11] According to him the senses deceive us only insofar as we pass uncritically from sense-perception to a judgment that things are exactly as they appear to the senses. If St. Augustine nevertheless shows a certain distrust toward the senses, he leaves no doubt as to the reliability of another source of information, namely of introspection, whose certainty he defends in a remarkable apology against all sorts of Sceptics. [12]

St. Augustine, therefore, does not deny every kind of natural certitude. And yet, throughout the whole of his works he persists in postulating the intervention of a higher authority or *light* which constitutes the ultimate basis of and the indispensable requisite for any exhaustive and infallible knowledge of truth. [13] It was

10. Geyser, *loc. cit.*

11. *De Trinitate*, XV, chap. 12; PL 42, col. 1075.

12. *De Trinitate* XV, chap. 12; PL.42, cols. 1073f.

13. Concerning the relation of this Augustinian "light of the soul" to the tenets of Plato and the Neo-Platonists cf. E. Gilson, *Introduction à l'étude de saint Augustin* (Paris, 1943), pp. 103 ff.

doubtless the inadequacy of our sense perceptions, which is due to the frequent illusions to which the senses fall prey and to the changeableness of all sensible things, that prompted St. Augustine to decide on a solution similar to that of Plato and Plotinus.[14] In fact, St. Augustine's whole theory of knowledge reflects the influence of the Platonic Essences. It is the Essences, or *rationes aeternae*, as St. Augustine calls them, which are the last guarantee of certitude. As a Christian thinker, he could of course not admit of a separate world of thought which exists independently of God. "He decidedly places the eternal Essences and truths in God Himself, Who is for him the First Truth and the repository of all truths."[15] Hence, if we ask St. Augustine for the ultimate foundation of all intellectual knowledge, and of certainty, he answers without hesitation: The foundation of all true knowledge can only be found in the Absolute Truth, or God Himself. He proves this in the following manner:[16] To be able to judge correctly about anything, a norm is required, according to which we may formulate our judgment. No correct judgment about anything is possible, unless there is a norm within us which helps us formulate the judgment. This norm must be absolutely unchangeable, for if it were subject to change, it would not be a reliable rule. Moreover, this rule must be present to our mind. Yet, it cannot be simply identical to the mind, since the mind is mutable, and since we must also judge ourselves and our actions according to that norm. Hence this immutable norm must be above our mind. Since there is nothing immutable and unchangeable but God, it follows that the mentioned norm must be God, the absolute Truth itself.[17]

St. Augustine adduces several other arguments to prove the necessity and the existence of such an absolute rule of knowledge. If someone tells me that he understands this and that, or that he loves one thing and hates another, I accept his statements as true

14. Geyser, *loc. cit.*, p. 167.

15. Geyser, *Ibid.*

16. For the following cf. Gilson, *op. cit.*, pp. 88 ff.; R. Arnou, art. "Platonisme des Pères" in *Dictionnaire de Théologie Catholique*, t. XII (Paris, 1935), coll. 2338 ff.

17. *De libero arbitrio*, II, chap. 8; PL 32, cols. 1251 ff.

because of his honesty and veracity. Facts of this kind, however, produce a quite imperfect degree of certitude, since they are warranted only by human authority, and cannot be ascertained through direct observation. But as soon as the speaker leaves the realm of purely personal experience and makes statements about the human mind in general, I can know immediately, and hence can approve of, or disprove of what he states, and this with absolute certainty. St. Augustine concludes that this second kind of knowledge must proceed from a source of truth which is radically different from and absolutely superior to that from which the first knowledge proceeds. Such perfect knowledge as is that which we have of the essence of the soul and of its faculties, he thinks, must be derived from Truth itself.[18] As Prof. Gilson explains, "no matter how great the number of observations by which we may know what men actually are, we cannot deduce from these observations what man should be to answer his own definition."[19] This can only be seen in absolute Truth itself.

The same transcendent principle of truth plays a role in the formation of our judgments about sensible and bodily things. For instance, I have seen the walls of Carthage. Based on this experience, I try to imagine how the walls of Alexandria, which I have not seen, should be. At the same time I am conscious that my memorative image of the walls of Carthage is more perfect than the image my phantasy has of the walls of Alexandria, since the latter have to conform to the former to be true walls. Whence do I know that one image is superior to the other, and that one has to conform to the other to be true? This judgment must be based on some immutable and incorruptible rules which are above the human mind and which direct and guide its thinking: "Viget et claret desuper judicium veritatis."[20] Hence, the Bishop of Hippo concludes that "when we inwardly approve or disprove something with right, we are convinced that we do it in conformity with other rules that are above our minds, and which remain perfectly unchangeable."

---

18. *De Trinitate,* IX, chap. 6; PL 42, cols. 965 f.
19. *Op. cit.,* p. 122.
20. *De Trinitate,* IX, chap. 6; PL 42, col. 966.

An analogous process can be observed in our mind when we are appreciating works of art, or studying geometrical figures. When we find ourselves in the presence of a work of art, two images, as it were, come together in our mind. One is the artistic object which impresses its image through the eyes on our imagination. At the same time we contemplate another exemplar according to which the object pleases or displeases us. For this exemplar plays the role of a prototype on which we can measure and evaluate the object before us as to its fidelity of representation. This standard-image, contrary to the first image, is seen by intuition of the rational mind: "Et illam cernimus rationalis mentis intuitu." It enables us to grasp "the ineffably beautiful art of such figures above the perception of the mind by simple intelligence."[21]

Reviewing his preceding considerations, St. Augustine concludes: "Therefore, in that eternal Truth, from which all temporal things proceed, through the vision of the mind we perceive the form according to which we perform anything with true or right reason, whether in ourselves or in outside bodies, and thence we have the true knowledge of things conceived as of a word within us."[22]

A similar thought is expressed by St. Augustine when he comes to speak of the differences between man and brute as to their cognitive powers. Contrary to the brute, man does not receive blindly (naturaliter) what comes into the range of his senses and phantasy, but he is in a position to retain consciously and deliberately (de industria) the data stored in his memory, and thus prevent them from falling into oblivion. He can combine the data of different perceptions into new images, and of these he can tell whether they are true images, or whether their truth is only one of appearance. For St. Augustine, however, such knowledge of truth is not yet satisfying, because it is based exclusively on mutable, sensible things, and therefore is insufficient for the formation of a sure and stable judgment. "It is of more sublime reason to judge these corporeal things according to incorporeal and eternal reasons," he writes. These alone are above the human mind and have the distinction of

21. *Ibid.,* col. 967.
22. *Ibid.,* chap. 7; col. 967.

immutability. Therefore, although something of our own is always and necessarily associated with cognition of corporeal things, our most certain judgments are ultimately based on "dimensions and figures which the mind knows to remain unchanged."[23] This distinction between true knowledge through sense perception and true knowledge in the *rationes aeternae* rests on the Augustinian distinction between a *ratio superior* and a *ratio inferior* in the soul. Both of these rationes are rational, although the *ratio inferior* is subordinate to the *ratio superior*. It is the privilege of the latter to establish contact with, and to give assent to, intelligible and immutable truth.[24]

St. Augustine explicitly admits the possibility of acquiring knowledge through human agencies. How is this communication of knowledge to be explained? The means of communication of ideas are external and sensible, and therefore insufficient to convey truth. How does it happen that nevertheless we do know the truth of the ideas and propositions transmitted to us by others? The communication of truth can take place only in the light of a higher source of truth, from which both the speaker and the hearer draw their certain knowledge: "If, then, there is the idea of wisdom that you see without my knowing it, and that I can see without your knowing it (and which we therefore cannot show to one another, although it is identical in all of us), this must be due to the fact that the idea is commonly accessible to all of us."[25] Therefore, all truth and certitude comes from on high: "If both of us see the true, you do not see it in me, nor I in you, but both of us in that immutable truth which is above the mind."[26]

From these considerations it follows that in the Augustinian concept of truth and certitude two important factors must be taken into consideration. On the one hand, we have the concepts and propositions known through experience of either the objective, sensible creation, or of our own internal acts. On the other hand,

23. *Ibid.,* XII, chap. 2; col. 999.
24. *Ibid.,* chap. 3. Cf. Gilson, *op. cit.,* pp. 114 f.; Gilson and P. Boehner, O.F.M., *Die Geschichte der christlichen Philosophie* (Paderborn, 1937), p. 178.
25. *De libero arbitrio,* II, chap. 28; PL 32, *col.* 1256.
26. *Confessiones,* XII, *chap.* 25; PL 32, col. 840.

there are the divine Ideas with which these natural cognitions must
be compared in order that their truth-value may become clear. What
the external or internal senses and the reflection upon our mind
represent to the inquiring intellect may be in accordance with reality.
But the knowledge of such accordance is not the entire truth. Truth
is perfect only if and when I reach the conclusion that both the
concept of the mind and the object represented by it are in harmony
with the Idea which the Creator Himself has of the object. This
applies to psychological, aesthetical, mathematical, physical, and
ethical concepts and judgments. However high the number of images
the senses convey to the mind, however keen our intellectual faculties, we will never be able of ourselves to discover an absolute and
necessary truth in any of these cognitions. The ultimate guarantee
of truth is not found in any of the purely human factors of knowledge.
There is no infallible knowledge of truth except in the light of the
divine Ideas, or *rationes aeternae.*

We have exposed St. Augustine's doctrine at considerable length
in order that the divergencies between the Augustinian and the
Scotistic views may become apparent. True, Scotus frequently tries
to reconcile his own doctrine with that of the bishop of Hippo. These
efforts to "save the authority" of St. Augustine have led some
historians to believe that the Franciscan Doctor still holds to the
theory of illumination. Thus Msgr. Grabmann, in one of his later
works, lists Scotus among the followers of this theory, along with
St. Bonaventure, Walter of Bruges, and Matthew of Aquasparta.[27] In
fact, however, Scotus has definitely abandoned the characteristi-
cally Augustinian doctrine of a special illumination of the mind by
the *rationes aeternae* as a requisite for certain knowledge of truth,
and has clearly adopted the main lines of the Aristotelian position.[28] There can be no doubt concerning this point if we keep in
mind Scotus' arguments against illuminationism as represented by
Henry of Ghent,[29] whose doctrine we shall now proceed to examine.

27. Martin Grabmann, *Die theologische Erkenntnis und Einleitungslehre des
heiligen Thomas von Aquin* (Fribourg, 1948), pp. 321 f.

28. Scotus' position regarding the doctrine of illumination is well described by
E. Gilson, "Sur quelques difficultés de l'illumination augustinienne" in *Revue néo-
scholastique de philosophie,* XXXVI (1934), pp. 321-331.

29. *Oxon.* I, d. 3, q. 4, nn. 5-6; IX, 168a-170a.

C. TRUTH AND ILLUMINATION ACCORDING TO HENRY OF GHENT

In the *Opus Oxoniense*, Scotus gives a faithful and very fair account of Henry of Ghent's position.[30] But since in that brief résummé the sequence of the Belgian philosopher's arguments is somewhat changed, we prefer to follow the original order of Henry's *Summa*.[31]

Henry of Ghent may be considered one of the last great Illuminationists. Although well acquainted with Aristotle's doctrines, he refuses to accept the Aristotelian theory of abstraction as a basis for true knowledge through the natural powers of the intellect. In his *Summa* Henry defines true knowledge as the knowledge of the conformity of the thing known with its exemplar.[32] He distinguishes two kinds of true knowledge, one which can be obtained naturally, and another which can be had only with the help of the "divine Light." The former extends only to "that which the thing is" (*id quod res est*), and is obtained through the senses and the simple intelligence. The senses can be said to be true inasmuch as they apprehend things as they are in themselves. Likewise, simple intellectual apprehension is true inasmuch as it shows things as they are. Henry remarks, however, that this first apprehension of the intellect is not sufficient to make the truth of the thing known. This is due to the intellect and to the thing itself. To the intellect, because it does not apprehend truth formally in the stage of simple intellection, formal truth being present only in compositions and divisions, i.e., in affirmative and negative judgments; to the thing itself, because to be is one thing, to be true is another (though these two things are always found together). Indeed, being, which is the first *intentio comprehensibilis*, can be grasped by the intellect regardless of other *intentiones*, due to its absolute nature. The *intellectio veritatis* of a thing, however, implies the apprehension of the relation of the thing to its exemplar or original idea. Hence perfect truth (*sincera veritas*) cannot be apprehended unless the conformity of the thing with its exemplar be apprehended as well.

30. *Ibid.*, nn. 2-4; 163a-165a.
31. Art. I, quaest. II et III (Paris, 1620), fol. III verso - XI recto.
32. Art. I, quaest. II, fol. V r, D. Cf. J. Paulus, "Henri de Gand et l'argument ontologique" in *Archives d'histoire doctrinale et littéraire du Moyen Age*, X (1936), pp. 269 ff.

According to Plato,[33] there is a double exemplar. One exists in the soul and is caused by things; the other is found in God, or, better, in the ideal reasons He has of all things.[34]

The first of the two mentioned exemplars, viz., that which is abstracted from things, permits the truth of the thing to be known to some degree, i.e., when the mind forms actual concepts which correspond to the exemplar which is already in the soul. These are Aristotle's universal concepts. By means of these, Aristotle maintains that we are able to know the truth of things, not excluding natural and mutable things. Thus with the help of a universal notion acquired through observation of various species of animals, we are in a position to decide about anything we see, whether it is an animal or not. Likewise, through the specific concept of a donkey, we can judge of any animal whether it is a donkey or not.[35]

Henry maintains against Aristotle that it is impossible with such abstracted exemplars to arrive at any infallible knowledge of truth. And this for a threefold reason. Firstly, there is no certain cognition of truth unless it be had under the aspect of immutability. The thing from which the exemplar is abstracted is subject to change. Therefore it cannot be the cause of certain cognition of truth. In support of his opinion Henry quotes St. Augustine, who writes that "pure truth is not found in sensible things,"[36] because sensible things change continually.[37]

33. We have not been able to locate Henry's reference to Plato. His words seem to be a rather general statement of the interpretation given to Plato's doctrine of the Ideas in the Middle Ages.

34. *Summa*, art. I, q. II; fol. Vr, E: "Primum exemplar rei est species ejus universalis apud animam existens, per quam acquirit notitiam omnium suppositorum ejus, et est causata a re. Secundum exemplar est ars divina continens omnium rerum ideales rationes, ad quod Plato dicit Deum mundum instituisse, sicut artifex ad exemplar artis in mente sua facit domum."

35. *Ibid.*, fol. V v, E.: "Unde per universalem notitiam quam in nobis habemus acquisitam de diversis speciebus animalis, cognoscimus de qualibet re quae nobis occurrit an sit animal an non; et per specialem notitiam asini cognoscimus de quolibet quod nobis occurrit an sit asinus an non."

36. *Liber LXXXIII Quaestionum*, quaest. 9; PL 40, col. 13.

37. *Summa, loc. cit.:* "Sed quod per tale exemplar acquisitum in nobis habeatur certa omnino et infallibilis notitia veritatis, hoc omnino est impossibile triplici ratione quorum prima sumitur ex parte rei de qua exemplar hujusmodi abstractum est...quia res naturales magis sunt transmutabiles quam mathematicae....Unde hanc

Secondly, the soul as such cannot be rectified nor prevented from erring by something more mutable than the soul itself. The exemplars of sensible things, however, are more mutable than the soul. Therefore these exemplars cannot prevent the soul from erring.[38] This again is said to be the opinion of St. Augustine when he writes: "Since the law of all arts is absolutely immutable, and since the human mind, to which it has been permitted to see such a law, can suffer the mutability of error, it is sufficiently apparent that there is above our mind a law which is called truth."[39]

Thirdly, no one has a certain and infallible knowledge of truth, unless he has that by which he can distinguish what is true from what is only apparently true. Indeed, if he cannot distinguish truth from falsity or from apparent truth, he can doubt whether he is deceived. Such a discernment, however, is not attainable by means of the created exemplar alone. Consequently it cannot give an infallible knowledge of truth. The minor premise of this syllogism can be thus proved. An abstracted species can represent itself as itself, i.e., as a mere representation, or can represent itself as object. If it represents itself as object, as is often the case in dreams, it is a false representation; if as itself, it is a true representation. Since there is nothing in the abstracted species which could show with sufficient distinctness whether it merely represents itself as itself, or whether it appears as real object, it follows that no distinction between truth and falsity is possible by means of the species alone.[40]

---

causam incertitudinis scientiae rerum naturalium ex sensibilibus acceptam Augustinus pertractans LXXXIII, q. IX dicit quod a sensibus corporis non est expectanda syncera veritas."

38. *Ibid.:* "Secunda ratio est quod anima humana quia mutabilis est et erroris passiva, per nihil quod mutabilitatis aequalis vel majoris est cum ipsa potest rectificare ne obliquetur per errorem et in rectitudine veritatis persistat. Igitur omne exemplar quod recipit a rebus naturalibus, cum sit inferioris gradus naturae quam ipsa, necessario aequalis vel majoris mutabilitatis est cum ipsa. Non ergo potest eam rectificare ut persistat in infallibili veritate."

39. *De vera religione,* ch. 30; PL 34, col. 147: "Lex omnium artium cum sit omnino incommutabilis, mens vero humana, cui talem legem videre concessum est, mutabilitatem pati possit erroris, satis apparet supra mentem nostram esse legem quae veritas dicitur."

40. *Summa, loc. cit.:* "Tertia ratio est quod hujusmodi exemplar cum sit intentio et species sensibilis rei abstracta a phantasmate similitudinem habet cum falso

Having rejected the abstracted species as a means of arriving at perfect and certain knowledge, Henry concludes that we must take recourse to the eternal exemplar, i.e., to the eternal reasons or ideas in God. This does not mean that Henry makes God Himself the direct object of our knowledge in the present state of life. God, he says, is simply the *ratio cognoscendi.* He explains his meaning by comparing intellectual knowledge with the process of sensible seeing, which for him is parallel to the intellectual contemplation of "sincere" or perfect truth. As in sensible seeing the eye must be illumined and "sharpened" by natural light, [41] so in the process of intellectual "seeing" the mind must be illumined and sharpened by Divine Light. Just as natural light, by shining upon colors, enables the bodily eye to perceive the objects, so Divine Light by illumining the species of the objects, enables the spiritual eye of the mind to know the *sincera veritas,* or perfect truth of things. This seeing of truth "in God" is to be taken in this sense: God impresses on the human mind the exemplars of things as they are in his own intellect. By virtue of these exemplars we are in a position to know the perfect truth of things, according to their conformity with the eternal and perfect exemplars of the same things. [42]

---

sicut cum vero. Ita quod quantum est ex parte sua internosci non potest; per easdem enim imagines sensibilium in somno et in furore judicamus imagines esse res ipsas: et in vigilia sani judicamus de ipsis rebus. Veritas autem syncera non percipitur nisi discernendo eam a falso; igitur per tale exemplar impossibile est certam haberi scientiam et certam notitiam veritatis." Our exposition follows Scotus' own formulation of Henry's argument. Scotus' text reads: "Notitiam veritatis certam et infallibilem nullus habet, nisi habeat unde possit verum discernere a verisimili; quia si non possit discernere verum a falso vel a verisimili, potest dubitare se falli: sed per exemplar praedictum creatum non potest discerni verum a verisimili; ergo, etc. Probatio minoris: talis species potest repraesentare se tamquam se, vel alio modo se tamquam objectum, sicut est in somniis. Si repraesentet se tamquam objectum, falsitas est: si se tamquam se, veritas est; igitur per talem speciem non habetur sufficiens distinctivum, quando repraesentat se ut se, vel ut objectum, et ita nec sufficiens distinctivum veri a falso" (*Oxon.* I, d. 3, q. 4, fol. 31 r, a; n. 3, IX, 163b s.)

41. *Summa,* art. I, quaest. III; fol. IX r, B: "Primum illorum quae requiruntur in visu corporali est lux illuminans organum *ad acuendum.*" Note how this concept of "light" as taken over from Plato, runs through the Augustinian school. Cf. Gilson, *op. cit.,* pp. 103 ff.

42. *Ibid.,* fol. IX v, F: "Sic autem illuminat secundum communem hujus vitae statum ad cognoscendum synceram veritatem rerum: primo diffundendo se super

From these considerations, according to Henry of Ghent, it follows that perfect truth is obtained with the help of a twofold exemplar or species, one taken from the thing itself,[43] the other from the Divine Intellect. These two exemplary species, by coming together in the mind, enable it to know perfect truth through comparison of the created or acquired species of the thing with the infused species or divine exemplar which represents the perfect image of what the created object is, or should be.

Scotus takes position toward the exposed doctrine of illuminationism in a special question of the *Opus Oxoniense*.[44] After a concise exposition of Henry of Ghent's views he proceeds to show that illuminationism gives no satisfactory explanation of true knowledge. Far from saving truth and certitude, the postulation of a special illumination from on high leads to the opposite extreme, namely, to universal doubt and absolute scepticism. These criticisms of Scotus constitute the subject matter of the following chapter.

---

species rerum, et ab illis in mentem ad formandum in ipso intellectu perfectum conceptum de re ipsa, ad modum quo lux corporalis primo diffundit se super colorem ad informandum visum perfectum oculi. Et ita sicut color est motivum visus secundum actum lucidi corporalis, sic res quaelibet intelligibilis per suam speciem est motivum visus mentis ad syncerae veritatis cognitionem secundum actum lucidi spiritualis. "

43. It follows that illumination is not required to furnish the elements of knowledge. It only enables the mind to a better and more penetrating knowledge. Cf. Paulus, *loc. cit.*, p. 274.

44. Book I, d. 3, q. 4; IX, 162a-207b.

CHAPTER II
ILLUMINATIONISM IS NOT THE BASIS OF CERTITUDE

Scotus' point of departure in discussing the problem of certitude is the weakness in Henry of Ghent's interpretation of St. Augustine. He shows first of all that far from saving the certitude of human knowledge, Henry's views lead to absolute scepticism. The gist of Henry's first objection to certain knowledge through our unassisted natural faculties can be had in the following line of reasoning. Any certain knowledge presupposes an unchangeable object. All things are changeable. Consequently, there is no certain knowledge of things, unless a special illumination be admitted.

Scotus argues back by saying that recourse to illumination is of no avail to safeguard the certainty of knowledge under the presuppositions of Henry's system. Indeed, a changeable thing cannot be represented as unchangeable. If it could be, it would no longer be known in its true nature. Hence there is no certitude in the cognition of a mutable thing as immutable:

> Istae rationes videntur concludere impossibilitatem cunctae cognitionis naturalis. Puta quia si objectum continue mutatur, nec potest haberi aliqua certitudo de ipso sub ratione immutabilis, imo nec in quocumque lumine posset certitudo haberi, quia non est certitudo quando objectum alio modo cognoscitur quam se habet; igitur nec est certitudo cognoscendo mutabile ut immutabile. (*Oxon.* I, d. 3, q. 4, fol. 31 r, b; Vivès ed., *ibid.*, n. 5, vol. IX, p. 168, col. a).

As Messner points out,[1] Henry of Ghent's position is vitiated by a radical dissonance between our thought-contents which are immutable, and things which are mutable. If the condition of unchangeable and true knowledge were to be looked for in the immutability of objects, then we would never be in a position to pass immutably true judgments on contingent things.

Scotus also shows that Henry's supposition itself is false and that it does not give St. Augustine's doctrine, but rather that of Heraclitus and his disciple Craytylus. The Heracliteans maintained,

---

1. R. Messner, O.F.M., *Schauendes und begriffliches Erkennen nach Duns Skotus* (Freiburg, 1942), pp. 208E.

according to Aristotle, that the whole world of nature is in continual movement, and that therefore no true statement can be made about anything. Cratylus drove this view to the extreme by refusing to say anything, because at the moment in which a proposition is uttered, the thing might have undergone a new change and the statement no longer be true: [2]

> Patet etiam quod antecedens hujus rationis videlicet quod sensibilia continue mutantur, falsum est; haec est enim opinio, quae imponitur Heraclito 4. *Metaphysicae (ibid.)*.

Even if we granted Henry's assumption that all things are mutable, there would be at least one certain and immutable truth, viz., the fact that all things are continually changing. This argument was already used by Aristotle against the extravagant opinions of the Heracliteans. Not everything is changing in nature, and hence we are in no way limited to such imperfect knowledge. Aristotle concedes that we can make no true statement about a thing precisely insofar as it is changing; yet he maintains that even in changing things there must be an element of constancy: "For that which is losing a quality has something of that which is being lost, and of that which is coming to be, something must already be. And in general if a thing is perishing, there will be present something that exists; and if a thing is coming to be, there must be something from which it comes to be and something by which it is generated, and this process cannot go on *ad infinitum.*" [3] And a little further we read: "Grant that in quantity a thing is not constant; still it is in respect of its form that we know each thing." When applied to the present problem, the Aristotelian reasoning serves to show that in spite of changing appearances the possibility of unchangeable, and therefore certain, knowledge can be saved. For in virtue of their unchanging nature even accidentally mutable things can produce, and produce in fact, immutable knowledge in our minds:

> Non sequitur etiam: si objectum est mutabile, igitur quod gignitur ab eo non est repraesentativum alicujus sub ratione immutabilis; quia mutabilitas in objecto non est ratio gignendi, sed natura ipsius objecti quod est mutabile, vel quia natura est immutabilis; genitum igitur ab ipsa repraesentat naturam per se....(*loc. cit.*, f. 32 r, a-b; Viv. n. 13, 181b).

2. Aristotle, *Metaphysics* IV, ch. 5; 1010a 6-14.
3. *Ibid.*, 1010a 15-25.

Lychetus[4] remarks that this text must be interpreted in the light
of Scotus' teaching on the intelligible species. The Franciscan
Doctor maintains that universal knowledge is impossible unless the
intellect possesses a species of its own.[5] The sensible species
alone does not account for universal concepts, since it is totally
caused by the singular object. In order that an object be known under
the aspect of universality another species must be admitted which
is not produced by the object or the species in the phantasy as by
its total cause, but by the object together with the agent intellect,
as two partial causes. This is the so-called intelligible species.
The universality of such a species is due to the fact that the *ratio
gignendi* is not the singularity of the sensible object, but its nature.
The intelligible species which is the common effect of the two
mentioned causes is similar to the object, not because it proceeds
from *this object,* but because the object has *this nature.* The intelligible species, therefore, owes its origin, not to the singular as
singular, but to the nature in which the singular participates:

> Cum ergo accipitur quod quaecumque species gignitur ab aliquo re-
> praesentat ipsum secundum illam rationem secundum quam gignitur ab
> eo, si intelligatur de ratione gignentis falsa est; si de ratione gignendi,
> concedi potest; et tunc non sequitur quod repraesentat ipsum sub ratione
> singularis, sed sub ratione naturae, quia ratio naturae est ratio gignendi
> (*Oxon.* I, d. 3, q. 6, f. 35 v, b; Viv. n. 15, IX, 255b).

From this text we can safely draw the conclusion that since objects
remain unchanged in nature, the intelligible species which proceeds
from the immutable nature can never produce a false cognition.

Messner tries to give a more acceptable interpretation to the
meaning of *natura* in this text. He comes to the conclusion that,
whether Scotus refers to the common nature as something immutable
and opposed to the *haecceitas* as something mutable, or to the
constant nucleus (*Kern*) which remains while the appearances come
and go, neither of the two alternatives is entirely satisfactory. For
this would seem to imply that only those judgments about reality
would be immutably true which are concerned with that unchangeable
nucleus. This Messner refuses to admit, for the knowledge of a

---

4. *Commentary,* n. 21; Vivès edition IX, pp. 184a f.
5. Cf. *Oxon.* I, d. 3, q. 6 *passim;* IX, 232a-335a.

passing event, he maintains, can very well remain immutably true.[6]

Needless to say, we fully agree with Messner that there is such a thing as a true and constant cognition of passing and past facts. But on the other hand, we think that Scotus does not deny what Messner would make us believe he denies, or at least calls in doubt. It should be kept in mind that in the text under discussion Scotus is fighting off an objection. It is unlikely that he would determine the whole course of his theory of knowledge in such a place, as Messner thinks he does.[7] For in answering an objection one does generally not say more than what is needed to invalidate the arguments of the opponent. Hence, what is said in such circumstances does not necessarily express the whole of one's own convictions. Moreover, in the present place, Scotus, to all appearances, is treating of abstractive knowledge, as is clear from such expressions as *repraesentat* and *exemplar,* which can only refer to cognition through a species. The latter is precisely what characterizes abstractive knowledge, in opposition to intuitive cognition.[8] As Day points out, abstractive knowledge is a cognition "in which the agent intellect abstracts the *species* of quiddity from the *species* in the phantasm; this *species* represents the object absolutely, without any reference to actual existence in time and location in place." Intuitive knowledge is a cognition "in which the object is apprehended precisely as present to the observer here and now – i.e., not absolutely (which means from the quidditative aspect alone) but existentially. This kind of cognition "co-operates" with the intellect in the causation of a habit in the intellect and, as a result of this co-operation, a habitual intuitive cognition is caused in the *intellective* memory. This habitual intuitive cognition does not regard the object in its absolute quidditative aspect any more than the initial perfect intuitive cognition does; it regards the known object existentially – i.e., with the qualification that it *was* existing when

---

6. *Op. cit.,* p. 210.

7. "Ist es zweckmaessig, die Lehre vom unwandelbaren Kern an die Spitze der Erkenntnislehre zu setzen? Ist es richtig, diese Lehre als Bedingung der Erkenntnissicherung ueberhaupt zu betrachten?" *Op. cit.,* p. 210.

8. Cf. also *Oxon.* I, d. 3, q. 6, n. 16; IX, 356a.

it was apprehended in the past."[9] In other words, what is said of the
mode of abstractive knowledge does not necessarily apply to intuitive cognition. In the latter, as the text just cited indicates, Scotus
does not demand any degree of immutability, contrary to what he
demands of abstractive cognition. The aforementioned "habitual
intuitive cognition" of things past, it seems, is a sufficient indication that a true and certain knowledge of contingent past events
is admitted, even under the assumption that they no longer exist or
that they have been subject to change.

Another argument Scotus adduces against Henry of Ghent is that
even mutable things can make something known under the aspect
of immutability. That this is not impossible is shown with the
help of an analogy taken from Natural Theology. We know that God
is immutable, and this not through an immediate contact with God
himself, but through the knowledge of natural things which are
continually changing:

> Patet etiam quod repraesentativum in se mutabile potest repraesentare
> aliquid sub ratione immutabilis, quia essentia Dei sub ratione immutabilis
> repraesentatur intellectui per aliquid omnino mutabile, sive illud sit
> species sive actus (*Oxon.* I, a. 3, q. 4, f. ·32 r, b; Viv. n. 13, IX, 182a).

The same is illustrated by a simile. Finite things can and do represent something under the aspect of infinity:

> Hoc patet per simile, quia per finitum potest repraesentari aliquid sub
> ratione infiniti (*ibid.*).

For instance, the species produced in the intellect by a finite
object represents the same object somehow under an infinite aspect.
For the species does not represent a single object but can stand
indifferently for any object of the same kind. As Lychetus remarks, [10]
the intelligible species represents the object *in ratione intelligibilis,* i.e., under its essential aspect, which is not the exclusive
property of any individual thing, but can pertain to an unlimited
number of objects.

Henry of Ghent's second objection against certain natural
knowledge appeals to the mutability of the species. The images of

---

9. Sebastian F. Day, *Intuitive Cognition a Key to the Significance of the Later
Scholastics* (St. Bonaventure, N.Y., 1947), pp. 80 f.

10. *Commentary* n. 25; IX, 225b. Vide also Messner, *op. cit.,* pp. 349 ff.

sensible things, he thinks, are unfit to produce true knowledge, since they are more mutable than the soul itself. [11]

Scotus brings out the weakness of this argument in the following reasoning. If all which is in the soul is said to be mutable, it follows that the act of understanding itself is mutable, and thus nothing at all is found in the soul by which it could be corrected or prevented from error. Not even the assumption of the Eternal Light is of any assistance. For its influence, if it is to enlighten the human mind at all, must evidently exert itself somehow through the intellectual faculty. But since mutability extends to the intellectual act itself it is clear that the only means that could have saved certain knowledge becomes entirely ineffective:

> Similiter, si propter mutabilitatem exemplaris quod est in anima nostra non posset esse certitudo, cum quidquid ponitur in anima subjective sit mutabile, etiam ipse actus intelligendi erit mutabilis et ita[12] sequitur quod per nihil in anima rectificatur anima ne erret. Sequitur etiam quod ipse actus intelligendi cum sit mutabilior quam ipsa anima in qua est, nunquam erit verus nec veritatem continebit. [13] *(Ibid.,* f. 31 r, b; Viv. n. 5, 168a f.).

Henry's attempt to save true knowledge by the concourse or agreement of two exemplars, one proceeding from the sensible object and the other infused by the Eternal Light, is also doomed to failure. Logic tells us that from two premises, one of which is contingent and one necessary, only a contingent conclusion can be drawn. Similarly in the process of cognition, if one element which is certain is combined with another that is uncertain, no certain conclusion follows:

> Similiter secundum istam opinoinem, species creata inhaerens concurrit cum specie illabente; sed quando aliquid concurrit quod repugnat certitudini, non potest certitudo haberi; sicut enim ex altera de necessario et altera de contingenti non sequitur conclusio nisi de contingenti, ita ex certo et incerto concurrentibus ad aliquam cognitionem non sequitur cognitio certa *(ibid.)*.

Scotus holds to a middle course regarding this question of the mutability of the soul. The soul is not absolutely immutable, nor is it altogether mutable. It is immutable in its nature, and mutable

11. *Supra,* p. 24.
12. Erit mutabilis et ita *add. Viv.*
13. Sequitur etiam.../ *om. Viv.*

insofar as its habits and acts are concerned. In the latter a double mutability is distinguished – one from a privation to a quality, e.g., from ignorance to knowledge; another from one contrary to the other, e.g., from correctness to deception and vice-versa. The soul is, and always remains, immutable in the first sense, i.e., in its nature. Regarding the second kind of mutability, a change can take place only in the case of propositions which are not known in virtue of their terms. Concerning propositions known in virtue of their terms (*propositiones per se notae*, self-evident propositions), the mind can never err, because the apprehended terms are both a necessary and evident cause of the conformity of the proposition to the terms themselves:

> Ad secundam dico, quod in anima potest intelligi duplex mutabilitas, una ab affirmatione in negationem et e converso, puta ab ignorantia ad scientiam, vel a non intellectione ad intellectionem. Alia quasi a contrario in contrarium, puta a rectitudine in deceptionem vel e converso. Ad quaecumque autem objecta est mutabilis anima prima mutabilitate, et per nihil formaliter in ea existens tollitur ab ea talis mutabilitas; sed non est mutabilis secunda mutabilitate nisi circa illa complexa, quae non habent evidentiam ex terminis. Circa illa vero quae sunt evidentia ex terminis mutari non potest secunda mutabilitate, quia ipsi termini apprehensi sunt causa necessaria et evidens conformitatis conformis compositionis factae ad ipsos terminos [14] *(loc. cit.* f. 32 r, b; n. 14, 182a).

Hence, although, absolutely speaking, the soul may fall into error after it has been in the possession of truth, it by no means follows that it cannot be corrected. For there are propositions about which the intellect never errs, once it apprehends the meaning of their terms:

> Ergo si anima est mutabilis a rectitudine in errorem absolute, non sequitur quod per nihil aliud a se potest rectificari; saltem rectificari potest circa illa objecta, circa quae non potest intellectus errare apprehensis terminis (*ibid.;* 182a f.).

In his third objection Henry of Ghent says that certain knowledge is impossible without a special illumination because we cannot always distinguish between objects and mere images of objects. [15] Scotus shows that this argument is inconsistent with Henry's own doctrine of knowledge. The Belgian philosopher admits the need of a species abstracted from the thing as a condition for knowledge.

14. Causa necessaria conformitatis compositionis ad ipsos terminos *Viv.*
15. *Supra*, p. 24.

Now, if we are unable to decide whether such a species represents itself as itself or as object, Scotus reasons, then we will never be in a position to discern the true from the mere appearance of truth, no matter by how many higher *rationes* the species may be accompanied:

> Item patet etiam de tertia ratione, quia si species ipsa abstracta a re concurrat ad omnem cognitionem, et non potest judicari quando illa repraesentat se tamquam se et quando se tamquam objectum, ergo quantumcumque aliud concurrat, non potest haberi certitudo per quam discernatur verum a verisimili (*loc. cit.*, f. 31 r, b; n. 5, 168b).

Henry's objection, Scotus remarks, would be valid against the theory which denies the intelligible species and maintains that the phantasm alone is sufficient to fulfill the role attributed by common opinion to the intelligible species. It is the species in the phantasy, the Franciscan Doctor points out, that is sometimes mistaken for the real object in dreams, for the activity of the phantasy is not suspended during sleep. The intelligible species, however, cannot be the object of such a mistake, for the intellect cannot operate with the mentioned species unless it is adequately disposed. In the state of sleep, however, this condition is absent. It follows that, since Scotus admits the existence in the mind of intelligible species, Henry's argument does not touch his position:

> Ad tertiam dico quod si aliquam apparentiam haberet, magis concluderet contra opinionem illam quae negat speciem intelligibilem, quia illa species quae potest repraesentare se tamquam objectum in somniis, esset phantasma, non species intelligibilis; igitur si intellectus solo phantasmate utatur per quod objectum est sibi praesens, et non alia specie intelligibili, non videtur quod per aliquod in quo objectum sibi relucet, posset discernere verum a verisimili. Sed ponendo speciem in intellectu non valet ratio, quia intellectus non potest uti illa pro se ut pro objecto, quia non contingit uti illa in dormiendo (*loc. cit.* f. 32r, b; n. 14; 182b).

In the *Commentary on Metaphysics* we find a text where Scotus considers the role of the species from a somewhat different angle. In the passage just quoted from the *Oxoniense* he describes the function of species in unconscious and abnormal states, as opposed to conscious and normal states. In the *Metaphysics* he draws a distinction between the species which proceeds from a present object and that which is only in the imagination. Someone had argued[16] against the reliability of sense-perception that according to St. Augustine the senses never perceive whether they are subject to the action of a real object, or of a mere species or image of an object. For this reason, the objector maintained, we can expect no certain truth from the senses. A faculty of apprehension which cannot distinguish between a true and a false object (i.e., between a real and an apparent object) is unable to produce true knowledge in the mind.

Scotus answers that the species by which we apprehend the objects cannot prevent the senses from distinguishing whether an object is present or not present.[17] This is especially true with regard to the particular senses (as opposed to the common sense). For these do not retain the species of absent objects. The mentioned illusion, therefore, cannot take place with regard to particular senses:

> Unde ad rationes illas, ut sunt rationes, dicendum quod nec sensibilia omnia continue moventur secundum omnia, nec ita imprimuntur species, ut ab ipsis phantasmatibus non possit discerni quando objectum est praesens, et quando non, praecipue de sensu particulari, qui non tenet speciem in absentia sensibilis. (*Metaph.* I, q. 4, n. 24; VII, 65a).

In fact, a sense-perception is had only of a present object. A sense-perception, therefore, always indicates the presence of a real object, whereas the absence of sense-perception indicates the absence of the object.[18] A more detailed discussion of the problems of sense-perception will be given in the third part of our dissertation, where we shall also consider the remaining points of Scotus' refutation of Henry of Ghent's third objection.[19]

Returning to the fundamental position of his opponent, Scotus tries to obviate his contentions, by examining the nature of what

16. *Quaestiones super libros Metaphysicorum Aristotelis*, lib. I, q. 4, n. 2; VII, 51b f.

17. What Scotus wants to say is, obviously, that the intellect is able to decide, through the service of the senses, whether an object is, or not, present.

18. Cf. Gilson, "Avicenne et le point de départ de Duns Scot" in *Archives d'hist. doctr. et litt. du m. â.*, II (1927), p. 119: "Si l'on s'en tient surtout aux sens particuliers, comme la vue ou l'ouie, et abstraction faite du sens commun, chaque sens distingue fort nettement la sensation que provoque la présence d'un objet réel, de l'absence de sensation qui résulte de l'absence d'un tel objet."

19. Cf. *Oxon.* I, d. 3, q. 4, nn. 14-15; IX, 182b ff.

Henry calls *veritas certa et sincera,* and by proving that whatever definition or description of this "certain and sincere truth" is proffered, a recourse to a special illumination is either superfluous or impracticable. Three different meanings can be connected with the expression just mentioned. Firstly, it may be taken in the sense of infallible truth, i.e., of a knowledge which excludes every doubt and deception. That we can obtain such knowledge by purely natural means has been proved in the second and third articles of question under discussion:[20]

> Circa quartum articulum contra conclusionem opinionis arguo sic: Quaero quid intelligit per veritatem certam et sinceram, aut veritatem infallibilem, absque dubitatione scilicet et deceptione, et probatum est prius et declaratum in articulo secundo et tertio quod illa potest haberi ex puris naturalibus (*Oxon.* I, d. 3, q. 4, f. 32 v, a; n. 16, IX, 185b).

Secondly, the expression *veritas certa et sincera* may be understood in the sense of a property of being (*passio entis*). If this is Henry's meaning he must admit that truth can be known naturally. For he states explicitly that we are able to know being naturally.[21] Hence, Scotus argues, we must also be in a position to know the qualities or properties coextensive with being, such as *true (verum).* It also follows that if *true* can be known as a property of being, then its abstract or *truth (veritas)* can also be known naturally:

> Aut intelligit de veritate quae est passio entis, et tunc cum ens possit naturaliter intelligi, ergo et verum ut est passio ejus; et si verum, igitur et veritas per abstractionem, quae quia quaecumque forma potest intelligi ut in subjecto, potest intelligi ut in se et in abstracto a subjecto (*ibid.*).

Thirdly, the expression may be taken in the sense of conformity with an exemplar. This exemplar, according to Scotus, is either created or uncreated. If it is created there will be no doubt that truth can be known. If an uncreated exemplar is meant, and the knowledge of truth is made dependent on the apprehension of the conformity of things with such an exemplar, then it is clear that true knowledge cannot be arrived at unless this exemplar itself is first known. For a relation is unintelligible without a previous knowledge of both extremes. It is unthinkable that the eternal ex-

---

20. For our treatment of these texts cf. *infra,* Part II, Chaps. I-III.
21. *Supra,* p. 22.

emplar be the *ratio cognoscendi*, though unknown in itself, as is maintained by Henry: [22]

> Aut alio modo intelligit per veritatem conformitatem ad exemplar; et si ad creatum, patet propositum; si autem ad exemplar increatum, conformitas ad illud non potest intelligi nisi in illo exemplari cognito, quia relatio non est cognoscibilis nisi cognito extremo; ergo falsum est quod ponitur exemplar aeternum esse rationem cognoscendi et non cognitum *(loc. cit.,* 185b f.).

SCOTUS REJECTS EVERY FORM OF ILLUMINATION

Scotus, contrary to Henry of Ghent, does not limit man's natural and unassisted faculties to knowing the *verum,* or that which is true. He holds that *veritas,* or certain and infallible truth, is also accessible to man. In other words, man's knowledge is not restricted to the imperfect apprehension of truth, such as it is had in simple apprehension. He is also able to know with absolute certainty the truth of many judgments, such as the first principles and other propositions. Scotus proves this by taking Henry's concession of a *confusa cognitio* of the *verum* as a starting-point. What can be known *confuse* can also be known *definitive.* In other words, unclear concepts can be made clear and distinct with the help of definitions. This is done by the simple intellect through the method of division. The distinct knowledge of concepts thus arrived at is the highest and most perfect cognition accessible to the simple intellect. Once the latter has seized these concepts, the *intellectus componens* is in a position to formulate certain basic principles, as well as any number of conclusions that can be drawn from the principles. It would seem, Scotus adds, that the knowledge of these principles constitutes the very peak of perfection in intellectual knowledge. For it renders superfluous any other mode of knowing the same truths. The certitude of the principles is so absolute that no intervention of an uncreated Light is needed to further convince us. The cognitions which we are able to acquire in this manner are fully sufficient in the realm of natural knowledge:

> Intellectus simplex omne quod intelligit confuse potest cognoscere definitive, inquirendo definitionem illius cogniti per viam divisionis. Haec cognitio definitiva videtur perfectissima pertinens ad intellectum

22. *Supra,* p. 25.

simplicem; ex tali autem cognitione perfectissima terminorum potest intellectus perfectissime intelligere principium, et ex principio conclusionem, et in hoc compleri videtur notitia intellectus, ita quod non videtur cognitio veritatis necessaria ultra veritates praedictas (*loc. cit.,* 186a).

Scotus then presents a detailed refutation of the various interpretations of which Henry's illuminationism is susceptible. At the same time he proves that any kind of knowledge allegedly obtained through illumination can be had by man's unassisted natural faculties. In his criticisms Scotus bases himself on the inconsistencies of Henry's own expositions.

Henry refuses to admit an infusion or substantial communication of any kind of "Uncreated Light" into the human soul. Furthermore, he rejects immediate and direct contemplation of truth in the Divine Intellect on the part of man. Hence Scotus concludes that the influence of Divine Light is necessarily accidental in character. In other words, it must be a real accident, which is either prior to the act of understanding or concomitant with it. If illumination is prior to the act, the Uncreated Light must create a convenient disposition, either in the objective concept, i.e., in the object as it exists in the intellect, or in the intellectual faculty itself. In the first case it would seem that Scotus is thinking of Henry's concept of the *verum* which is had in the act of simple intelligence and which remains imperfect until through illumination the *sincera veritas* itself is apprehended. [23] This, however, is impossible, Scotus objects, because concepts do not belong to the real but to the intentional order, and therefore can never be modified by real accidents:

> Aut lux aeterna quam dicis necessariam ad habendam sinceram veritatem causat aliquid prius naturaliter actu, aut non. Si sic, aut igitur in objecto, aut in intellectu. Non in objecto, quia objectum inquantum habet esse in intellectu non habet esse reale, sed tantum intentionale; igitur non est capax alicujus accidentis realis (*ibid.*).

If the said disposition is placed in the intellectual faculty, it likewise follows that the cognition of infallible truth is brought about by means of an accidental effect of the Uncreated Light. To this theory, which implies an intervention of the Divine Light before each and every new act of knowledge, Scotus opposes what he calls

23. *Supra*, pp. 21 f.

the common opinion. For the latter accounts in a much more satisfactory manner for the knowledge of truth. The common opinion,
moreover, also lays claim to a mode of knowledge "in the Uncreated
Light," and that in a more perfect sense than in Henry's own opinion.
For the agent intellect, which, according to the common opinion
takes the place of the Uncreated Light, is itself an effect of the
same Uncreated Light. And furthermore, the agent intellect is a more
perfect principle of operation, as far as the human act of understanding is concerned. For the agent intellect belongs to the very
nature of the human soul. Its action is not merely accidental as is
the action of the created light which, according to Henry, would have
to be infused by the Uncreated Light:

> Si[24] in intellectu, igitur lux increata non immutat ad cognoscendum
> sinceram veritatem nisi mediante effectu suo, et ita aeque perfecte
> videtur opinio communis ponere notitiam in lumine increato, sicut ista
> opinio, quia ponit eam videri in intellectu agente, qui est effectus lucis
> increatae et perfectior quam esset illud lumen accidentale creatum
> (*ibid.*).

Since there is no illumination prior to the act, it remains that
true knowledge must be traced, either to the Uncreated Light alone,
or to the Uncreated Light together with the intellect and the object.
The first alternative must be excluded, for to attribute the act of
knowledge to the Uncreated Light alone would be running counter to
the commonly accepted doctrine on the agent intellect and its
functions in the process of knowledge. If the knowledge of truth
were the exclusive effect of the Uncreated Light, then the intellect
would be merely a passive recipient of an external influence of the
Divine Intellect. Since the latter is no more determined toward one
intellect than toward another, we would have to assume that it im-
parts knowledge of truth on its own free determination and regardless
of personal human activity. In other words, the agent intellect which
is the noblest principle of intellectual operation would be excluded
from every participation in one of our most characteristic and personal acts. It goes without saying that this is highly incongruous.
Aristotle[25] gives a more satisfactory, because more exact, expla-

---

24. In this paragraph we quote from Vivès (with the exception of the very last
word), in view of several obscurities in the *Assisi Ms.* version.

25. *De anima*, III, chap. 5; 403a 10-17.

|

nation of the process of knowledge by describing the act of understanding in terms of a twofold intellectual activity. Between this
twofold activity[26] a mutual correlation and completion can be
observed. The first is of the possible intellect which is thus named
in virtue of "becoming all things;" the other is of the agent intellect which owes its name to the fact that it "makes all things"
which are received in, and retained by, the possible intellect:

> Si autem nihil causat ante actum, aut ergo sola lux causat actum, aut
> lux cum intellectu et objecto. Si sola lux, ergo intellectus agens nullam
> habet operationem in cognitione sincerae veritatis, quod videtur incon-
> veniens, quia ista operatio est nobilissima intellectus nostri; igitur
> intellectus agens, qui est nobilissimus in animo, concurret aliquo modo
> ad istam actionem.
>
> Et item, actus intelligendi non magis diceretur unius hominis quam
> alterius, et sic superflueret intellectus agens, quod non est dicendum,
> cum ejus sit omnia facere, sicut possibilis omnia fieri.
>
> Similiter etiam secundum Philosophum tertio *de anima* intellectus
> agens correspondet in ratione activi, possibilis in ratione passivi; ergo
> quidquid recipit possibilis, ad illud aliquo modo se habet active intel-
> lectus agens.[27] (*Loc. cit.;* 186a f.).

The opponent may seek to escape the incongruities that follow
from his position by granting that although the agent intellect
cooperates in the genesis of the act of true knowledge, this is due,
not to its own intrinsic energy, but to the fact that it is used by
the Divine Light as a means or instrument for the production of
knowledge in the possible intellect. This is a useless and invalid
argument. For, no matter how perfect an agent is in itself, if it acts
through the medium of an instrument, it is not in a position to produce an effect which is more perfect than that which is proper to the
instrument itself. Hence, if the agent intellect cannot attain perfect
truth of itself (as the objector maintains), it will not be able to do
so when acting as an instrument of the Uncreated Light. It follows
that no other way out of the difficulty is left but to admit the second
alternative, i.e., that the Uncreated Light is the cause of knowledge

---

26. We say: "twofold activity," because, according to Scotus, the possible intellect is not merely passive. It has its own operation in the process of knowledge.
Cf. *Oxon.* I, d. 3, q. 7, n. 38; IX, 387b ff.

27. In the *Assisi Ms.* the last two paragraphs are accompanied by the marginal
note: "Non in libro Scoti." If we make use of these texts it is because they are
quoted in the very body of the MS., which seems to speak for their value.

of sincere truth together with the intellect and the object. This solution, however, does not differ substantially from the common opinion which, though admitting unhesitatingly a natural knowledge of truth, nevertheless also ascribes every certain cognition of truth to the Eternal Light as to its remote cause:

Et hoc etiam inconveniens quod illatum est ibi concluditur ex opinione praedicta per aliam viam, quia secundum sic opinantem agens utens instrumento non potest habere actionem excedentem actionem instrumenti; ergo cum virtus intellectus agentis non possit in cognitionem sincerae veritatis, lux aeterna utens intellectu agente non poterit in cognitionem vel in actionem istius cognitionis sincerae veritatis,[28] ita quod intellectus agens habeat ibi rationem instrumenti. Si dicas quod lux increata cum intellectu et objecto causat istam veritatem sinceram, haec est opinio communis quae ponit lucem aeternam, sicut causam remotam causare omnem certam cognitionem vel veritatem; vel ergo erit ista opinio inconveniens, vel non discordabit a communi opinione (*loc. cit.;* n. 17, 186b).

28. Lux aeterna.../ *om. Viv.*

CHAPTER III
EVIDENCE AS THE BASIS OF CERTITUDE

Having considered the negative aspects of Scotus' doctrine on certain knowledge, we must now pass on to his own positive teachings on certitude and its foundation, i.e., evidence. As a prerequisite for the understanding of the nature and function of the latter it is first necessary to consider briefly Scotus' conception of truth. This will be followed by a description of evidence and its functions in general. The role of evidence in particular kinds of knowledge will be considered in Part II and III of this dissertation.

A. THE NATURE OF TRUTH

The goal of all intellectual endeavor is the knowledge of truth. The knowledge of truth is the result of a complex operation. One can distinguish two main operations of the intellect. The first, which the Scholastics call simple apprehension or simple intellection, furnishes the material for thought by apprehending simple concepts from either the sensible world or from internal experience.

The second operation is composition and division, i.e., the affirmation of agreement or disagreement between the predicate and the subject, the expression of the former being an affirmative, and of the latter a negative proposition:

> Intellectus secundum Philosophum, tertio *de Anima,* [1] habet duplicem operationem, scilicet intelligentiam simplicium, et intelligentiam compositorum, scilicet componere et dividere intellecta (*Quodlibeta,* quaestio XIV, n. 3; XXVI, 5a).

A third operation may be added, viz., the reasoning process which is a combination of several judgments, from which a conclusion is derived:

> Prima operatio intellectus, ut habetur tertio *de Anima*...est apprehensio simplicium, quam consequitur compositio ut actus secundus, et argumentatio ut tertius actus (*Quaestiones subtilissimae in Metaphysicam Aristotelis,* lib. I, quaest. 4, n. 4; VII, 53a).

Formal truth is found only in the second and third operations of

---

1. Book III, chap. 6; 430a 26-b 5.

the intellect, never in simple apprehension. Material truth, however, is present even in sense-apprehensions and simple intellections. Scotus states repeatedly that simple apprehension is always true, whether it follows upon a true or a false sense-apprehension:

> Prima operatio intellectus semper vera est, licet sequens sensum errantem; ita enim concipitur albedo, si visus apprehendit illud esse album, quod est nigrum, sicut si albedo conciperetur a sensu vere vidente album, quia sufficit quod species vere repraesentativa albi veniat ad intellectum, ad hoc ut simplici apprehensione album vere apprehendatur (*ibid.*, n. 14; 59a).[2]

But he never omits to call attention to the fact that the simple intellect does not know or apprehend truth. In his commentary on *Perihermenias*[3] Scotus describes truth as the conformity between things as measures, and the intellect as that which is measured. He adds that the simple intellect and the senses may be said to be true, because they conform to their measure. Nevertheless it would be false to say that they know truth. To know truth means to know the conformity of knowledge with the thing known, which neither the senses nor the simple intellect can do. It is reserved to judgment to decide whether the thing is in reality as it is perceived. For this reason the intellect cannot know truth except through composition or division:

> Licet autem sensus dicatur verus, et intellectus similiter, propter conformitatem ad suam mensuram, tamen sensus secundum se non cognoscit conformitatem sui ad id, quod cognoscit, nec cognoscit se conformem suo cognoscibili. Similiter est de intellectu simplici... Intellectus simplex est verus, licet non cognoscat verum, quia cognoscere verum est cognoscere conformitatem intellectus ad rem. Intellectus autem hoc non facit, nisi quia judicat ita esse in re, et propter hoc componit vel dividit; propter. quod nullus intellectus praeter componentem vel dividentem verum cognoscere potest (*In duos libros Perihermenias, operis secundi, quod appellant, quaestiones octo,* q. 3, n. 1; I, 588a-b).[4]

Simple apprehension may be compared with the image produced

---

2. Cf. *loc. cit.* VI, q. 3, n. 6; 338a: "Intellectus circa quod quid est semper est verus, sicut sensus circa proprium sensibile."

3. Although the authenticity of this work is not yet established beyond every doubt, it shows indubitably a genuinely Scotistic trend of thought.

4. Fr. Messner, in *Schauendes u. begriffliches Erkennen,* p. 72, points out that Scotus ascribes truth and error to the judicative act, whereas objectivity or non-objectivity can already be spotted in the simple thought-contents. He adds a warning against the identification of truth with objectivity, and of error with non-objectivity.

by an object in a mirror. The mirror represents the object as it is, and can therefore be said to render a true image of the object. However, it does not perceive the conformity of the image with the object. Likewise simple apprehension is always true materially, but never formally. It contains something that is true, but the truth itself is not apprehended by the intellect. [5]

The knowledge of truth in the formal sense is the exclusive privilege of the composing and dividing intellect:

> (Intellectus simplicis) non est errare, nec verum dicere; istae sunt enim tantum conditiones intellectus componentis et dividentis (*Oxon.* II, d. 6, q. 1, f., 122 r, a; n. 6, XII, 336b f.). [6]

Judgments are either affirmative (*compositio*) or negative (*divisio*), according to whether the predicate is attributed to, or denied of, the subject. A composition, therefore, is a judgment in which it is affirmed that this particular predicate belongs to this particular subject; a division is a judgment in which it is affirmed that this particular predicate does not belong to this particular subject.

The reason why truth in the strict sense is found in affirmative and negative judgments only may be described in the following manner. To say that the intellect composes or divides is equivalent to saying that the intellect judges that "it is so in reality," or that "it is not so in reality." It is only in such judgments that truth, i.e., conformity of the intellect with the thing, is present in the sense described above. Affirmative judgments are true if that which is said to be is; negative judgments are true if that which is said not to be is not. For the intellect does not formulate a judgment by stating that one intelligible species is another intelligible species, but by affirming its own conformity with the objective state of affairs. Whatever the intellect judges to be, it judges it to be as it

---

5. Modern text-books of Epistemology present essentially the same doctrine. Cf., for instance, Fernand van Steenberghen, *Epistémologie* (Louvain, 1947), 2. ed., p. 154: "La vérité se trouve déjà d'une certaine manière, inchoativement, dans l'idée ou le concept; elle s'y trouve même nécessairement, car le concept est nécessairement la représentation d'un objet d'expérience: un concept qui ne représenterait rien est une contradiction dans les termes; le concept est donc toujours vrai, c'est-à-dire conforme au réel qu'il représente. Mais cette conformité est encore statique et inaperçue."

6. Cf. *Oxon.* I, d. 3, q. 3, n. 12; IX, 110b ff.

is in reality. And this is why only the judging intellect knows the truth:

> Intellectus componens cognoscit illam conformitatem sui ad rem. Unde intellectum componere vel dividere non est nisi intellectum judicare ita esse in re, vel ita non esse, sicut res conformatur intellectui. Non enim intellectus componit per hoc, quod dicit unam speciem intelligibilem esse aliam, sed per hoc quod judicat ita esse in re, sicut intellectus conformatur rei. Quidquid enim judicat esse componit ut in re est; et ideo nullus intellectus nisi componens cognoscit verum *(Op. II Perihermen.*, q. 3, n. 3; I, 588b).

The composing or dividing intellect, therefore, depends for its truth on the objective order. If the object is in reality such as it is intellectually apprehended, then the composition or division is true. If the objective state of affairs differs from what is expressed in the composition or division, then the latter are false:

> Veritas intellectus non dependet nisi a solo objecto, quod objectum si ita se habeat sicut intelligitur, verus est intellectus *(Oxon.* I, d. 48, quaest. unica, f. 96 r, a; n. 2, X, 780b).
>
> Ab eo quod res est vel non est, dicitur oratio vera vel falsa. Potest etiam poni circa rem quae intelligitur, et sic: intelligens rem aliter quam est fallitur *(Oxon.* IV, d. 50, q. 6, f. 290 v, a; n. 10, XXI, 567b).

Wherever Scotus describes truth he insists on its objectivity. He does not consider the intellect as a merely passive faculty in the process of knowledge;[7] yet he never goes to the extreme of maintaining that the intellect creates truth. For him, as for the Scholastics in general, true knowledge is essentially a relation. To be true, the act of knowledge must conform with the objective state of affairs, i.e., it must express the relation existing between subject and predicate in reality. In fact, as an act of knowledge is unthinkable without an object of knowledge, so likewise a relation apprehended in any act of knowledge is incomprehensible except on the basis of an objective relation between subject and predicate.

Let us examine more closely in what this objectivity of truth consists. The truth of an act of knowledge (at least of a perfect act of knowledge, as in an affirmative or negative proposition) is not something of an absolute nature, but is the result of a comparison of one simple concept with another. This act is followed by a *relatio rationis* between the two extremes. It is this relation which

---

7. Cf. *Oxon.* I, d. 3, q. 7; IX, 335b-398a.

can be either true or false:

> Videtur quod actus secundus (i.e., the act of composition or division) non est alicujus absolute, sicut primus (i.e., simple apprehension); sed est actus comparativus unius conceptus simplicis ad alterum, ut ejusdem in affirmativa, vel diversa in negativa; hunc autem necessario sequitur vel concomitatur relatio rationis in utroque extremo ad alterum...quae nata est esse vera *(Metaph.* VI, q. 3, n. 13; VII, 344a).

By calling the result of the act of comparison of the extremes a *relatio rationis* Scotus does not mean that we have here a relation that exists only in the intellect. He wants to say that the relation can be called true only as it is conceived by the intellect. Although a relation may occasionally exist in the intellect independently of a real relation, Scotus always insists that even such a *relatio rationis* is ultimately based on a virtual relation in the objective order. This concept of virtual relation will be briefly discussed a little further.

As Messner remarks, Scotus does not demand a strict image-likeness *(Bildaehnlichkeit)* between knowledge and the object of knowledge. Knowledge is the common effect of two causes, viz., of the knowing subject and the object known.[8] On the part of the knowing subject the resulting knowledge is basically different from the object, because there is a fundamental difference between the order of thought and the order of reality. This difference does not exclude a cognitive coordination between knowledge and object. As the greatest possible likeness between A and B does not justify one in stating a cognitive relation between B and A, so likewise no degree of difference between B and A can by itself prevent one from establishing a cognitive relation between them.[9] Indeed, while the sensible species in the phantasy may be said to be similar to the object, inasmuch as it faithfully represents the object, the same cannot be said of the intelligible species which conditions the judgment. The intelligible species which is the result of the co-causation of the phantasm and the agent intellect is obviously of a more undetermined or general nature than the species in

---

8. *Oxon.* I, d. 3, q. 7, nn. 20-23; IX, 361a-364a.
9. *Schauendes u. begriffliches Erkennen,* p. 51.

the phantasy. It is in virtue of this universality of signification to which the sensible species is transferred that universal judgments are made possible:

> Phantasma quidem gignit speciem sibi similem, et reprehensivam vel repraesentativam objecti [10] similitudine determinationis vel indeterminationis; nam ista similitudo potest auferri ratione intellectus agentis communicantis vel concausantis qui potest tribuere effectui maiorem indeterminationem quam potuit habere a solo phantasmate, ita quod similitudo est naturae repraesentatae, sive phantasma sit causa partialis sive totalis (*Oxon.* II, d. 9, q. 2, f. 128 v, b; n. 34, XII, 507b f).

Scotus, therefore, does not place knowledge in a strict similarity between thing and concept, or in an exact reproduction in the intellect of the object known. It is sufficient that there be "likeness through imitation, such as is the likeness between an idea and its object:"

> Ulterius ad propositum, cum aliquid possit multipliciter participare perfectionem ab alio, actus cognoscendi sic participative se habet respectu objecti, sicut similitudo respectu cujus est. Non dico similitudinem per communicationem ejusdem formae, sicut est albi ad album, sed similitudo per imitationem sicut est ideati ad ideam (*Quodl.* q. 13, n. 12; XXV, 526a).

Accordingly, Scotus describes the relation of truth, not in terms of strict image-likeness, but in terms of conformity between a sign and that which is signified. This concept of truth is developed in the commentary on *Metaphysics*. Among other significant texts we read the following:

> Verum in signo dicit significatum esse id, quod manifestatur per signum, et in hoc signum manifestare illud quod est, et ita conformitatem signi ad signatum (*Metaph.* VI, q. 3, n. 8; VII, 340b).

As Boehner [11] remarks, this definition of truth is ambiguous, as it fails to distinguish between the sign-relation of simple concepts and that of complex concepts or propositions. "The difference between these two relations is this," writes Boehner, "that the meaning (the *signatum*) of the simple concept has no other existence than to be the object of this conceptual act, i.e., it is as it is conceived, and hence no difformity can enter into this sign-relation. On the other hand, the sign-relation of a complex concept (i.e., here,

---

10. Similitudine naturali, sed non *add. Viv.*

11. Philotheus Boehner, O.F.M., "Ockham's Theory of Truth" in *Franciscan Studies*, V (1945), p. 157.

of a proposition) *presupposes* the sign-relation of the simple concept; in other words, the sign-relation of the simple concept naturally precedes the sign-relation of the proposition and thus is the basis for the agreement or disagreement, for conformity or difformity of the sign which is the proposition with the signs which are the simple concepts. The objects or the meanings of the simple concepts thus measure the proposition and account for its truth or falsity.... Truth considered in itself and not considered as object of the intellect is the conformity of a complex concept or a proposition with the relation virtually given by the extremes or the simple concepts. If the proposition is in conformity with the *significatum* (meaning) of its elements, the proposition is true; if it is in difformity, it is false." [12]

This broad concept of truth makes it possible for Scotus to apply it in the most extensive fashion, even to those propositions where an image-likeness or *adaequatio* is absent. This is probably one of the reasons why in his description of truth, Scotus, as a rule, avoids such terms as "adaequatio" and "similitudo" which could be understood ambiguously. He gives preference to the expressions "relatio mensurati ad mensuram, correspondentia," etc. [13] As Boehner puts it, Scotus' description of truth is "stated so generally that it comprises all the possible relations, given in any...proposition." [14] It is this concept of true knowledge as a diminished sort of likeness which accounts for our ability to formulate and apprehend the truth of such propositions as "homo est homo" or "Deus est Deus," where no real relation is found between the terms *in re*. The relation between the extremes exists actually only in the intellect. However, this does not mean that the proposition is false or that there is nothing in the object corresponding to the proposition. To be sure, it would be difficult to adapt to such propositions the definition which places truth in a *similitudo imaginis* or strict ade-

12. *Loc. cit.*, p. 157 f.

13. *Loc. cit.*, p. 158.

14. Cf., for instance, *Op. II Periher.*, q. 3, n. 2; I, 588a: "Verum dicitur unumquodque, ex hoc quod est adaequatum suae mensurae;" *Quodl.*, q. X, nn. 8 ss, XXV, 243 ss, where Scotus elaborates upon the concept of relation in knowledge.

quation. But there is not the least difficulty that it fits exactly with Scotus' definition of truth as a *correspondentia*. All that is required for the relation to be true is that it correspond to the thing. And it corresponds to the thing if it is such as to be virtually contained in the thing, i.e., such as the thing itself would produce in the intellect, were it to produce that relation:

> Ulterius ista habitudo rationis conformis est rei, non quod oporteat in re esse relationem aliquam inter extrema, ut in re similem isti rationis, quae est inter extrema ut intellecta, imo ut ab intellectu invicem comparata, nam tunc esset haec falsa, *homo est homo*...Sed tunc hic habitudo correspondet rei, quando est talis, qualem res virtualiter continet, sive qualem res de se nata esset facere in intellectu, si faceret relationem illam *(Metaph.*, VI, q. 3, n. 13; VII, 344a f).[15]

A proposition, therefore, is known as true if we know its conformity with the relation which is included in the extremes or simple concepts, irrespective of whether this relation is real or merely virtual. We shall see later that a relation can be included in the extremes in three different ways. Accordingly, three kinds of knowledge can be distinguished, viz., self-evident propositions and principles, conclusions derived from self-evident propositions and principles, and contingent propositions.

Presently we shall proceed to examine the criterion of truth, and the conditions required so that the mentioned objective relations may be apprehended by the intellect. In other words, we shall try to answer, according to Scotus' teachings, the crucial question: "What enables the human intellect to know truth?"

B. NATURE AND FUNCTION OF EVIDENCE IN GENERAL

1. *Evidence, the Ultimate Criterion of Truth and Motive of Certitude*

It has been said that truth, in the proper sense of the word, viz., logical truth or truth of judgments, is of an essentially relative nature. In other words, the formal knowledge of truth presupposes the presence of two terms, namely of the intellect and the object. Although truth first appears formally in the intellect, it is not the intellect that creates or produces truth.[16] True knowledge presup-

15. Vide Boehner, *loc. cit.*, pp. 158 f, where a more exhaustive treatment of this and other related texts is offered.

16. Cf. Donato Zuchherelli, O.F.M., "Il pensiero del B. Giovanni Duns Scoto sulla contingenza dell'ordine etico" in *Studi Francescani*, II (1915), p. 385: "I Dot-

poses the existence of an objective regulative norm to which the intellectual judgment has to conform. Scotus calls this norm "evidentia rei in se." For the Franciscan Doctor, evidence is first of all an objective property of things and propositions. Not that he ignores the concept of what we call "subjective evidence." The very expression "evidentia rei in se" suggests that it is taken as the counterpart of subjective evident knowledge. In fact, we find that the phrase "notitia evidens" is frequently used throughout Scotus' works. It is important to note, however, that for him subjective evidence is made possible only through a previous objective evidence. Objective evidence can be considered either as something absolute or as something that is actually or at least potentially related to the human intellect.

2. *Objective Evidence, an Absolute Property of Things*

If we look at things in an absolute manner, i.e., if we disregard their relation to a particular intellect, we can say that their evidence is in exact proportion to their entity. Aristotle [17] writes that things are related to truth as they are to entity. This saying must be interpreted in the sense that everything is knowable in the same measure as it has entity. This knowability of things "in themselves" is called by Scotus "evidentia rei in se:"

> Et ita debet intelligi veritas de qua loquitur Philosophus *II. Metaph.* [18] pro evidentia rei in se, sive pro intelligibilitate eius ex parte sui. *(Oxon.* I, d. 3, q. 2, f. 28 r, a; n. 30, IX, 83b).

The same thought is expressed in another passage where Scotus explains the various meanings of *certa et sincera veritas*. It can be considered from three different viewpoints. Firstly, it can be considered from the part of the knowing (created) intellect, i.e., as actual infallible knowledge (logical truth); secondly, truth can be viewed as *passio entis* or as a property of being (ontological truth). It is in virtue of this transcendental property that every being is true and knowable as such to every intellect, due to the knowability of being itself; thirdly, truth can be seen as a relation of conformity:

tori Scholastici mettendo a base della filosofia il principio della distinzione del soggetto dall'oggetto, dell'*io* dal *non-io*, dell'ordine della realtà dall'ordine della cognizione, hanno pure ammesso che la mente non crea ma scopre la verità."

17. *Metaphysics* II (alias I Minor), chap. 1; 993b 30-31.

18. Sicut res se habent ad entitatem, ita ad veritatem *add. Viv.*

Quid intelligit per veritatem certam et sinceram? Aut veritatem infallibilem, absque scilicet dubitatione et deceptione... Aut intelligit de veritate quae est passio entis, et tunc cum ens possit naturaliter intelligi, ergo et verum ut est passio ejus... Aut tertio intelligit per veritatem conformitatem ad exemplar... (Oxon. I, d. 3, q. 4; f. 32 v, a; n. 16, IX, 185b).[19]

As Albanese points out, the second mode of truth, contrary to the first and third modes, prescinds from every actual relation of being and intellect. It considers only the knowability (manifestabilità) of being, or that property by which being is capable of being known by all intellects in general, and abstracting from every actual knowledge.[20]

Evidence, therefore, is always present in the thing in consequence of its very being. Entity and truth being convertible concepts, everything is susceptible of being known by the very fact that it has being. Even under the assumption that no intellect at all were actually existing, the knowability of things would in no wise be diminished:

Si nullus esset intellectus, adhuc quaelibet res secundum gradum suae entitatis esset nata se manifestare; et haec notitia est qua res dicitur nota naturae, non quia natura cognoscat illam, sed quia propter manifestationem maiorem vel minorem nata esset, quantum est de se, perfectius vel minus perfecte cognosci (Metaph. VI, q. 3, n. 5; VII, 337b).

To say that something is absolutely evident is not equivalent to denying every relation to an intellect. It would be meaningless to speak of evidence, while denying every relation, including a potential relation, to a knowing intellect. To do so would be to render unintelligible the very concept of evidence. Albanese goes as far as to state that essential evidence of things or their manifestabilità is necessarily relative, i.e., in the sense that it cannot absolutely disregard the intellect as the term of potential knowledge.[21] Hence,

19. Cf. supra, pp. 44-46 for a more detailed description of these three concepts of truth.

20. Cornelio Albanese, O.F.M., "Intorno alla nozione della verità ontologica" in Studi Francescani I (1915), p. 275: "Nel terzo caso (Fr. Albanese considers transcendental truth in the third place and truth as conformity in the second) invece si prescinde da qualunque relazione attuale tra l'ente e l'intelletto, e si considera soltanto la manifestabilità dell'ente, cioè quella proprietà (passio transcendentalis) per cui l'ente è capace d'esser conosciuto da qualsiasi intelletto, fatta astrazione da ogni conoscenza attuale."

21. Loc. cit., p. 278.

by saying that every being is absolutely evident, Scotus wants to denote that, as far as the thing is concerned, it can be known according to the grade of its perfection or entity. It need not, however, be actually known by any particular intellect. [22]

3. Objective Evidence in Relation to the Human Intellect

There is only one intellect which apprehends all things perfectly, viz., the Divine Intellect. The Uncreated Intellect knows all things according to their proper degree of intelligibility, or in other words, according to their absolute objective evidence. Created intellects apprehend only those things that fall under their proper object, or in other words, those things that are proportionate to them. Thus the human intellect (at least in its present state) is set in motion mainly by sensible objects:

> Non autem oportet quod res sicut se habet ad entitatem, sic se habeat ad cognosci, nisi [23] cognosci ab intellectu illo qui respicit intelligibilia omnia secundum gradum proprium cognoscibilitatis eorum, qualis non est noster, sed maxime cognoscit sensibilia (Oxon. I, d. 3, q. 2, f. 28r, a; n. 30, IX, 83b).

The remark, "at least in the present state," is added because, according to Scotus, the adequate object of the human intellect as such, i.e., of the intellect considered as potency, is Being in the broadest sense of the term and without any kind of restriction. [24] Everything that essentially includes the *ratio entis,* and for this reason, everything that is contained in something including the *ratio entis,* is, absolutely speaking, an adequate object of our intellect. [25] Hence, considered as potency, the human intellect is able to know any being, regardless of its nature or perfection. During mortal existence, however, its intellections are limited to, or at least conditioned by, the quiddities of material things:

> Ei pro statu isto adaequatur in ratione motivi quidditas rei sensiblis; et ideo pro isto statu non naturaliter intelliget alia quae non continentur sub isto primo motivo (Oxon. I, d. 3, q. 3, f. 30r, b; n. 24, IX, 148a).

22. Cf. Allan B. Wolter, O.F.M., *The Transcendentals and their Function in the Metaphysics of Duns Scotus* (St. Bonaventure, N.Y., 1946), pp. 117 f., where Fr. Wolter studies *"Truth as a Coextensive Attribute."*

23. Itelligatur *add. Viv.*

24. *Oxon.* I, d. 3, q. 3, n. 8; IX, 108b f.

25. Albanese, *loc. cit.,* p. 279. For further explanation of this point of doctrine cf. A. Wolter, "Duns Scotus on the Natural Desire for the Supernatural" in *The New Scholasticism* XXIII (1949), esp. pp. 283-301.

4. *Subjective Evidence or Evident Knowledge*

Although evidence is primarily an objective property of things, it is always considered in relation to a knowing, or as Scotus puts it, a seeing intellect. Even what we have called "absolute evidence" has been described in terms of knowability, i.e., of a potential relation to a knowing intellect. It is plain that as soon as we proceed to stress the function of evidence in *actual* knowledge, the subjective side comes into prominence. The subjective element in evidence is clearly expressed in the phrases "evident knowledge," "evident certitude," which Scotus uses in the texts we are about to analyse. The sense of such expressions can be interpreted thus. Any subjective knowledge is evident insofar as it owes its whole content and truth-value to the thing insofar as it presents itself to intellect in its objective knowability. For this reason the subjective act by which the object is apprehended can be called with full right an act of evident knowledge. To say that knowledge is evident, therefore, means that it is formulated on the basis of, and dependent on, objective evidence. We shall now examine in detail the conditions which have to be fulfilled on the part of both object and intellect so that truly evident knowledge may be produced.

C. DEFINITION AND DESCRIPTION OF EVIDENT KNOWLEDGE

What is the definition of evident knowledge? Scotus gives no *ex professo* treatment of evidence, and hence we look in vain for an explicit definition of it. However, there is at least one text from which we are able to gather a more or less satisfactory notion of what he considers to be the essential traits of evident knowledge. Let us quote this significant passage:

> Ad auctoritatem Augustini dicendum quod illa scientia est distincta notitia, sed non evidens simpliciter, quia non attingit ad notitiam distinctam subjecti in se praesentis *(Reportatio Exam.*, prol. q. 2, cod. Vien. 1453 fol. 7 v; Viv. n. 18, XXII, 43b).

In order to obtain a definition of evident knowledge it suffices to reiterate this text positively as follows:

> Notitia evidens est distincta notitia subjecti in se praesentis.

As is implicit in this definition, evident knowledge presupposes several conditions on the part of the object and of the subject.

1. Conditions for Evidence on the Part of the Object

For evident knowledge two conditions are required on the part of the object. First, the object must be *present;* second, it must be present *in se.*

The object must be present

First, let it be noted that the word "object," when used in an epistemological sense, is to be taken in a very broad sense, so as to include not only really existing or concrete things, but also logical structures, first objects of speculative sciences, and the like. According to these different meanings of object we must distinguish various kinds of presence. When we deal with logical structures or first objects of certain sciences, for instance, it is sufficient that they be present in the mind. Objects of this kind cannot be present in a material, concrete sense, for the simple reason that they are of an immaterial nature, or at least are considered in a sense which transcends the material order, as for instance, the objects of mathematical sciences. In these, the presence of the object consists simply in its being apprehended with sufficient clearness by the mind. For these sciences proceed, not on the basis of experience, or *a posteriori,* but from the mere analysis of concepts. The conclusions that are evidently contained in the first object are drawn from it in a purely logical process of deduction:

> Quando habitus est in aliquo intellectu habens evidentiam ex objecto, tunc primum objectum illius habitus ut est illius, non tantum continet virtualiter illum habitum, ita quod notitia objecti in isto intellectu continet evidentiam habitus, in isto intellectu; quia intellectus cognoscens tale objectum potest elicere omnem conclusionem hujus habitus[26] *(Oxon.* prol. q. 3, f. 5r, a; Viv. quaest. 2. lateralis, n. 12, VIII, 150b).[27]

In sciences which deal with contingent things, however, such a mode of presence is not sufficient to produce evident knowledge. These sciences do not fulfill the two conditions of *a priori* sciences,

---

26. Quia.../ add. Viv.

27. Cf. *ibid.,* n. 4; 122b-123a: "Ratio primi subjecti est continere in se primo virtualiter omnes veritates illius habitus cujus est. Quod probo sic: primo, quia objectum primum continet propositiones immediatas, quia subjectum illarum continet praedicatum, et ita evidentiam propositionis totius. Propositiones autem immediatae continent conclusiones..."

i.e., they have no first object which virtually contains the *habitus*, so that the knowledge of the first object alone would render possible the knowledge of all the conclusions contained in it:

> In habitu vero non habente evidentiam ex objecto, sed causatam ali-unde,[28] non oportet dare primum objectum ejus habere duas dictas con-ditiones, immo neutram oportet dari, quia perinde est habitui ut in hoc, ac si esset de contingentibus, quae neutro modo habent objectum primum *(ibid.,* 150b-151a).

What, then, is required for contingent propositions to be known evidently? The reason why contingent propositions are not evident *ex objecto* is that their subject does not include the predicate in such a way that the latter is known through a mere analysis of the former. If the subject is indifferent to one or another predicate,[29] it is impossible to formulate any true proposition about it, unless a direct and immediate apprehension of the actual concrete relation between subject and predicate is had.[30] It was the realization of this fact that led Scotus to develop his theory of intuitive knowledge. He holds that, through intuitive cognition, the human intellect is capable of apprehending existing objects, not only in an absolute manner, or quidditatively, but also under their exist-ential aspect. As Day points out,[31] "when some sensible object" – and it is with sensible objects that we are now concerned – "is present to our senses, a double cognition can be cause in the intel-lect...: 1. *abstractive cognition,* in which the agent intellect ab-

---

28. Quam ab objecto suo *add. Viv.*

29. "Dico hic contingens... cujus oppositum posset fieri quando istud fit" *De primo principio,* cap. 4, quarta conclusio (Revised text ed. by Evan Roche, O.F.M., St. Bonaventure, N.Y., 1949), p. 84. The true nature of contingent truths could hardly be better characterized than has been done by Dr. Klein, who calls them "neutral." Vide Joseph Klein, "Der Glaube nach der Lehre des Johannes Duns Skotus" in *Franziskanische Studien* XII (1925), pp. 197 f.

30. It is true that Scotus also speaks of a first object in contingent science: "Contingentium est ordo, quia aliqua est prima vera contingens, et ita subjectum primum multarum veritatum contingentium..." *(Ibid.* n. 13, 156a). But such first objects do not contain all the truths of the whole science. They only contain certain primary truths: "subjectum primum...cui immediate insunt veritates primae illius habitus" *(ibid.).* Moreover, Scotus states expressly that such first subjects, contrary to the first subject of demonstrative sciences, cannot be known except through intuition of the extremes: "Primum notum in contingentibus nihil est nisi per intuitionem extremorum" *(ibid.).*

31. *Op cit.,* pp. 81 f.

stracts the *species* of quiddity from the *species* in the phantasm; this species represents the object absolutely, without any reference to actual existence in time and location in space; 2. *intuitive cognition*, in which the object ·is apprehended precisely as present to the observer here and now – i.e., not absolutely (which means from the quidditative aspect alone) but existentially." A little further in the same author we read that "without intuitive cognition our intellects could not be certain of the existence of *any* objects: cognitio quae dicitur intuitiva, potest esse intellectiva, alioquin intellectus non esset *certus* de aliqua existentia alicujus objecti (*Oxon.* IV, d. 45, q. 3, n. 17; XX, 348b-349a)." [32]

These facts leave no doubt as to the indispensability of intuitive cognition as a presupposition for evident knowledge of contingents. In fact, how could we formulate a true proposition concerning contingent things, unless we first grasped the objects as they are actually existent and present to us? Scotus does not fail to furnish explicit and implicit statements regarding this intimate connection between intuitive and evident knowledge. He observes that it is by reason of the distinct presence of the object that a distinct and evident knowledge of the same is obtained:

> Objectum naturale est in se et distincte praesens...et ideo movet ad notitiam distinctam et evidentem ex evidentia objecti (*Rep. Exam.* prol. q. 2, f. 8r).

As we have just seen, it is precisely the knowledge of present objects *as present* that constitutes one of the distinctive characteristics of intuitive cognition. Scotus goes further. For him, presence and evidence, and hence intuitive and evident knowledge, are equivalent terms:

> (Fides infusa) quamvis firmiter inclinet intellectum in objecta, tamen non facit ea praesentia ex evidentia rei, nec aliquid aliud facit ea sic evidenter presentia (*Oxon.* III, d. 23, q. un., f. 165v, b; n. 11, XV, 17a). [33]

The same thought is brought out in a negative, but nonetheless emphatic formulation in the *Reportatio Examinata*. While describing the knowledge of the Prophets, Scotus calls it non-intuitive and non-evident, precisely because it does not proceed from a present object, but is produced immediately by God:

32. *Ibid.*, pp. 82 f.
33. In the Vivès text the mentioned equivalence appears in even stronger formulation: "nec aliquid aliud facit ea sic evidentia *vel* praesentia."

Talis notitia dicitur locutio Dei, qualis in Prophetis, non tamen clara et intuitiva, et non est immediate evidens ab objecto... Unde iste gradus (cognitionis) est objecti non praesentis intellectui nec in se nec in aliquo repraesentativo, sed immediate causata a Deo, quae tamen non est evidens ab objecto *(Rep. Exam.* prol. q. 2, f. 7v; cf. *Rep. Par.* n. 17; XXII, 43a).

In the following question of the same work, Scotus again juxtaposes clear and intuitive knowledge. "Clear" knowledge, as is apparent from the analogy with *visus*, is here obviously used as a synonym of evident knowledge:

Perfectionis est in potentia inferiori sensitiva apprehensiva cognoscere suum objectum clare et intuitive in existentia ejus, sicut patet in visu; ergo hoc non repugnat intellectui respectu sui objecti...*(Rep. Exam.* prol. q. 3, f. 8v).

To exclude every possible doubt concerning the mentioned connection between the two kinds of knowledge, we quote a last text where Scotus describes evident knowledge as the natural consequence of intuitive cognition:

Si res ipsae de quibus Scriptura tractat essent clare apprehensae et *intuitive,* generarent notitiam certam absque omni dubitatione, et haec notitia, quia *evidens* est, diceretur scientia [34] *(Oxon.* III, d. 24, q. un., f. 167v, a; n. 17, XV, 47b).

It was his failure to grasp the role of intuitive and evident knowledge in the epistemology of Scotus that prompted Mr. Harris to deny the existence of any criterion in the Scotistic theory of truth.[35] Without detaining ourselves with the contradictory statements of Harris' exposition[36] we want to point out that he did not realize that Scotus in no way limits true knowledge to statements about universals, or essential properties of things. That the Franciscan Doctor not only admits, but strenuously defends, the possibility of contingent knowledge is obvious to anyone who is familiar with his classical treatises on certitude and evidence in the *Oxoniense* and in the commentary on *Metaphysics,* as well as to anyone who knows about the importance he attaches to intuitive knowledge. Scotus does not consider the universe as something "neatly arranged into classes fitting into each other like Chinese boxes." Nor does he

34. Et haec notitia.../ *om. Ass. MS.*
35. C.R.S. Harris, *Duns Scotus* (Oxford, 1927), II, p. 39
36. "Of any criterion there is here no question," he writes. And a little further: "The actual criterion was after all not so difficult a thing to find." *(Ibid.).*

maintain that 'all that was necessary to the discovery of truth was 'experience' [37] and a knowledge of the rules of the syllogism." It seems unnecessary to adduce any particular text at this place to refute Harris' assertions, as our whole dissertation, and especially the chapters on evident knowledge of contingents, will show their gratuitousness.

The object must be present in itself

This is another condition which shows the close connection between evident and intuitive cognition. As intuitive cognition is opposed to abstractive cognition by the fact that the latter is of an object that is indifferent to presence or absence, existence or non-existence, while intuitive knowledge is exclusively of objects existent and present, [38] so likewise evident knowledge is incompatible with abstractive knowledge and any other kind of cognition that is not intuitive. This, of course, refers only to contingent cognition. In analytical sciences the object itself is present by the very fact that it is in the intellect. In contingent knowledge, on the contrary, a concrete and real presence is required. The most perfect presence of this kind is that of the internal acts and states of both the intellectual and emotional spheres. [39] Scotus maintains that many of these acts and states are not only evident but immediately evident [40] in a way similar to the first principles.

As to extramental or trans-subjective facts and states of affairs it is obvious that they cannot be apprehended unless they are actually present to the senses of the knower. This follows from the nature of the senses, which normally react to actual outer or physical stimuli:

37. By "experience" Harris means here merely a "sense-stimulation."
38. Day, *op. cit.*, p. 73.
39. *Oxon.* I, d. 3, q. 4, n. 15; IX, 183a-b.
40. Although Scotus applies (at least once, namely, in the place last cited) the term "self-evident" to our knowledge of internal acts, we prefer to substitute the phrase "immediately evident" in order to prevent misunderstandings concerning this "self-evidence." We shall see later that the expression "per se notum" has a very specific sense in Scotus. He applies it to denote the manner in which first principles are known. The occasional application of the term to internal acts only indicates that these are apprehended in the same *immediate* manner as first principles.

Sensus enim non percipit nisi praesens, et ideo non cognoscit ex se aliquid se habere, nisi dum praesens est, et non semper praesens est sensui corporali... (*Metaph.* I, q. 4, n. 23; VII, 65a).

It is objected that the presence of the object to the senses is not a sufficient criterion for infallible (*sincera*) and certain truth, because the senses often perceive as present something not present at all. This frequently happens to the sense of taste in the state of fever, and to the sense of sight in the state of anger. [41] Scotus does not dispute the fact that occasional mistakes occur. He also admits that the senses cannot by themselves decide whether or not they are stimulated by an object or by a mere image or species of an object, due to their lack of reflexive power. However, we are always in a position to distinguish between the proper or improper functioning of the senses with the assistance of a faculty that is superior to the senses:

Dicendum quod forte sensus non reflectitur supra speciem, et ideo non discernit utrum tantum specie informetur, vel utrum objectum sit praesens specialiter de phantasia...sed est alia virtue superior ipsa sensitiva, quae semper judicat de bona et mala dispositione sensus (*Metaph.* I, q. 4, n. 24; VII, 65a).

In a later chapter it will be shown that we have immediate knowledge of whether our faculties are well disposed. This immediate awareness, in turn, enables us to judge the value of the sense-perceptions of abnormal states.

The *praesentia rei in se* required by Scotus for evident knowledge should become clearer by following him through a few questions that deal with the differences between evident knowledge and several other kinds of knowledge where the object is absent either in space or in time. The two main kinds of non-evident knowledge are historical knowledge of past facts, and knowledge through belief. Let us consider them briefly and by way of corollaries to our preceding expositions.

First corollary. Absence of evidence in past facts.

Knowledge of the past or historical knowledge does not reach the facts themselves directly and immediately. It has to rely exclusively on the testimony of persons who have actually witnessed the facts.

41. *Loc. cit.*, n. 25; 66a.

Hence historical knowledge does not grasp its objects *in se* as present and existent, or, in other words, it does not fulfill the second condition of evidence. This fact accounts for the profound difference between philosophical and historical knowledge. Philosophy concerns itself primarily with propositions known in virtue of their own terms. Such propositions lose nothing of their evidence, irrespective of when, where, or by whom they are apprehended. For this reason the student of philosophy is always in a position either to refuse or to accept the assertions of his masters, according as they are evident or not. The student of history, however, cannot contradict his master, for history deals with contingent facts of the past, which cannot be verified by the hearer. He has to accept them on the authority and veracity of his master:

> Non evidentia tradiderunt priores, ideo posteriores non potuerunt eos per rationem improbare, et noluerunt eis discredere nisi possent pro se rationem. cogentem habere, reverentes eos ut magistros veraces; sed philosophi discipuli per rationem potuerunt magistros improbare, quia materia circa quam altercabantur potuit habere rationes sumptas ex terminis. Exemplum: non ita contradicit discipulus historiographus magistro historiographo sicut philosophus philosopho, quia historiae de praeteritis non possunt esse evidentes, ut avertant discipulum a magistro, sicut possunt esse philosophicae rationes (*Oxon.* prol. q. 3, f. 3r, b; n. 4, VIII, 78a).

It is true that historical knowledge (and for the same reason any knowledge of absent facts) produces a high degree of certainty, and therefore stands above opinion. But it does not produce a strict *scientia* or demonstrative knowledge. For while the conclusions of a *scientia* proceed from evident premises, past facts are non-evident forasmuch as they are knowable only through acceptance of another's testimony:

> Concedo mundum non incepisse mecum, non quia scio ipsum praecessisse me, quia praeteritorum non est scientia secundum Augustinum, nec opinor mundum praecessisse me, sed adhaereo firmiter huic, mundum praecessisse me, per fidem acquisitam ex auditu aliquorum, quorum veracitati credo firmiter. Nec dubito...partes mundi esse quas non vidi, quia non dubito de veracitate narrantium talia mihi et asserentium haec vera esse... (*Oxon.* III, d. 23, q. un., f. 165r, b; n. 5, XV, 8b).

Second corollary. Absence of evidence in belief.

Scotus explicitly sets evident knowledge in opposition to belief, on the grounds that in natural and evident knowledge the object itself is distinctly present (except in some abstractive concepts) and consequently produces a distinct knowledge *ex evidentia objecti*. Such is not the case with regard to the object of faith:

> Objectum naturale est in se et distincte praesens, nisi in quibusdam conceptibus abstractis a creaturis, et ideo movet ad notitiam distinctam et evidentem ex evidentia objecti; non sic est de objecto fidei (*Rep. Exam.* prol. q. 2, f. 8r; cf. *Rep. Par. ibid.,* n. 21, XXII, 45b).

This text treats primarily of the difference between the object of natural cognition and supernatural faith. However, we can legitimately conclude that the same also applies to those objects of belief based on human authority. For, both supernatural faith (*fides infusa*) and natural faith (*fides acquisita*) have this in common, that their objects are not present *in se*. [42] And since presence *in se* is one of the conditions for evident knowledge, we can conclude that acquired faith, no less than infused faith, is incompatible with evidence.

On the other hand, Scotus is well aware of the fact that, despite the lack of evidence, belief cannot be dispensed with as a source of knowledge. The necessity of belief extends not only to past facts but also to those things which, though actually existing, cannot be perceived *hic et nunc* because of their distance. All these things are not evident, and therefore we must accept what others relate about them. In other words, we must rely on the veracity or truthfulness of the witnesses who assert that it is so. Thus, due to our limited personal experience, belief is the only reliable substitute for evidence. This is true particularly of those facts and things for which we have the authority of society. To refuse to accept the testimony of our fellow men unconditionally, would render life socially impossible:

> Aut nulli credes de contingenti quod non vidisti, et ita non credes mundum esse factum ante te, nec locum esse in mundo ubi non fueris, nec istum esse patrem tuum, et illam matrem; et ista incredulitas destrueret omnem vitam politicam. Si igitur vis alicui credere de contingenti

---

42. Cf. Joseph Klein, "Der Glaube nach der Lehre des Johannes Duns Skotus" in *Franziskanische Studien,* XII (1925), p. 204: "Der Glaubenshabitus neight zwar den Intellekt hin zu den Glaubenswahrheiten als fu seinen Objekten aber er vergegenwaertigt sie ihm keineswegs als erkannte durch sachliche Evidenz; auch nichts anderes verleiht ihnen diesen Charakter evidenten Vergegenwaertigkeitseins."

quod tibi non est nec fuit evidens, maxime credendum est communitati, sive illis quae tota communitas approbat (Oxon. prol. q. 2, f. 3v, a; n. 6, VIII, 84b-85a).[43]

It is interesting to note, however, that belief itself also is ultimately based on evidence, i.e., on the evident knowledge which the witness has or has had of the facts or objects of which he gives testimony. This is stated in a text of St. Augustine, according to whom things removed from the senses are the object of belief. We believe these things on the testimony of those witnesses from whose senses these same things are not or were not absent:

> Profecto, inquit (S. Augustinus), ea quae remota sunt a sensibus nostris, quoniam testimonio nostro scire non possumus, de his alios testes requirimus, eisque credimus, a quorum sensibus remota esse vel fuisse non credimus[44] (Oxon. III, d. 24, q. un., f. 167r, b; n. 13, XV, 44a).

Thus we find that all certitude, whether of actual or past, of present or absent things and facts, rests in the final analysis on evident knowledge.

2. Conditions for Evident Knowledge on the Part of the Subject
Evident knowledge must be distinct

We have seen that according to Scotus' definition evident knowledge must be *distinct*. How is this to be understood? In the *Reportatio* Scotus describes distinct and evident knowledge as a consequence or effect of a distinct presence of the object:

> Objectum naturale est in se et distincte praesens...et ideo movet ad notitiam distinctam et evidentem ex evidentia objecti (Rep. Exam. prol. q. 2, f. 8r; cf. Rep. Par. ibid., n. 18, XXII, 43b).

It is unlikely that the expressions *distincte praesens* and *distincta notitia* are taken here in the strict sense of a definition of the object, i.e., in the sense of a distinct subjective apprehension of all the essential components of the object. This would contradict many of Scotus' statements regarding the evidence of propositions composed of terms known confusedly.[45] Moreover, no definition of the terms is required for evident knowledge of contingent propo-

---

43. Cf. *Oxon.* III, d. 23, q. un., n. 11; XV, 17a; d. 38, q. un., n. 3; 865b.
44. Cf. St. Augustine, *De videndo Deo*, n. 5; PL 33, col. 598.
45. Vide *infra*, Part II, chap. I.

sitions. In fact, what distinguishes contingent propositions from necessary propositions is precisely that they are known, not through analysis of their terms, but through direct and immediate contact with the object. How, then, is the word *distinct* to be understood in the present context?

An attentive examination of a few related texts has convinced us that Scotus does not always take the words *distincta notitia* in the sense of a *notitia per definitionem*. He frequently gives them a less strict signification. Thus, when speaking of our knowledge of God he states that we do not apprehend Him by a distinct concept, but merely under certain general notions, such as concepts *common* to God and creatures. [46] Similarly, he says that a perfect artist knows distinctly beforehand every detail of his work, whereas a less perfect artist has only a *general* or vague idea of what he is going to produce. [47] These and many other passages indicate that *distincta cognitio* is not always a *cognitio definitiva* in opposition to a *cognitio non-definitiva*. It can also have the sense of *undetermined* knowledge as against *determined knowledge*. In other words, distinct knowledge can mean the grasping of a particular or individual object, as opposed to the apprehension of the same object in a more or less vague or universal way. [48] At times Scotus contrasts the *distincta cognitio* with the *indistincta* or *imperfecta cognitio*. In this sense a cognition is distinct if the object is grasped in its own proper form and shape, so as to be discerned from every other object:

> Una intellectione perfecta et distincta existente in intellectu, multae intellectiones indistinctae et imperfectae possunt inesse. Patet in exemplo de visu, qui in pyramide et infra basim videt unum punctum in cono distincte; et tamen in eadem pyramide et infra eandem basim videt

46. *Oxon.* I, d. 2, q. 2, f. 15r, b; n. 8, VIII, 408a: "Ex creaturis possumus cognoscere Deum esse, saltem in rationibus *generalibus;* subdit ibi...de cognitione Dei sub rationibus *communibus* convenientibus sibi et creaturis... Quod autem non loquatur de cognitione actuali et *distincta* Dei patet..."

47. *Ibid.,* f. 17r, a; n. 24, 460a: "Artifex perfectus *distincte* cognoscit omne agendum antequam fiat... Contra istam instatur de arte, quod ars *universalis* sufficit..."

48. *Oxon.* I, d. 3, q. 3, f. 28r, b; n. 3, IX, 189b: "Desiderium naturale est in intellectu...cognoscente causam in *universali*...ad cognoscendum illam in particulari et *distincte.*"

multa imperfecte et indistincte (*Oxon.* II, d. 42, qq. 1-5, n. 10; XIII, 460b). [49]

It follows that an object is distinctly present if it shows a sufficiently sharp delineation against the surrounding objects, so that it can be clearly or distinctly perceived in the sense described above. Every object, therefore, which is more or less "mixed" with other objects so that its shape and contours cannot be distinguished from them, is not distinctly but indistinctly present. This indistinct presence prevents a distinct apprehension of the object. As a consequence evident knowledge of the same object is also excluded. Needless to say, the distinctness of a perception, whether sensible or intellectual, very often depends not so much on the object itself as on the higher or lower degree of attention on the part of the apprehending subject to one rather than to another aspect of the object present. [50]

D. EVIDENCE, THE SOURCE OF SUBJECTIVE CERTITUDE.

1. *Necessary Apprehension*

Since the intellect is a natural faculty, i.e., a faculty that acts of necessity and not on free determination, it is clear that the intellect, when confronted with a proportionate object as described above, will be forced to apprehend it. All that is required for such a necessary apprehension is that the mentioned object be present to the intellect:

Concedo quod..intellectus naturali necessitate videat objectum praesens proportionatum...Neque etiam illa necessitas videndi est simpliciter necessitas, sed tantummodo necessitas si objectum praesens noveat (*Oxon.* IV, d. 49, q. 6, f. 279v, a; n. 9, XXI, 187b-188a).

This necessary reaction to a present and proportionate object is a consequence of the principle that every cause that is sufficient to produce an effect will produce it as soon as it is put in contact with a proportionate recipient of that effect:

49. This text is absent from the *Ass. Ms.* The question from which we are quoting belongs to those parts of the *Oxoniense* that are not in Scotus' *Ordinatio* in its original form, but were supplied later from other works of Scotus. Vide Carl Balić, O.F.M., *Relatio a Commissione Scotistica exhibita Capitulo Generali Fratrum Minorum Assissii A. D.* 1939 (Rome, 1939), pp. 141 ff.

50. Cf. *Oxon.* II, d. 42, q. 4, n. 11; XIII, 461b.

> Illud quod sufficienter est in actu primo respectu alterius[51] effectus potest illum causare in receptivo proportionato et approximato (*Oxon.* II, d. 9, q. 2, f. 127r, b; n. 15, XII, 446b).

The objects of knowledge play the role of true causes in the process of cognition. Every object sufficiently present to the human intellect, whether in a sensible or in an intelligible species, produces the most perfect effect of which it is capable. In other words, it produces an effect adequate to itself, or a proper concept, as well as a concept of everything essentially or virtually contained in the object:

> Objectum quodcumque, sive relucens in phantasmate, sive in specie intelligibili cum intellectu agente vel possibili cooperante, secundum ultimum suae virtutis facit, sicut effectum sibi adaequatum, conceptum suum proprium, et conceptum omnium essentialiter vel virtualiter inclusorum in eo (*Oxon.* I, d. 3, q. 2, f. 26r, a; n. 9, IX, 19b).

While describing the objective causality in the act of knowledge, Scotus does not overlook the activity of the intellect. As is well known, the Franciscan Doctor describes the act of cognition as the result of a double causality, viz., of the object and of the intellect, the former being subordinated to the latter. The same is the case with evident knowledge. Evident knowledge is not the result of the object alone, but of the object together with the intellect.[52] Any intellect faced with an objective evidence (i.e., with an object that is intelligible and proportioned to the intellect) reacts necessarily and to the utmost of its power to that evidence.[53] The intellect apprehends the object in the same measure as it manifests itself. Acting, as it does, in the manner of a non-free agent, the intellect is directly determined by the objective state of affairs, and it is not in its power to choose to apprehend one aspect of the object in preference to another:

> Cum intellectus de se sit potentia naturalis et non libera, agente objecto, intellectus agit quantum potest; ergo si objectum ex parte sui

51. Alicujus *Viv.*

52. Cf. *Oxon.* I, d. 3, q. 7, n. 20 ss; IX, 361a ss.

53. Note that in the present state the human intellect does not always react to the utmost of its power. For by divine disposition its activity is limited to certain objects only. Cf. A. Wolter, "Duns Scotus on the Natural Desire for the Supernatural" in *The New Scholasticism*, XXIII (1949), pp. 290-294. However, the human intellect does react in the described manner to all objects proportionate to it.

agit manifestando...non est in potestate intellectus ut videat aliquid ostensum et aliquid non videat[54] *(Oxon.* I, d. 1, q. 2, f. 11r, a; n. 9, VIII, 334b-335a).

As Belmond[55] writes, "the affirmation of being, in virtue of its very presence, bars the alternative, 'being is or is not' as out of place. For the presence of being to itself and to the mind gives rise to the affirmation of the same presence. Unable to escape the obsession of that presence, the mind, whether willingly or unwillingly, is compelled to surrender to evidence. Hence proceeds the highest degree of certitude....When we say: 'I am, the sun is, these flowers are,' we undoubtedly express the truth. For we assert nothing but what is evident at first sight, viz., the presence of being." In addition to underscoring the role of the object in evident knowledge Belmond's remarks also reveal two further effects of evidence, viz., necessary assent and absolute certitude.

2. Necessary Assent

Just as the apprehension of truth is determined by evidence, so also the assent which immediately follows in the intellect is determined by objective evidence of truth as perceived by the intellect:

Intellectus assentit cuilibet vero secundum evidentiam ipsius veri[56] quam natum est facere de se in intellectu *(Oxon.* I, d. 1, q. 1, f. 10r, b; n. 6, VIII, 311a).

The intellect assents to truth according as the latter manifests itself in the thing, or according to the evidence of the thing. If objective evidence is conclusive the intellect is compelled to give its assent. It is not in the power of the intellect to regulate the intensity of its assent which is necessarily in strict proportion to the evidence or intelligibility of the object:

Non est in potestate intellectus firmius vel minus firmiter assentire vero, sed tantum secundum proportionem ipsius veri moventis intellectum *(ibid.).*

In this the assent of the intellect differs profoundly from the assent of the will. While the assent of the intellect is irresistibly

54. Aliquid.../ *om. Ass. Ms.*
55. Séraphin Belmond, O.F.M., "Le fondement de la certitude" in *Etudes Franciscaines,* LI (1939), p. 415.
56. Rei *Viv.*

determined by objective evidence, the will has the power to assent
with more or less intensity to its object (the good), and this regardless of the imperfection or perfection of knowledge. This difference of assent is due to the fact that the will, contrary to the intellect, is a free potency[57] which is not determined by external factors.
It is entirely free to adhere to a higher or lower good:[58]

> In potestate voluntatis est intensius assentire bono,vel non assentire,
> licet imperfectius viso (ibid.).
> Nec est assensus similis hinc inde, quia necessitas est in intellectu
> propter evidentiam causantem assensum vel propter evidentiam objecti
> necessario causantis assensum in intellectu; non autem bonitas aliqua
> objecti causat necessario assensum voluntatis, sed voluntas libere
> assentit cuilibet bono et ita libere assentit maiori bono sicut minori
> (Oxon. I, d. 1, q. 4, f. 12v, b-13r, a; n. 16, VIII, 372a-b).

The necessity of assent on the part of the intellect is particularly apparent in propositions that are evident in virtue of their own
terms, and in conclusions derived from such propositions. Here,
more than anywhere, the strict proportion between subjective assent
and objective evidence is apparent:

> Non est in potestate intellectus moderari assensum suum veris, quae
> apprehendit; nam quantum veritas principiorum ex terminis, vel conclu-
> sionum ex principiis, tantum oportet assentire propter carentiam liber-
> tatis (Oxon. II, d. 6, q. 2, f. 123r, a; n. 11, XII, 355b).[59]

The character of the evidence of principles and conclusions will
be discussed at greater length in the second part of this dissertation.

3. Infallible Certitude

The necessary assent to evidence is accompanied by certitude.
Certitude is a quality of knowledge which excludes deception and
doubt. In other words, it excludes both objective falsity or error,
and such modes of knowledge that fail to produce a subjective
assurance of actual possession of truth:

> Certitudo nata est inesse intellectui de actu suo excludens non

57. Scotus calls it a "potentia libera per essentiam." Oxon. I, d. 1, q. 4, n. 9;
VIII, 359a.
58. Cf. J. Auer, Die menschliche Willensfreiheit im Lehrsystem des Thomas v.
Aquin und Johannes Duns Scotus (Munich, 1938), pp. 238-254. For parallel passages
see: Oxon. I, d. 1, q. 3, n. 2; VIII, 344-345a; also q. 4, n. 9; 359a; Metaph. IX, q.
15, n. 4; VII, 609a.
59. Cf. also Oxon. II, d. 7, q. un., n. 27; XII, 407b s.

tantum deceptionem sed etiam dubitationem *(Quodl.* q. 17, n. 11; XXVI, 220b).

By characterizing certitude as a quality of knowledge Scotus does not identify certitude with subjective assurance. Certitude is not merely a subjective disposition, or a feeling of security resulting from the possession of truth or from what is considered to be the truth. Such feelings may accompany the act of knowledge. But they are not the only distinctive mark of certitude. For a feeling of security does not necessarily guarantee the knowledge of truth. And truth is an essential condition for genuine certitude, as is clear from the cited description of certitude. Such a subjective state may easily be the result of illusions of the senses, of fallacious reasonings, of mistakes on the part of relating witnesses, and other similar deceptions and errors. According to Scotistic teaching, only that knowledge is certain which is capable of rendering account of its conformity with the objective order of things. In other words, only that knowledge is certain which is true and which realizes that it is true:

> Certitudo numquam est in apprehendendo verum, nisi talis sciat illud esse verum quod apprehendit *(Metaph.* I, q. 4, n. 12; VII, 58a).

In the *Quodlibeta,* Scotus shows that the same relation that constitutes the truth of knowledge, viz., the "relatio mensurabilis ad mensuram" is also responsible for certitude. To say that something is measured is equivalent to saying that the intellect is made certain of the size or quantity of the measured thing through something else. "To be measured" implies a relation both to the intellect which is made certain, and to the measure by means of which certitude is procured:

> Aliquid mensurari est intellectum de ejus quantitate determinata per aliud certificari, ita quod mensurari importat respectum ad intellectum cui fit certitudo, et ad mensuram per quam fit certitudo *(Quodl.* q. 13, n. 12; XXV, 525b).

Scotus is here using the language of Aristotle[60] who compares the relation of the knowable to the knower with that of the measurable to its measure. The meaning of the figure is clear. If the knowledge

---

60. *Metaphysics* V, chap. 15; 1020b, 26-32: "Things are relative...as the measurable to the measure, and the knowable to knowledge, and the perceptible to perception."

we have of a thing measures up with the thing itself, then our knowledge not only is true but it also produces genuine certitude in virtue of its very truth. In other words, certitude is the effect of the conformity of knowledge with the thing known.

The objective character of certitude is also stated (at least implicitly) in the question on the univocity of being where it is said that certitude cannot be had of anything false. Scotus observes that the ancient philosophers who admitted of a first principle (whether they considered it to be fire or water or some other element) were certain that this first principle was a being. But they were not certain whether this being was created or uncreated, first or not first in the order of being. Scotus maintains that no philosopher could have been certain that anyone of the named elements was the first being. For if he had been, he would have been certain of something false, and what is false is not knowable. [61] Nor could anyone of them have been certain that his principle was *not* the first being. On the contrary, the ancient philosophers would not have posited their principles as first beings:

> Quilibet Philosophus fuit certus illud quod posuit primum principium esse ens, puta unus de igne, et alius de aqua, certus erat quod erat ens... non autem fuit certus quod esset ens creatum vel increatum, primum vel non primum. Non enim erat certus quod erat primum, quia tunc fuisset certus de falso, et falsum non est scibile; nec quod erat ens non primum, quia tunc non posuisset oppositum *(Oxon.* I, d. 3, q. 2, f. 25v, b; n. 6, IX, 18b).

That this text contains a confirmation of our assertion that Scotus' concept of certitude is essentially objective can be shown thus. On the one hand, Scotus says of the Ancients that they posited one of the aforementioned elements as first principle; on the other hand, he states that they were not certain it was first, although they pretended that one or the other of their principles was first. Scotus implies that they could not have been certain of this, for if they had been, then they would have been certain of something false; something false, however, cannot produce genuine certitude, since in any false cognition an essential element of certitude is absent,

---

61. It seems that the phrase "Falsum non est scibile" is not to be understood as if that which is false is not at all knowable, but rather that it is not knowable with genuine certainty such as it results from a true *scientia*.

viz., the *exclusio deceptionis*. Scotus does not deny, therefore, that these thinkers may have been subjectively convinced that what they considered to be the first principle was such in fact. A subjective conviction, however, is not yet a guarantee of truth which in Scotus' mind is required in order that genuine certitude may be had.

A further confirmation of the objective character of certitude is found in a passage where Scotus writes that the intellect can "in some way" apprehend contradictory propositions, i.e., as long as the contradiction remains hidden to it. But he adds that the intellect cannot conceive them with certainty:

> Potest dici...quod contradictoria latentia, quamdiu non percipitur contradictio evidens in eis, possunt aliquo modo apprehendi ab intellectu, non tamen certitudinaliter *(Oxon.* II, d. 1, q. 3, f. 99v, b; n. 15, XI, 79a).

The remark, "quamdiu non percipitur contradictio evidens in eis," suggests the reason for the absence of certitude. One of the contradictory statements is false, and therefore, although they may be apprehended as being both true at one and the same time, this is due to the fact that the contradiction involved in the statements is not perceived by the intellect. Since the illusion, however, must sooner or later come to light, it follows that the temporary conviction produced by it cannot be considered as genuine certitude, for it is not the result of objective truth.

His insistence on the objective character of certitude notwithstanding, Scotus does not exclude its functions as a subjective qualification of knowledge. The very definition of certitude bears witness to this fact. Inasmuch as certitude excludes doubt it can safely be called a qualification of the subjective act of assent. Scotus repeatedly hints at the intensity and firmness of the act of knowledge in connection with its certitude.[62] Such expressions unmistakably refer to the subjective act of assent. This is particularly true in reference to first principles, the certitude of which the Franciscan Doctor so energetically defends. For to these principles the intellect assents without any doubt whatsoever:

---

62. Cf. *Oxon.* II, d. 6, q. 2, n. 11; XII, 355b; III, d. 24, q. un., n. 17; XV, 47b; *Quodl.* q. 17, n. 11; XXVI, 220a.

Intellectus virtute sui et terminorum assentiet indubitanter isti complexioni *(Oxon.* I, d. 3, q. 4, f. 31v, a; n. 8, IX, 175b).[63]

The subjective aspects, therefore, are not excluded from Scotus' concept of certitude. In point of fact, it is one of the specific functions of certitude to assure the intellect of the truth of the cognitive acts. Since true cognitions alone, however, can produce a lasting subjective assurance, it is necessary that they be true in themselves. Perfect certitude, therefore, contains an objective and a subjective element, the latter being produced by the former. In other words, perfect certitude can be had only in reference to propositions which are both true in themselves and known as true. This is Scotus' genuine doctrine, as it can be seen from a few texts where he stresses the subjective aspects of certitude, i.e., the firmness of assent as opposed to those states of mind where an imperfect cognition of truth leaves the intellect in doubt or produces a merely opinionative assent:

> Certitudo enim nata est inesse intellectui de actu suo excludens non tantum deceptionem sed etiam dubitationem. Et hoc non est nisi intellectus percipiat id a quo actus habet quod sit certus, quia si nihil potest percipere unde sit certus, videtur quod possit dubitare *(Quodl.* q. 17, n. 11; XXVI, 220b).

The possibility of doubt remains as long as the intellect does not perceive the very foundation or basis of certitude. In other words, the intellect cannot be certain except by apprehending the truth of its knowledge:

> Certitudo numquam est in apprehendendo verum, nisi talis sciat illud esse verum quod apprehendit *(Metaph.* I, q. 4, n. 12; VII, 58a).

Even a first principle, Scotus remarks, would fail to produce certitude if the intellect were to overlook its truth:

> Si opinando apprehendam primum principium, licet illud quod verum est necessario apprehendam, tamen non sum certus *(ibid.).*

The most important question, however, still remains to be answered: how can the intellect ascertain the truth of its own knowledge? Scotus tries to solve the problem by an appeal to reflection. Truth, he thinks, can be ascertained by comparing the relation expressed in the proposition with the simple concepts. If there is conformity or agreement between proposition and simple concepts, then the proposition is true:

63. Cf. *Metaph.* I, q. 4, *passim;* VII, 51a ss.

Neutra veritas[64] est in intellectu objective,[65] nisi reflectente se super actum suum, comparando illum ad objectum *(Metaph.* VI, q. 3, n. 6; VII, 338b).

Objecta conceptus complexi[66] quae sunt extrema...mensurant illum conceptum complexum, cui esse priori conceptum complexum conformari est verum esse, difformari est falsum esse... *(loc. cit.,* n. 9, 340b-341a).

Scotus is well aware of the difficulties that can be raised against this solution. Among the objections he raises against himself he even anticipates Montaigne's famous diallelus.[67] Another weighty argument is the following. In simple concepts things are perceived *absolute,* i.e., irrespective of any actual or possible relationship. How can the relation expressed in the proposition be ascertained through comparison with such simple apprehensions?

Si converto ad rem nude conferendo, per hoc non potero judicare de veritate compositionis, quae est actus collativus *(ibid.,* 341a).

In his answer Scotus adduces the argument of virtual inclusion. The composition formulated by the knower, he observes, is preceded by a mutual inclusion (or "natural identity") of the extremes. To be true, the act of the intellect must be in agreement with that natural inclusion as with its measure:[68]

Complexum est verum quia complexionem quae est a ratione praecedit naturaliter identitas extremorum; et alia habitudo virtualiter inclusa in ipsis, cui actum rationis conformari ut mensurae, est ipsum verum esse *(ibid.,* 341b).

Hence, Scotus, in the final analysis, makes certitude dependent on immediate contact with the object of knowledge. He believes that the object has an intrinsic capacity of making itself known. This must be admitted if we are to have any true knowledge at all. Indeed, the only means of avoiding complete scepticism is to stop at some sort of irreducible factor of truth and certitude. For as we have seen, in order to obtain perfect truth, we must make the act of composition or division the object of a new act or reflection, which examines whether or not the composition or division renders the

---

64. Scotus distinguishes two *veritates;* the *prima veritas* is that of simple apprehension; the *secunda veritas* is that of compositions or divisions.

65. *Objective* in medieval language, is equivalent to the modern *subjective.*

66. *Conceptus complexus* is here taken in the sense of proposition.

67. *Loc. cit.,* n. 7; 339a-b.

68. Cf. Boehner, "Ockham's Theory of Truth" in *Franciscan Studies,* V (1945), pp. 156 ff.

objective state of affairs. This new act either leads to the unquestionable possession of truth or not. If not, another reflection
must follow, after which the same dilemma will again be posed.
Hence we must choose between two alternatives: either falling back
on an infinite regress - which would mean scepticism - or stopping
at an ultimate and unquestionable criterion of truth. Scotus maintains that there is such an absolutely reliable foundation for truth
and certitude which needs no justification other than itself. This
criterion is what he calls evidence.

4. Evidence is at the Basis of All Truth and Certitude

Certitude, according to Scotus, is had only in acts of cognition
strictly proper to the intellect, i.e., in affirmative and negative
judgments:

> Certitudo proprie non est nisi circa compositionem et divisionem,
> quae ad intellectum tantum proprie pertinet (Metaph. I, q. 4, n. 14; VII,
> 59a).

Scotus gives an exhaustive enumeration of the various classes
of propositions in which true and infallible knowledge may be had
on the basis of objective evidence. In order to apprehend the truth
of a proposition, he explains, we must know that it expresses the
relation which exists between its extremes. The apprehension of
this conformity between proposition and terms differs from proposition to proposition just as the relations between the extremes
themselves differ from case to case. Sometimes the conformity is
in the very nature of the extremes and not in something prior to
them; sometimes it is perceived as included in something prior to
the proposition; sometimes, finally, it is seen neither in the nature
of the terms, nor through inclusion, but by means of an external
cause which conjoins or separates the terms:

> Dico quod complexionem cognosco esse veram, cognoscendo confor-
> mitatem ejus ad illam habitudinem virtualiter inclusam in extremis, quae
> quandoque includitur in extremis ex natura extremorum, non per aliud
> prius; quandoque per aliud prius includens; quandoque nullo modo ex
> natura terminorum vel includentium ipsos, sed a causa extrinseca con-
> jungente ipsa vel disjungente (Metaph. VI, q. 3, n. 10; VII, 341b).

Accordingly, Scotus distinguishes three ways of knowing truth,
viz., principles of demonstration, conclusions derived from principles of demonstration, and contingent propositions:

Primo modo est in principio demonstrationis. Secundo modo in conclusione... Tertio modo est in propositione contingente *(ibid.)*.

In explaining the principles of demonstration Scotus points out that the extremes of these principles have the property of making their relation known at once and by themselves to the intellect. As soon as the intellect unites these terms in a judgment, it sees the conformity of its act to the relation existing between the extremes:

> Itaque in primo modo extrema absolute intellecta, statim nata sunt facere ex se in intellectu illius notitiam habitudinis ipsorum, sicut et alia absoluta relationis consequentis; quando ergo intellectus conjungit terminos illos componendo, statim *videt* conformitatem actus sui ad illam habitudinem quam prius natura habuit notam ex terminis *(ibid.)*.

In conclusions, however, – and in this they differ from first principles – something prior is needed in which the truth of the conclusion is intuited. For in formulating a conclusion, the intellect does not perceive the conformity of its act with the objective relation between the terms except by first perceiving the relation as it is present between the terms in the premises:

> Quando autem componit terminos conclusionis non videt illum actum esse conformem habitudini reali terminorum, donec *videat* illam habitudinem terminorum, cujus notitia non fuit impressa sibi ex terminis conclusionis, nec imprimitur nisi ex notitia habitudinis terminorum principii quae includit illam *(ibid., 342a)*.

In contingent propositions the conformity between the act of the intellect and the objective relation between the terms cannot be seen unless the relation between the terms is apprehended in reality, i.e., in things as they really exist. For, since the relation between the extremes is brought about by an extrinsic cause, it exists only insofar as the extremes have a real existence, and never insofar as they are considered as mere concepts of the mind. Hence, in order to formulate a true judgment about contingent things the intellect must be able to see the extremes as they are united or separated in reality:

> Quando autem componit terminos propositionis contingentis, non videt actum esse conformem, nisi *videndo* habitudinem terminorum in re, quia causa extrinseca si facit eam, facit circa terminos ut in re, non ut in conceptu, et tunc oportet *videre* intellectualiter terminos in re conjungi vel dividi *(ibid.)*.

The reader will have noticed that, in spite of their differences, the three kinds of knowledge have this in common, that in each one of them the conformity between proposition and terms is due to a *visio* of the relation. The term "videre" expresses here the reaction of the knowing intellect to the evidence of the relation between the terms and to the evidence of the present object. Hence there is no doubt that we are here in the presence of three cases of evident knowledge.

It must be added, however, that Scotus does not intend herewith to ascribe the same degree of scientific certitude to each and every one of the aforementioned kinds of knowledge. He constantly distinguishes between the scientific value of necessary and contingent propositions. For Scotus as well as for Aristotle,[69] the ideal of knowledge is that in which certitude is produced by objects that are not only evident but necessarily evident. In fact, any proposition, in order to be strictly scientific, must have a necessary object. Only necessary objects can yield a knowledge which is certain and valid everywhere and at all times.

Considerably less perfect is our knowledge of those contingent propositions for which we have to rely mainly or exclusively on the data of the external senses.[70] Contingent things, as the term implies, can exist or not exist. They are subject to more or less unexpected changes; moreover, they often lack the necessary proportion to our limited sense-faculties. Therefore, all knowledge based on the external senses as its exclusive source of information is not only contingent or non-necessary, but is frequently of a very questionable character, at least as far as the *sensibilia communia* are concerned. It was Scotus' awareness of these shortcomings of sense-cognition that induced him to give a remarkably prominent place to the privileged certainty proper to intellective and introspective knowledge. On the basis of these two kinds of absolutely infallible cognitions he tries to correct the deficiencies of sense knowledge. Thus the self-evident principles furnish him with a re-

69. *Posterior Analytics* I, chap. 6; 74b 6-75a 37.

70. We want to stress the words "on the data of *external senses*" because for Scotus there is a category of contingent propositions which are as evident and certain as the first principles themselves. We are referring to the propositions concerned with subjective internal acts and states of which we have a direct or intuitive cognition. Cf. Day, *op. cit.*, pp. 123 ff.

liable basis both for his theory of induction, and for the appraisal and correction of conflicting sense perceptions. Introspection, on the other hand, is assigned a still more fundamental role, namely, that of warranting the subjective certainty of the very principles of knowledge.

The evidence of the principles or self-evident propositions will be studied in the first two chapters of Part II of this dissertation. In the concluding chapter of this part we shall present a brief analysis of the evidence proper to conclusions. Introspective evidence will be considered in the first chapter of Part III. The remaining chapters of this last part will be devoted to an examination of the various functions which intellective and introspective evidence are called to perform in the different provinces of knowledge.

PART TWO
EVIDENCE OF PRINCIPLES
AND CONCLUSIONS

CHAPTER I
DEFINITION AND DESCRIPTION
OF SELF-EVIDENT PROPOSITIONS

A. DIFFERENT TYPES OF PRINCIPLES

Aristotle, when speaking of *immediate propositions,* distinguishes between the *axiom* "which the pupil must know if he is to learn anything whatever," and the *thesis* which, 'though it is not susceptible of proof by the teacher, yet ignorance of it does not constitute a total bar to progress on the part of the pupil."[1] No essential difference is found between these two Aristotelian propositions, since both are known in an immediate manner, i.e., through no other proposition prior to them.[2]

In like manner, Scotus makes use of two denominations when referring to principles of sciences, namely, *first principles (prima principia* and *self-evident propositions (propositiones per se notae).* Here also, no essential difference can be established, for both of these propositions are evident in virtue of their terms alone.[3] This accounts for the fact that the expression "self-evident proposition" is often applied to first principles, and vice versa. However, just as Aristotle distinguishes between axiom and thesis according to their degree of accessibility, so we can also distinguish between Scotus' principles of science according as they are known with a greater or lesser effort. The *prima principia,* which in general seem to be identical with the axioms or "basic and common truths" of

---

1. *Posterior Analytics* I, chap. 2; 72a, 15-18.

2. *Loc. cit.,* 72a, 5-7.

3. That there is no essential difference between the two kinds of propositions is clear from the following text where Scotus uses the terms "propositio per se nota" and "principia prima" synonymously: "Propositio per se nota non est exclusiva notitiae terminorum, quia prima principia cognoscimus inquantum terminos cognoscimus" *(Oxon.* I, d. 2, q. 2, f. 14v, a; n. 2, VIII, 396a).

Aristotle,[4] are presupposed in, and applicable to, every science. They must be known to everyone who wants to study any particular science. They are the most immediate, the highest, and most universal rules of all intellectual activity. For the same reason they are easily accessible to every normal mind.

Not so with the *propositiones per se notae*. These need not be known in their entirety to every student. Only those must be known which constitute the principles of the particular science in which the student is actually engaged. It is in this sense that they are often called first principles, in spite of what has been said about the more general character of the *prima principia*. It should be noted, however, that Scotus, although he uses the two denominations interchangeably, does not intend to attribute the same degree of accessibility to the first principles and to the self-evident propositions. First principles (in the more universal sense of the word) are, as a rule, easily grasped even by the more limited minds, because the meaning of their terms is apprehended without any particular effort. The terms of self-evident propositions, however, admit of various degrees of distinctness, and may, therefore, be known only to a few. [5]

All these distinctions, however, do not reach the internal structure of the first principles and self-evident propositions. For this reason we shall treat them conjointly as to their constitution and evidence.

B. DEFINITION OF A SELF-EVIDENT PROPOSITION

Like most of the Scholastics, Scotus discusses the problems connected with the self-evident proposition in his question on the cognoscibility of the existence of God. This question is found in the *Opus Oxoniense* under the title: "Utrum aliquid infinitum esse sit per se notum, ut Deum esse." [6] In addition to this basic question

---

4. *Loc. cit.*, chap. 11; 77a, 24-33.

5. The preceding considerations are meant to be an introduction to Scotus' treatment of self-evident propositions. It will soon become clear that they are sufficiently substantiated by Scotus' own texts.

6. *Ass. MS.* Lib. I, d. 2, q. 2; ff. 14v, a-18r, b; *Viv.* VIII, 395a-486a. In the Vivès edition the title reads: "An aliquod infinitum, sive an Deum esse sit per se notum?"

we shall make extensive use of the important parallel texts of the
Reportatio Examinata. [7]

Before giving his definition of a self-evident proposition, Scotus
explains the meaning of the expression *per se* when used in this
connection. When it is said that a proposition is known *per se* this
does not mean to exclude any and every causality. It is clear that
we cannot dispense with the knowledge of the terms, for no proposition is knowable except through a previous apprehension of the
terms. The terms of self-evident propositions, however, differ from
those of any other proposition in that they are not merely a necessary but also a sufficient cause for the formulation of the proposition. No other causality apart from the terms is needed to produce
the evidence of these propositions:

> Primo assigno rationem propositionis per se notae. Et dico sic: cum
> dicitur propositio per se nota non excluditur per ly *per se* quaecumque
> causa, quia non excluduntur termini propositionis. Nulla enim propositio
> nota est exclusa notitia terminorum. Ergo propositio per se nota non est
> exclusiva notitiae terminorum, quia prima principia cognoscimus inquan-
> tum terminos cognoscimus; sed excluditur quaecumque causa et ratio
> quae est extra per se conceptum terminorum propositionis per se notae
> (*Oxon.* I, d. 2, q. 2, f. 14v, a; n. 2, VIII, 396a).

Hence *per se* does not indicate an innate knowledge in the human
intellect, i.e., a knowledge impressed on the mind without any
activity on its part. Scotus does not admit of propositions or of
simple apprehensions which are innate to the intellect. All our
knowledge starts somehow from sense perception. Not even first
principles are grasped unless their terms are received from the
sensible world without:

> Intellectus noster...ante omnia intelligere est sicut tabula rasa (*Oxon.*
> II, d. 23, q. un., n. 5; XIII, 160b). [8]
>
> Pro tanto (principia) dicuntur nobis naturaliter nota sive cognita, quia
> praescita compositione simplicium terminorum, statim ex lumine natu-
> rali intellectus acquiescit vel adhaeret illi veritati; tamen cognitio
> terminorum acquiritur ex sensibilibus (*Metaph.* II, q. 1, n. 2; VII, 97a).

Sense perception, however, is in no way the *cause* of the *propositio per se nota.* It is simply a *conditio sine qua non* by which the
terms become subjectively known. This sense activity need not

---

7. *Cod. Vienn.* 1453, Lib. I, d. 3, q. 2, ff. 21v-22r.
8. We give here only the version of the Vivès edition, since this question is
missing in the Assisi Ms.

even be true in order to produce a true principle in the mind. "Therefore," writes Mastrius de Meldula,[9] "the expression *per se* excludes everything by which the intellect would be moved, as through a middle term, to give its assent to the aforesaid proposition. As soon as the intellect apprehends the terms of that proposition, it knows evidently their mutual connection by virtue of the apprehension. In this sense the proposition is said to be evident by its own proper terms."

The only constituent of the self-evidence of a proposition, therefore, are the terms of which it is constituted. Scotus specifies the function of the terms in his definition of a self-evident proposition:

> Dicitur igitur propositio per se nota quae per nihil aliud extra terminos proprios qui sunt aliquid ejus[10] habet veritatem evidentem *(Oxon. I, d. 2, q. 2, f. 14v, a; n. 2, VIII, 396a).*
>
> Hic primo ostendo quid est propositio per se nota, scilicet quae est quae habet evidentem veritatem ex suis terminis ut sui sunt. Unde in propositione per se nota non excluditur terminorum notitia, quia nulla propositio est nota sine cognitione terminorum; sed in ratione causae vel veritatis evidentiae illius propositionis per se notae excluditur quaecumque alia veritas complexa. Illa est enim nota per se quae non habet evidentiam ex alia propositione notiori in veritate, sed ex suis terminis intrinsecis ut sui sunt *(Rep. Exam. I, d. 3, q. 2, f. 21v).*

According to these texts a proposition is self-evident if it is known in virtue of its terms alone; or as the *Reportatio* puts it, if it is evidently known to be true "ex suis terminis ut sui sunt." This shows the difference between the self-evidence of propositions and conclusions. Conclusions are evident if deduced from evident premises, the truth of which is better known than that of the conclusions themselves, and which for this reason serve as a means to make the conclusions known. This is why conclusions are said to be known, not *per se* but *per aliud;* although truly evident (if deduced from evident premises), yet they are never *self*-evident. Self-evident propositions, on the contrary, are known, not by means of some higher or more evident truth, but simply and solely in virtue of the terms *ut sui sunt,* i.e., as they stand in the propo-

9. *Cursus philosophicus* (Venice, 1708), tom. I, disput. XIII, quaest. III, art. I, n. 49; pp. 359a s.
10. Quae ex terminis propriis qui sunt aliquid ejus, ut sunt ejus *Viv.*

sition, and independently of any other truth or proposition. As Mastrius remarks, a proposition is said to be known in virtue of its terms *ut sunt ejus* "when the terms are taken in the precise sense in which they are used to integrate the proposition."[11]

The example used by the Vivès edition to illustrate is a clear case of a perfectly self-evident proposition in the sense described. Although this example is not found in the Assisi MS it is within the Scotist line of argument. In point of fact, it is cited in the parallel text of the *Reportatio* and also occurs elsewhere in the works of the Franciscan Doctor.[12] The example is presented as follows:

> Et (propositio per se nota) non propter aliquid aliud quod sit extra terminos proprios habet evidentiam, sed ex se tantum, ut omne totum est majus sua parte (*Oxon*. I, d. 2, q. 2, n. 2; VIII, 396a-b).

From the sole apprehension of the meaning of the terms "whole" and "part" and their comparison, the mind can immediately formulate the proposition, "Every whole is greater than its part." The mutual inclusion of the two terms is so obvious that by comparing one and the other, the mind immediately perceives their relationship, and that independently of any other factor apart from the terms themselves. The grasping of this relationship is, of course, accompanied by the apprehension of the truth of the proposition, as well as by a most certain assent in the mind. A more detailed discussion of these subjective aspects of the self-evident proposition is reserved for the next chapter.

The *propositio per se nota* has been defined as evident in virtue of its terms. In order to be able to appreciate its epistemological importance, we must first examine the nature and function of the terms.

C. THE FUNCTION OF THE TERMS IN
SELF-EVIDENT PROPOSITIONS
1. *Distinct and Confused Terms*

In his description of the terms and their function in the *propositio per se nota*, Scotus begins by establishing a distinction be-

---

11. *Loc. cit.*, p. 360.
12. *Rep. Exam.* I, d. 3, q. 2; f. 21v-22r: "Propositio est per se nota intellectui habenti distinctam notitiam terminorum...sicut ista: omne totum est majus sua parte." Cf. also *Oxon.* I, d. 2, q. 2, n. 9; IX, 609a.

tween the terms which may enter a self-evident proposition. First
of all, one and the same thing can be designated by two different
terms, one of which represents the definition of the thing in
question, while the other simply stands for the thing defined, without expressing its definition. This distinction applies both to vocal
terms, or words, and to concepts in the mind which are signified
by words. Thus "man" is a defined thing *(definitum)* and "rational
animal" is a definition *(definitio):*

> Ulterius, qui sunt illi termini proprii ex quibus debet esse evidens? -
> Dico quoad hoc: alius terminus est definitio et alius definitum, sive
> accipiantur termini pro vocibus significantibus sive pro conceptibus
> significatis *(Oxon.* I, d. 2, q. 2, f. 14v, a; n. 2, VIII, 396b).

The important point to note in this text is that the term (or group
of terms) which expresses the definition is not at all identical in
meaning with the term which simply stands for the thing defined,
even though both terms stand for, and signify, one and the same
thing. This difference is brought out more emphatically in the *Reportatio*, where Scotus distinguishes between distinct and confused
concepts in the self-evident proposition:

> Hic primo ostendo quid est propositio per se nota, scilicet quae est
> quae habet evidentem veritatem ex suis terminis ut sui sunt... Et dico
> "ut sui sunt" vel conceptus confusi ut confuse sunt, vel distincti ut
> distincte sunt; non enim idem termini definitio et definitum, quia defi-
> nitum prius notum est quam definitio eo quod confusum et confusa sunt
> prius nota...et ideo aliquid potest esse per se notum secundum unum
> terminum, scilicet secundum definitum quod non erit notum secundum
> definitionem *(Rep. Exam.* I, d. 3, q. 2, f. 21v).

A term is called distinct when it expresses the essential components which constitute the object. In other words, an object must
be defined as to its genus and specific difference in order to be
distinctly known:

> Nihil concipitur distincte nisi quando concipiuntur omnia quae inclu-
> duntur in ratione ejus essentiali *(Oxon.* I, d. 3, q. 2, f. 72v, a; n. 24, IX,
> 49b).

A term is said to be confused if it expresses a merely nominal
acquaintance with the thing. In other words, a confused term stands
for the thing as it is apprehended before the definition is established:

> Confuse dicitur aliquid concipi quando concipitur sicut exprimitur per
> nomen. - Distincte quando concipitur per definitionem *(Loc. cit.,* f. 27r,
> b; n. 21, IX, 48a).

Therefore the phrase "confused knowledge" as used in this connection does not mean that the concept expressed by the term is
blurred or unclear, but simply that its essential definition is unknown. For I can know very clearly what is a man and distinguish
him from what is not a man, while still ignoring the essential definition of man. [13]

Scotus proves this distinction between *definitio* and *definitum*
by calling attention to the different functions exercised by the two
terms in the demonstrative process. According to Aristotle[14] the
quod quid est or essential definition of one of the extremes of a
demonstrated proposition (or conclusion) occurs as middle term in
the demonstration. Thus the definition, "animal rationale," is the
middle term of this syllogism: "Omne animal rationale est risibile;
Homo est animal rationale; Ergo homo est risibilis." Although the
conclusion differs from one of the premises (i.e., the first premise)
only as the defined term differs from its definition, the premise
nevertheless is self-evident, whereas the conclusion is demonstrated. Therefore, the *definitum (homo)* is not the same as the
definitio (animal rationale); for if it were, then the proposition,
"Homo est risibilis," would need no demonstration, because it would
be as evident as the premise, "Animal rationale est risibile." Moreover, it would follow that the *potissima demonstratio* – the most
obvious kind of demonstration – would be a fallacy, inasmuch as
it would suppose as previously evident the very thing it pretends
to demonstrate. Furthermore, such a "demonstration" would have
only two terms. For if the *definitio* is identical with the *definitum,*
then *animal rationale* and *homo* represent only one concept; this
leaves *risibile* as the only other term in the syllogism. The logical
consequence of the aforesaid identification, therefore, would mean
nothing less than a complete repudiation of the Aristotelian concept
of demonstration:

> Quod probo ex primo *Posteriorum,* quia quod quid est alterius extremi
> est medium in demonstratione; ergo altera praemissa non differt a con-
> clusione nisi sicut definitum differt a definitione, et tamen praemissa
> est principium per se notum, conclusio autem non est per se nota, sed
> demonstrata. Ergo quantum ad rationem propositionis per se notae alius

13. Cf. A.B. Wolter, O.F.M., *The Transcendentals and their Function in the
Metaphysics of Duns Scotus* (St. Bonaventure, N.Y., 1946), pp. 61 f.

14. *Post. Anal.* II, chap. 4; 91a, 13-16.

est conceptus definitionis [15] a definito; quia si idem conceptus definitionis et definiti, in demonstratione potissima esset petitio principii. Item, tunc essent ibi tantum duo termini, quod est falsum *(Oxon.* I, d. 2, q. 2, f. 14v, a; n. 2, VIII, 396b).

The distinction between distinct and confused terms can also be proven thus. Aristotle [16] writes that the same relation exists between a *nomen* or word as is found between a whole and its parts. As a whole is best known to sense perception (though confusedly) so also the *nomen* is more easily grasped by the mind than the definition. For the concept of a quiddity as expressed in the *nomen* contains confusedly what the *definitio* contains distinctly through an exact analysis of the constituent parts of that quiddity. Thus it is easier to know what a circle is if it is apprehended in a more vague or general manner, than if it be presented in an essential definition:

> Hoc probatur secundo sic per Aristotelem primo *Physicorum,* quod nomina sustinent ad definitionem hoc quod totum ad partes, id est, quod nomen confusum prius est notum definitione. *(ibid.)*

Another (and perhaps more convincing) argument can be drawn from the cited Aristotelian reasoning. If we admit to Aristotle that the *nomen* is known prior to the definition, then we must also admit that the *nomen* and the definition are not identical. To maintain that they are identical is to say that one and the same concept is simultaneously prior and posterior, or that it can be had and not be had at one and the same time. Actually we conceive first the confused term "man," and only after analyzing this confused concept into its essential components "rational" and "animal" do we arrive at the definition of man. In view of this successive apprehension it must be admitted that we are here in the presence of two different concepts:

> Ex hoc arguitur: impossibile est eundem conceptum esse priorem et posteriorem, haberi et non haberi de eadem re; sed idem potest prius concipi secundum nomen quam secundum definitionem; [17] nomen autem confuse importat quod definitio distincte, quia definitio dividit in singularia; ergo conceptus quidditativus vel quidditatis ut importatur per nomen confuse est prior notus naturaliter quam conceptus ejus ut importatur distincte per definitionem; et ita alius conceptus et aliud extremum *(loc. cit.).*

This somewhat lengthy exposition of the two concepts was necessary to enable us to follow Scotus' discussion of the conditions

15. Alius terminus est definitio *Viv.*
16. *Physics* I, chap. 1; 184a 21-b 11.
17. Ex hoc.../ *om. Assisi MS.*

for self-evidence in propositions the terms of which are confused.

2. Self-Evidence in Propositions with Confused Terms

In the following texts, Scotus deals mainly with propositions composed of confusedly known terms. We must not wonder at this, for propositions with distinctly known terms present little difficulty. For the relation between the terms is brought out by a definition which analyzes the subject in terms of its essential components and thus shows the relation between subject and predicate without further effort on the part of the knower. In propositions with confused terms, however, such an essential definition is not given; therefore the relation between the terms is not always evident. Hence Scotus subjects them to close investigation, laying down the conditions by which these propositions can be called self-evident.

After recalling his distinction between confused and distinct terms and his definition of a self-evident proposition, Scotus remarks that *a proposition where the quiddity is confusedly conceived is not self-evident if we have to define quiddity first:*

> Ex hoc ultra: Cum propositio sit per se nota quae ex propriis terminis habet evidentem veritatem, et alii termini sunt conceptus quidditatis distincte ut importatur per definitionem, et conceptus quidditatis confuse ut importatur per nomen, sequitur quod propositio non erit per se nota de quidditate confuse accepta, quae non est nota nisi per definitionem distincte concipiatur (Oxon. I, d. 2, q. 2, f. 14v, a; n. 3, VIII, 398b).

This text must be considered in connection with those which precede and follow, lest its peculiar formulation lead us astray. Scotus says that no proposition with confused terms is self-evident if we have to give a definition of quiddity first. As Bettoni[18] remarks, "quiddity" may be referred to either subject *or* predicate or to both subject *and* predicate of the proposition. It has been stated that a proposition is self-evident in virtue of its own terms. Moreover, it has been proven that terms differ according as they imply a distinct quidditative concept as expressed in the definition, or as they involve a confused quidditative concept as expressed in the *nomen* or word. Hence no proposition whose subject (or predicate) needs to be defined in order to become self-evident can be considered

---

18. Efrem Bettoni, O.F.M., *L'ascesa a Dio in Duns Scoto* (Milan, 1943), p. 21: "Se per rendere evidente una data proposizione occorre definire, e quindi conquistare il concetto preciso di uno o di tutti e due i termini, questa proposizione non è piu immediatamente evidente."

as self-evident as long as the subject is only confusedly conceived. For to say that a proposition with confused terms becomes evident only after the quiddity (of either subject or predicate, or both) is defined, is equivalent to saying that the said proposition is not self-evident in virtue of its own terms.

Scotus proceeds to adduce three arguments in support of the doctrine just exposed. The interpretation of these arguments presents some difficulty. It is our opinion that they cannot be rightly explained unless we interpret them as a threefold refutation of an objection that is implicit in the text. This is indicated by the little word "alias" which obviously aims at a real or supposed objector. In fact, Scotus' doctrine appears to be open to objection. It may be said, for instance, that even if Scotus' contention is granted that a proposition with confused terms is not self-evident as it stands, nevertheless it may be called self-evident because *it becomes self-evident as soon as the terms are defined,* or at least, because the terms are susceptible of being defined. This, it seems, is the objection Scotus has in mind in the following text (which also contains the first of the three arguments he himself produces to corroborate his own position):

> Haec etiam eadem conclusio probatur: quia alias quaelibet propositio alia quae est necessaria et per se primo modo,[19] ut homo est animal, et corpus, usque ad substantiam, esset per se nota. Nam si ratio utriusque extremi assignatur ex rationibus extremorum distincte conceptis, apparet manifeste quod unum extremum includit alterum (*Oxon.* I, d. 2, q. 2, f. 14v, b; n. 3, VIII, 398b-399a).

In other words, if it were true that every proposition with confused terms is to be considered self-evident because it becomes so through the definition of the terms, then every necessary proposition of the first mode would *eo ipso* be self-evident. For in all propositions of the first mode of predication the predicate is contained in the subject in such a way that, through the analysis of the subject, one arrives at the knowledge of the predicate. Hence from the standpoint of the objector it would have to be said that a proposition of the first mode, and formulated with confused terms, can be called self-evident with the same right as that in which the terms are distinct. Thus it would seem that the proposition, "Homo est animal," is to be considered to be as self-evident as the propo-

19. Quae est vera in primo modo *Viv.*

sition, "Animal rationale est risibile," in which the predicate is known as contained in the subject by reason of the distinct knowledge of the terms.

From the formulation of the text already quoted we can conclude that Scotus does not admit this reasoning. According to him, not all propositions of the first mode are *eo ipso* self-evident. They are self-evident only if it is evident *per se* (i.e., here, both necessarily and in virtue of the terms) that the component parts of the subject are actually united, as we read in another passage of the *Oxoniense*.[20] In the case of confused terms, however, the union of the parts is not always self-evident. True, such union can be manifested through the definition of the subject and thus a self-evident proposition may be obtained. This proposition, however, is no longer the same as before. For, if a definition is needed to render it self-evident, it is no longer known through its own terms. It follows that the inclusion of the predicate in the subject is not sufficient to make a proposition self-evident, unless this inclusion is known in virtue of the terms as they stand in the proposition. The inclusion of *animal* in *homo* is doubtless self-evident as soon as *homo* is substituted by the definition *animal rationale*. But it would be false to conclude that the proposition, "Homo est animal," is also self-evident. This proposition is not known in virtue of the terms as they appear in the proposition.[21]

Scotus' second argument is similar to the first. If a proposition with confused terms were to be considered self-evident because it becomes self-evident when the terms are defined, then it would follow that every proposition that is self-evident to the metaphysician - in virtue of the definition of the terms - would also be so in the special sciences. This, however, is not the case; for even though in geometry, for instance, a confused concept is sufficient for the formulation of the self-evident principle that a line is a "longitudo sine latitudine," this does not imply that the geometrician as geometrician is also in a position to conceive the self-

20. I, d. 2, q. 2, f. 15r, a; n. 5, VIII, 405b: "Nihil est per se notum de conceptu non simpliciter simplici, nisi sit per se notum partes illius conceptus uniri."

21. Belmond obviously goes too far when he concludes on the basis of the text cited above that for Scotus no analytical proposition is "nota per se, au pied de la lettre." (*Dieu, existence et cognoscibilité*, Paris, 1913, pp. 9 f.). All Scotus says is that such propositions are not self-evident through their confused terms.

evidence of the metaphysical definition of a line. The metaphysician defines line as a "specific instance of extended quantity, in contradistinction to surface and body." However evident such a definition may be to the metaphysician, no geometrician will ever consider it as self-evident to him. For the geometrician does not apprehend the terms of a metaphysical definition in their proper or distinct meaning:

> Similiter alias quaelibet propositio esset per se nota in scientiis specialibus, quam Metaphysicus posset habere per se notam ex definitionibus extremorum, quod non est verum, quia Geometer non utitur aliquibus principiis tamquam per se notis nisi quae habent evidentem veritatem ex terminis confuse conceptis, puta concipiendo lineam confuse, evidens verum est quod linea est longitudo sine latitudine, non concipiendo aliquid[22] distincte ad quod genus pertineat linea, sicut considerat Metaphysicus. Alias autem propositiones quas Metaphysicus posset concipere, puta quod linea est quanta[23] et hujusmodi, tales propositiones non habet Geometer per se notas (ibid.).

In his third argument, Scotus shows that a proposition with confused terms is not self-evident if it is known only with the help of a definition, by pointing out the different manner in which the predicate of a demonstrated proposition (i.e., of the conclusion of a syllogism) is known of the defined subject according to where it stands in the syllogism:

> Patet ergo tertio quod vere stat demonstratio alicujus praedicati de definito cum hoc quod illud praedicatum sit per se notum de definitione, sicut habere tres est demonstrabile de triangulo, cum tamen notum sit per se de ejus definitione quod omnis figura plana, etc. Est igitur omnis et sola illa propositio per se nota quae ex terminis sic conceptis ut sunt ejus termini nata est habere evidentem veritatem complexionis (ibid.)[24]

The first premise in the demonstrative process contains as predicate the definition of the subject. And for this reason the premise

22. Adhuc Viv.

23. Linea est species quantitatis continuae distincta contra superficiem et corpus Viv.

24. Sicut habere tres.../ om. Ass. MS. Although we are unable, at present, to appraise the critical value of this passage, we have cited it, because of the example it contains as well as of the concise and exact summary it presents of all that has been previously treated. Moreover, in the Reportatio the same instance occurs, although in a somewhat modified form. Instead of referring to the concept of triangle purely and simply, it sets out from the definition of triangle in genere and proceeds to the particular kinds of triangle in specie: "Per naturam trianguli ...possumus demonstrare particulariter de figura habere tres...et de ysocele et de omni contento sub triangulo" (Rep. Exam. I, d. 3, q. 2, f. 22r).

is self-evident, or in other words, the predicate is self-evidently known of the subject. It does not follow, however, that the same predicate is self-evidently known of the confused or undefined subject. It is only through demonstration that the predicate can be made known of such a subject. This is done by means of the definition which is used as middle term, as the following syllogism shows:

> Omnis figura plana tribus lineis contenta habet tres angulos aequales duobus rectis; atqui triangulus est figura tribus lineis contenta; ergo triangulus habet tres angulos aequales duobus rectis.

The definition of the triangle must first be given in order that the predicate ("habet tres...") may become known of the *definitum* (i.e., of the triangle). Hence the proposition, "Triangulus habet tres angulos aequales duobus rectis," is in no way self-evident. If it were, then all demonstrative reasoning would become superfluous. Demonstration and self-evidence being incompatible, nothing that is self-evident needs to be, or can be, demonstrated. Actually the inclusion of the predicate in the subject is not always self-evidently known through the confused concept of the subject, as the above considerations on the nature of the demonstrative process show. It is known only by means of the distinct concept of the subject as through a middle term. Therefore, no proposition with confused terms in which a definition is necessary to reveal the relationship between the terms can be considered self-evident. For it is not known *ex suis terminis ut sui sunt.*

Thus the conditions for self-evidence are clearly established. Only those propositions are self-evident which produce evident truth through their terms as found in the proposition. Or to say the same thing in other words: whether composed of distinct or confused terms, a proposition is self-evident only when, and as often as, it gives evident truth in virtue of its own distinct or confused terms as they stand in the proposition.

The detailed analysis of the three arguments enables us to avoid several misunderstandings of which Scotus' statements about the self evidence of propositions with confused terms has been the occasion. The somewhat obscure text[25] of the Franciscan Doctor

25. We are referring to the passage quoted *supra*, p. 137.

has given rise to two extreme interpretations. Belmond [26] maintains that Scotus denies self-evidence to all analytical propositions, i.e., to propositions "dont le prédicat évoque le sujet." According to Belmond, not even a definition of the terms can render such a proposition self-evident, and therefore the so-called evidence of metaphysics and other particular sciences "restent objectivement... des inévidences;" only the "axioms" which are known through their confused terms would fall under the definition of self-evident proposition. Schmuecker, [27] on the contrary, thinks that (apart from propositions with irreducibly simple concepts) only those propositions whose terms are previously defined can be called self-evident. For only a definition of the subject enables the mind to apprehend the inclusion of the predicate in the subject.

Both of these interpretations seem to fall short of Scotus' conception of the self-evident proposition. By saying that a proposition with confused terms is not self-evident if we must give a distinct definition of the quiddity first, Scotus does not imply either that propositions with distinct terms are not self-evident, or that propositions with confused terms cannot be (or at least become) self-evident. All he says is that propositions with confused terms are not always self-evident, viz., if the relation between subject and predicate is not known in virtue of the confused terms as they stand in the proposition. Nothing, however, prevents such a proposition from *becoming* self-evident. For by a subsequent definition the mutual relationship of the terms may become evident.

Schmuecker remarks in a footnote [28] that although Scotus occasionally speaks of self-evident propositions with confused terms, this is a rather rare case, for his allusions to this subject appear to be little more than cursory remarks. And thus the case of the confused

26. S. Belmond, O.F.M., *Dieu, existence et cognoscibilité* (Paris, 1913), pp. 9 ff. For an excellent criticism of Belmond's views see P. Raymond, O.F.M. Cap., "La philosophie critique de Duns Scot et le criticisme de Kant" in *Etudes Franciscaines*, XXII (1909), pp. 536 ff. The difference in dates is no indication of a prophetic charisma on the part of Fr. Raymond. Belmond's book is a compilation of articles published from 1908 to 1913 in *Revue de Philosophie* and *Etudes Franciscaines*.

27. Rainulf Schmuecker, O.F.M., *Propositio per se nota, Gottesbeweis und ihr Verhaeltnis nach Petrus Aureoli* (Werl i. Westf., 1941), pp. 116 ff.

28. *Op. cit.*, note 87, p. 117.

terms is dismissed as one which has no special bearing on Scotus' synthesis of the self-evident proposition as a whole.

We cannot agree with this oversimplification. First of all, we are dealing here, not with a "rare case," but with a notion which determines and runs throughout Scotus' entire conception of the hieraschy of sciences. This conception must be understood from the old theory of sciences which the Middle Ages inherited from Aristotle.

The Aristotelian and Scholastic scheme of sciences admits of a scale of subordinating and subordinate disciplines, each of which occupies a higher or lower place, according to the greater or lesser extension of its object and principles. Thus Scotus always distinguishes between a general or universal science on the one hand, and a special or particular science on the other. The former is Metaphysics, which treats of the most universal object, Being. All the other sciences are concerned with more or less particular and limited objects of study. Metaphysics is called a general science not only because it considers all things from a higher point of view than any other science, but particularly because its principles direct, if not immediately, at least remotely and implicitly, all thinking and all the conclusions of the particular sciences. This is done through the *dignitates* or axioms, which are the most universal of the self-evident principles.

A similar relationship of subordination is also present in the particular sciences. Thus the science of optics is subordinated to geometry, and the science of music to arithmetic, because optics and music accept their principles from geometry and arithmetic. Note that it is not said that the same principles are used in both sciences but that the principles of the subordinated science are the conclusions of the subalternating science from which they derive their evidence. [29]

Not all the principles of the particular sciences, however, need to be taken from higher sciences. There is a second alternative, namely, the formulation of self-evident principles from concepts obtained by experience. Although their terms are confusedly known, these principles are nevertheless truly self-evident. This is what we want to make clear with the help of texts gathered from several

29. Cf. Mastrius, *Cursus philosophicus*, tom. I, disp. XII, q. 4, pp. 338 ss.

of Scotus' works. First, however, a study of the various kinds of concepts in Scotus is necessary.

Schmuecker bases his contention that only distinct terms can enter a self-evident proposition on the allegedly exhaustive subdivision of concepts into irreducibly simple concepts on the one hand, and composed concepts on the other. While the irreducibly simple concepts are distinctly apprehended by one simple glance of the intellect, the composed concepts cannot be distinctly apprehended unless they appear in the form of definitions. In other words, composed concepts must first be analyzed into their elements or parts. A distinct cognition of the parts of the concepts is indispensable for self-evidence in propositions with composed concepts, because self-evidence consists in the evident inclusion of the predicate in the subject. In order that this inclusion may become evident, it is required, first of all, that the possibility of the association of the parts of the composed subject be evident. If it is not evident, then the subject cannot possibly enter a self-evident proposition. Indeed, let it be assumed that the association were impossible; in this case the composed concept would also be impossible; it would be false in itself. But a false concept, when put together with another concept (i.e., here, with a predicate) cannot yield a true proposition. The possibility of the association of the parts of a concept is evident only if the concept appears in the form of a definition. Hence, Schmuecker concludes, a composed concept cannot enter a self-evident proposition unless it is first defined.[30]

According to Schmuecker, the distinct apprehension of the terms, besides guaranteeing self-evidence *ex terminis,* fulfills at the same time another function - it shows the logical immediacy of the composition. Logical immediacy, or evident inclusion of the predicate in the subject, is that characteristic which distinguishes the self-evident proposition from the conclusion. In a conclusion the relation expressed between subject and predicate is known through the intervention of a third term, whereas in the self-evident proposition the inclusion is evident immediately, i.e., in virtue of the terms alone. In the case of propositions with composed terms this immediacy can be safeguarded only by the definition of the composed terms. For it is only by ascertaining the evident association of the composing

30. *Op. cit.,* pp. 117 f.

parts that any further proof of the same association is rendered superfluous. [31]

As convincing as Schmuecker's expositions may appear at first sight, they rest on an incomplete evaluation of Scotus' classification of concepts. It is true that the Franciscan Doctor says in the question under discussion that in the case of composed terms no self-evident proposition can be had unless it is evident that their parts are united. [32] But he does not state that the evidence of association of the parts appears only in the definition. Scotus, it should be kept in mind, admits a third kind of concept, which can be apprehended by "one glance of the mind" in the same manner as the irreducible concept. Yet, this third type of concept is not irreducibly simple but composed. Let us quote Scotus' own words: "I call irreducibly simple that concept which cannot be resolved into several other concepts, e.g., the concept of being and of the ultimate differences. Simple, though not irreducibly simple, is every concept which can be apprehended by the intellect in an act of simple intellection, although it is susceptible of being broken down into several other concepts which can be conceived separately; such are, for instance, the concepts of a *definitum* or of a species." [33]

> Conceptus simpliciter simplex est qui non est resolubilis in plures conceptus, ut conceptus entis vel ultimae differentiae. Conceptum vero simplicem, sed non simpliciter simplicem voco quicumque potest concipi ab intellectu actu simplicis intelligentiae, licet possit resolvi in plures conceptus seorsum conceptibiles, sicut est conceptus definiti vel speciei[34] *(Oxon.* I, d. 3, q. 1, f. 27r, b; q. 2, n. 21; IX, 47b s).

Here, then, we are clearly told that there are concepts which are not irreducibly simple, the parts of which can be known as united without an actual definition of the terms, or in other words, without a distinct resolution into the composing parts. [35] To say that such

31. *Op. cit.,* pp. 118 f.

32. *Oxon.* I, d. 2, q. 2, n. 5; VIII, 405b: "Nihil est per se notum de conceptu non simpliciter simplici, nisi sit per se notum partes illius conceptus uniri."

33. Cf. Wolter, *The Transcendentals and their Function,* p. 81: "A concept is said to be irreducibly simple if it is incapable of further analysis, that is to say, it cannot be broken down into two simpler concepts, one of which is determinable, the other determining."

34. Sicut est.../ add. Viv.

35. Cf. Wolter, *op. cit.,* p. 81: "A *simpliciter simplex,* or irreducibly simple concept is opposed, on the one hand, to a composite concept and, on the other, to those simple concepts which contain a number of intelligible elements, each of

a simple apprehension is not sufficient for the formulation of a self-evident proposition, offers little objection. For in formulating first principles, the intellect needs nothing besides the simple apprehension of the terms, which is followed by the act of composition of the terms, which in turn is followed by the assent of the intellect to the proposition thus obtained:

> Primo movetur sensus ab aliquo simplici, non complexum, et a sensu moto movetur intellectus et intelligit simplicia, quod est primus actus intellectus; deinde post apprehensionem simplicium sequitur alius actus qui est componere simplicia ad invicem; post illam autem compositionem habet intellectus ex lumine naturali quod assentiat illi veritati complexorum, si illud complexum sit principium primum *(Metaph.* II, q. 1, n. 2; VII, 96b).

No more clarity is required of the concept than that which enables us to distinguish it from other concepts. That this degree of clarity is had in simple apprehension not only of irreducibly simple concepts but also of simple concepts as the ones described above, is a fact of daily experience. We can, for instance, easily distinguish the concept "man" from any other simple concept, even before knowing the essential definition of man.[36]

Hence distinctness must not be equated with evidence. Schmuecker seems to proceed on the supposition that evidence and distinctness are always found together, not only in the sense that everything that is distinctly conceived is evident (which might be true), but also that nothing is evident unless it is distinctly conceived. However, the very definition of the self-evident proposition excludes such identification. We have found that the expression, "ex suis terminis ut sui sunt," is precisely intended to signify that both distinct and confused terms can constitute a self-evident proposition. The doubts left by the *Oxoniense* are easily dispelled by a quotation from the *Reportatio* where Scotus writes:

> Illa est enim nota per se quae non habet evidentiam ex alia propositione notiori in veritate, sed ex suis terminis intrinsecis ut sui sunt. Et dico ut sui sunt vel conceptus confusi ut confuse sunt, vel distincti ut distincti sunt...[37] *(Rep. Exam.* I, d. 3, q. 2, f. 21v).

---

which could be conceived distinctly but which de facto are grasped in a single act."

36. "Intelligitur aliquid per se, etiam in particulari, sed adhuc quodammodo confuse, sicut intelligo hominem antequam intelligam definitionem" *(Quodl.* q. 7, n. 7; XXV, 289b).

37. Version of MS *Merton College* 59 reads: "vel conceptus confusi ut confusi sunt, vel distincti ut distincti sunt."

That a confused concept can produce the same evidence as a distinct concept is again brought to view by a comparison between the respective function of the *definitum* and the definition in the demonstrative syllogism. A definition which appears as a middle term in the demonstration is not, as such, more evident to us than the *definitum*. It is not denied that the premise in which the definition appears is more evident *in relation to the conclusion*. For it is through the definition that the conclusion is drawn from the premises as through a middle term. It does not follow, however, that the premise which contains the definition is *more evident to us* than it was before we knew the definition. For the mutual relation between the terms of that premise is seen without the definition of the subject (at least confusedly):

> Definitio est medium in demonstratione et definitum erit conclusum, et ideo dixi *ut sui sunt,* scilicet confuse, si sunt concepti confuse, et distincte, si sunt concepti distincte. Unde definitio ut est medium non est ut sic declarativum vel magis evidens quoad nos quam subjectum definitum, sed propositio major vel minor est magis evidens conclusione *(ibid.).*

An important addition to Scotus' doctrine on self-evidence is found toward the end of the same question of the *Reportatio,* where the propositions of the first mode of predication are contrasted with those of the second mode. [38] Scotus points out that the propositions of the first mode, in spite of their greater degree of necessity, are not by that fact self-evident or better known than those of the second mode. They become self-evident only through definition of the terms, while many propositions of the second mode, though less necessary and composed of confusedly known terms, are perfectly evident to anyone who apprehends the terms. This is due to the fact that although the concept as presented in the definition is better known in itself *(in se)* than the undefined concept *(nomen),* yet the latter is better known to us *(nobis).* Thus the relation of the terms "whole" and "part" is immediately evident, although they may be apprehended in a confused manner only and accidentally *(secundum quid et confuse),* whereas many propositions with composite concepts are less well known to us, although the concepts

---

38. In predication *per se secundo modo* "the notion of the subject is found in the definition of the predicate, whereas in predication *per se primo modo* the predicate is either the whole or a part of the definition of the subject." Wolter, *op. cit.,* p. 87.

are apprehended distinctly and in their essential nature (*simpliciter et distincte*):

> Omnes propositiones de primo modo dicendi per se sunt magis necessariae quam de secundo, non tamen sunt magis notae, sive quod sint per se notae, quia nulla nisi resolvendo terminos in suas definitiones quae est magis in se notus conceptus quam conceptus nominis; sed nobis magis notus confusus, I. *Physicorum*. [39] Unde talis conceptus evidenter ostendit unionem sui et habitudinem ad entitatem sui, quando scilicet termini concipiuntur secundum quid et confuse, ut in toto et in parte, unde statim notum est quod omne totum majus est sua parte. Sed non est de terminis compositis simpliciter et distincte, licet sint magis necessariae, non tamen magis nobis notae (*loc. cit.*, f. 22r).

Hence it is clear that (at least as far as self-evident propositions are concerned) distinctness is by no means synonymous with evidence, [40] and that a proposition can well be evident without its terms being known through a distinct analysis into all the components.

3. Self-Evident Propositions with Confused Terms
as Principles of Particular Sciences

We have said before [41] that many of the principles used in particular sciences are not taken from a higher science, but won simply through experience. These are the principles which are self-evident through confused concepts, in opposition to the principles of metaphysics, which are always distinctly conceived, and in opposition likewise to those principles of the higher sciences whose concepts are already known distinctly:

> Principia dupliciter possunt esse nota: uno modo confusa notitia, ut si termini apprehendantur per sensum et experientiam; et hoc sufficit ad scientiam terminorum in scientia qualibet speciali, ut quod linea sit longitudo, ignorando utrum quidditas ejus sit substantia, quantitas vel qualitas, etc. Alio modo possunt cognosci notitia distincta, sciendo ad quod genus pertineat quidditas eorum... (*Reportatio Exam.* prol. q. 2, f. 6r; cf. *Rep. par. ibid.*, n. 5; XXII, 36a) [42]

39. Aristotle, *Physics* I, chap. 1; 184a 16-22.
40. Raymond comes to the same conclusion in his interpretation of Scotus' texts: "La connaissance des termes, requise, n'est pas nécessairement la connaissance distincte qui est exprimée dans la définition. La connaissance confuse, qui, sans atteindre les raisons essentielles et les natures spécifiques, manifeste cependant la nécessité d'un lien objectif entre les termes, peut suffire. Dès lors qu'une proposition a cette aptitude de produire l'évidence par ses propres termes, elle mérite le nom de *per se nota*." (*loc. cit.*, p. 537).
41. *Supra*, p. 149.
42. Cf. also *Oxon.* III, d. 3, q. 3, nn. 6-7; IX, 103a-b; q. 4, n. 22; 190b-191a.

Scotus repeatedly insists on the evidence of these principles known from experience. Far from assigning them an inferior degree of evidence, he places them on the same level with the principles derived through demonstration from subalternating sciences:

> Scientia subalternata...sua principia ut sibi evidentia...cognoscit... quia sunt nota per experientiam aut quia reducuntur in principia superioris scientiae (Report. Exam. prol. q. 3, f. 9v).

Despite the fact that their terms are only confusedly known these propositions are so evident that they dispense with every proof or confirmation on the part of the subalternating sciences; they are evident of themselves:

> Etsi Metaphysicus cognoscens distincte quidditatem lineae vel totius, perfectius cognosceret aliquod principium immediatum de linea vel de toto, quam Geometer tantum confuse cognoscens lineam vel totum, tamen Geometrae est illa propositio immediata per se nota, nec probatur per istam Metaphysici, si[43] ex conceptu confuso terminorum sit[44] complexio vel connectio evidenter vera (Oxon. prol. q. 6, f. 6r, b; Viv. q. 3, n. 29, VIII, 189b-190a).

This applies not only to one or the other particular science but to all of them. On several occasions, when contrasting metaphysics and special sciences, Scotus says, without specification or restriction of any kind, that the principles of the latter are self-evident through the confused apprehension of their terms:

> Sicut patuit ex quaestione illa de propositione per se nota, principia aliarum scientiarum sunt per se nota ex conceptu terminorum confuso (Oxon. I, d. 3, q. 2, f. 27v, a; n. 25, IX, 50a).[45]

Thus, on the one hand, there are self-evident propositions which are known as such only in that science in which the terms are conceived distinctly. These are metaphysical definitions. On the other hand, there are many propositions with confusedly known terms which are self-evident, not because their terms are defined, or capable of being defined by a superior science, or metaphysics, but merely and simply by their own confused terms. It is not without good reasons that Scotus insists so strongly on the distinction between principles of particular sciences and metaphysics. If the terms of every principle in particular sciences had to be defined to become self-evident, then no scientific knowledge would be possible unless it were preceded by a perfect knowledge of meta-

43. Sed Viv.
44. Fit Viv.
45. Cf. Metaph. VI, q. 1, n. 18; VII, 316a-b.

physics. However, just the opposite takes place in the actual order of cognition. For we acquire a distinct or metaphysical knowledge of things only subsequently to the less perfect knowledge of the particular sciences which proceed on the basis of principles composed of confused terms. [46] This is also the reason why Avicenna [47] places metaphysics last in the order of method, and first in the order of distinct knowledge:

> Metaphysica secundum Avicennam...est prima secundum ordinem sciendi distincte, quia ipsa habet certificare principia aliarum scientiarum; igitur ejus cognoscibilia sunt prima distincte cognoscibilia. Nec in hoc contradicit sibi Avicenna quod ponit eam ultimam in ordine doctrinae et primam in sciendo distincte, quia sicut patuit ex quaestione illa de propositione per se nota, principia aliarum scientiarum sunt per se nota ex conceptu terminorum confuso; sed ex Metaphysica scita postea est possibilitas inquirendi quidditatem terminorum distincte, et hoc modo termini scientiarum specialium non concipiuntur, nec principia earum intelliguntur ante Metaphysicam. Sic etiam multa possunt patere metaphysico geometrae, quae non erant prius nota geometrae ex conceptu confuso *(Oxon.* I, d. 3, q. 2, f. 27v, a; n. 25, IX, 50a).

It may be objected that, since these principles of particular sciences are said to be known as self-evident through experience, they fail to fulfill the requirement laid down in the definition of a self-evident proposition, namely, that they must be evident in virtue of their terms alone. To this we answer that Scotus, as the texts show, derives the evidence of these principles from the relation between the terms as such, and not from their actual relation in reality. For since self-evidence, according to definition, is essentially a relation between concepts, it cannot be produced by something merely extrinsic or experimental. What is taken from sense experience is not the self-evidence of the proposition, but the knowledge of the terms. Once the terms have been apprehended in their proper meaning, the intellect no longer regards the experimental data; it merely considers the relation between the terms as they stand in the proposition. This point, however, will be considered more extensively in our treatment on the truth-value of first principles. The rules we shall establish there for first principles or axioms are also applicable in their essential implications to the self-evident propositions in general.

46. Cf. Basil Heiser, O.F.M. Conv., "The *Primum Cognitum* According to Scotus" in *Franciscan Studies,* II, (1942), pp. 200f.
47. *De Philosophia Prima,* tract. III, cap. III.

D. INADEQUATE DISTINCTIONS REJECTED

As a consequence of his definition of the self-evident proposition, Scotus discards certain subdivisions, because they are incompatible with his interpretation of the function of the terms. In the mind of Scotus self-evident propositions are essentially objective structures[48] and therefore independent of actual apprehension on the part of any intellect.

For this reason Scotus first rejects the distinction between *propositio per se nota* and *propositio per se noscibilis*[49] on the grounds that they are simply identical. A proposition is self-evident, not because it is known as such by some intellect (in this case there would be no self-evident proposition unless an intellect were actually conceiving it), but rather because its terms contain evident truth, and because in virtue of these terms it can be conceived as true and evident by every intellect that apprehends the terms. A proposition loses nothing of its self-evidence because it is not actually conceived by some intellect:

> Patet quod distinguere non est inter propositionem per se notam et per se noscibilem, quia idem sunt. Nam propositio non dicitur per se nota quia ab aliquo intellectu per se cognoscitur; tunc enim si nullus intellectus actu cognosceret, nulla propositio esset per se nota; sed dicitur propositio per se nota, quia quantum est de natura terminorum nata est habere evidentem veritatem contentam in terminis, etiam in quocumque intellectu concipiente terminos; si tamen aliquis intellectus non concipiat terminos, et ita non concipiat propositionem, non minus est per se nota quantum est de se, et sic loquimur de per se nota *(Oxon.* I, d. 2, q. 2, f. 14v, b; n. 3, VIII, 399a-b).[50]

Likewise, the distinction between *propositio per se nota in se* and *propositio per se nota in nobis*[51] is meaningless. Every self-evident proposition, although it may not be actually known, is and remains simply self-evident. Since the evidence resides in the terms, the proposition is always evident as far as the terms are concerned. If I apprehend the terms, I also know the self-evident

48. Cf. Schmuecker, *op. cit.*, pp. 131 f.

49. St. Thomas, *Summa Theologica*, I, q. 2, a. 1, c.

50. *Report.* I, d. 3, q. 2, f. 21v: "Distinctio autem non est ad propositum qua dicitur quod propositio potest esse nota per se vel per se noscibilis; sufficit enim quod sit per se noscibilis in terminis, quantum est de se, licet accidentaliter non cognoscatur."

51. *Summa Theologica, loc. cit.*

proposition; if I do not apprehend them, I do not grasp the self-evident proposition. This subjective knowledge or ignorance of the self-evident proposition obviously is no reason for a distinction between a *propositio in se* and *in nobis,* since the whole difference between the two subjective states lies in the apprehension or non-apprehension of the *terms,* neither of which affects the proposition itself. A proposition does not cease to be self-evident because it is ignored, nor does it become self-evident because it is known:

> Ex his patet quod nulla est distinctio de per se nota in se et in nobis, quia quaecumque est in se et per se nota cuicumque intellectui est per se nota, licet non actu cognita; tamen quantum est ex terminis est evidenter nota si termini concipiantur *(ibid.).* [52]

Again, Scotus sees no reason to distinguish between propositions self-evident to the learned and propositions self-evident to the unlearned. Neither of these distinctions (and the same holds true of all the preceding and following distinctions) has any bearing on the intrinsic constitution of the propositions themselves. All of these distinctions are based on the merely extrinsic and accidental factor [53] of the actual apprehension or non-apprehension of the terms, which conditions subjective apprehension: [54]

> Propter idem non valet distinctio quod aliquid est per se notum sapientibus et insipientibus, [55] quia hoc tantum pertinet ad conceptionem terminorum, quae supponitur ad intellectum propositionis per se notae *(ibid.).*

Scotus also extends his objections to the subdivision based on the *communes animi conceptiones* of Boëthius [56] and to the dis-

---

52. *Report., loc. cit.:* "Similiter de nota quoad nos et in se, quia sufficit quod propositio sit de se nota, si sit intellectus cognoscens, evidentia enim patet ex habitudine terminorum."

53. Cf. *supra,* note 59: "...licet *accidentaliter* non cognoscatur."

54. Cf. Raymond, *loc. cit.,* p. 539: "Duns Scot enseigne que la proposition *per se nota* est exposée en termes capables de produire l'évidence en toute intelligence qui les conçoit suffisamment. Mais encore faut-il concevoir ces termes suffisamment. Or les esprits peu cultivés en auront, le plus souvent, une connaissance trop incomplète pour percevoir l'évidence de leur rapport. Pour eux, comme pour les savants, cependant, la proposition *per se nota* est réellement telle. La différence des deux situations ne change rien à la nature de la proposition *per se nota,* toujours identique à elle même: elle a trait seulement à la conception des termes, condition prérequise pour l'intellection actuelle."

55. St. Thomas, *loc. cit.*

56. *Quomodo substantiae bonae sint liber,* PL 64, col. 1311a, B: "Communis animi conceptio est enunciatio quam quisque probat auditam."

tinction between two different orders of self-evident propositions. Some of the Boëthian common conceptions which St. Thomas Aquinas adduces as a justification for his own distinctions are said to be commonly or universally known, whereas others are self-evident only to the wise. These common conceptions of Boëthius, says Scotus, either are not identical with the self-evident propositions in our sense, or else Boëthius, in establishing this subdivision, does not refer to them as actually apprehended, but merely as conceptions which may be apprehended by means of the terms. In this sense Scotus would grant a certain distinction, for terms admit of a more or less perfect degree of distinctness according as they are conceived by an unlearned or by a learned person. The metaphysician often has distinct concepts by which he apprehends certain propositions as self-evident which are not grasped as such by the man in the street who has only confused concepts:

> ...licet sic distinguat Boethius *De Hebdomadibus* communem conceptionem; sed vel non est idem propositio per se nota et communis conceptio, vel ipse intelligit de concepta, non de conceptibili sub ratione terminorum distincte *(ibid.).*

Finally, the distinction between a superior and an inferior order of self-evident propositions, too, is out of place.[57] Every genuinely self-evident proposition is such in virtue of its own terms, and therefore in an unqualified sense. Hence a proposition is either self-evident or it is not self-evident. It cannot be more or less self-evident:[58]

> Nec illa distinctio valet, quod aliquae sunt per se notae primi ordinis, aliquae secundi; quia quaecumque propositiones sunt per se notae conceptis terminis propriis, sicut sunt termini, habent evidentem veritatem in ordine suo *(ibid.).*

In view of the preceding texts it is quite surprising that Claverie[59]

---

57. Lychetus tells us in his commentary (Vivès ed. of Scotus, VIII, 401a) that this distinction proceeds from William of Ware.

58. Cf. H. Straubinger, "Evidenz und Kausalitaetsgesetz" in *Philosophisches Jahrbuch*, XLIII (1930), p. 17: "Mit einer halben oder Viertel-evidenz, wenn es eine solche ueberhaupt gibt, ist nichts gewonnen. Es bleibt wohl bei dem Dilemma: Entweder sind die ersten Grundlagen der Erkenntnis (unmittelbar) evident, oder sie sind nicht evident."

59. A.-Fr. Claverie, O.P., "L'existence de Dieu d'après Duns Scot" in *Revue Thomiste*, XVII (1909), p. 89. Raymond (*loc. cit.*, pp. 536 ff) sees an attenuating circumstance for Claverie's misconceptions in the fact that his remarks were made

could have seen in the rejection of the aforementioned subdivisions an indication that Scotus interprets the self-evident proposition in a subjective sense, as if to be self-evident a proposition would have to be actually evident to the intellect. Far from making it subjective, Scotus safeguards the objectivity of self-evidence by placing it in the terms alone. To Scotus, a proposition is self-evident not because it is actually apprehended by some particular intellect, but because it can be apprehended by any intellect which grasps the proper meaning of the terms.

E. FURTHER CLARIFICATIONS AND APPLICATIONS

1. No Proposition is Apprehended as Self-Evident
Unless its Terms are Apprehended in their Proper Meaning

The remainder of Scotus' discussion centers about the question whether or not it is self-evident that God exists. This problem gives the Franciscan Doctor the opportunity to discuss from new angles the important question of the function of the terms in self-evident propositions.

Scotus maintains that if the proposition, "Deus est," is taken in the sense of the *esse Dei in se,*[60] then it is self-evident. When the terms, "this divine Essence," and "exists," are combined, they constitute a proposition in which all the requirements for self-evidence are satisfied. For it is a proposition of the first mode of predication the terms of which are distinctly conceived. It is not, however, asserted that man in his present state is able to know this proposition evidently, for he does not grasp the terms in their proper meaning, as they are perceived by God and the Blessed:

> Propositio illa est per se nota quae conjungit extrema ista esse et essentiam divinam ut haec est, sive Deum et esse sibi proprium quomodo Deus videt illam essentiam et esse sub propriissima ratione qua est in Deo hoc esse. Quomodo nec esse a nobis nunc intelligitur, nec essentia, sed ab ipso Deo et a Beatis, quia propositio illa ex suis terminis habet evidentem veritatem intellectui, quia illa propositio non est per se se-

---

at the occasion of an article by Belmond ("L'existence de Dieu" in *Revue de Phil.,* Sept.-Oct. 1908) whose interpretations of Scotus are not "tout à fait *ad litteram,* et les notes critiques du R.P. Claverie en reproduisent les particularités."

60. *Report.* I, d. 3, q. 2, f. 21v: "(Propositio) 'Deus est'...intelligendo de Deo in se et de esse Dei in se...est per se nota." ›

cundo modo, quasi praedicatum sit extra rationem subjecti, sed per se primo modo immediata ex terminis est evidens *(Oxon.* I, d. 2, q. 2, f. 14v, b; n. 4, VIII, 402b-403a).

Scotus admits that man is able to formulate several concepts of God which do not apply to God and creature, as, for instance, the concepts of Necessary and Infinite Being, of Highest Good, etc. But if it is asked whether existence is self-evidently implied in such concepts, Scotus' answer is negative. His reasons are, first, that propositions formulated of such concepts can be demonstrated; secondly, that they can either be demonstrated or believed; thirdly, that the parts of the mentioned concepts do not constitute a self-evident unity. First, then, the said propositions can, at least absolutely speaking, be demonstrated. According to the rules of demonstrative sciences everything contained in and conceivable of the Divine Essence can be demonstrated of it as through a middle term, at least by those who know Divine Essence *ut haec.* Scotus does not say that such a demonstration is actually made either by the human intellect or by the Blessed. The former is unable to make it, and the latter most probably have no need of it. Yet such a demonstration is possible. This is sufficient to establish the non-evidence of the propositions in question, for no proposition that admits of a demonstration is self-evident:

> Si quaeratur an esse insit alicui conceptui quem nos concipimus de Deo, ita quod talis propositio sit per se nota...puta potest in intellectu nostro esse aliquis conceptus dictus de Deo, tamen non communis sibi et creaturae, puta necessario esse, vel ens infinitum, vel summum bonum... Dico quod nulla talis est per se nota propter tria. Primo quia quaelibet talis est conclusio demonstrabilis [61] et propter quid. Probatio, quidquid primo et immediate convenit alicui, de quolibet quod est in eo potest demonstrari propter quid per illud cui primo convenit tamquam per medium...Nulla igitur complexio...de Deo est primo vera sed per aliud vera et per consequens non est primo et per se nota *(Oxon.* I, d. 2. q. 2, f. 15r, a; n. 5, VIII, 405a-b).

Secondly, a self-evident proposition should be evident to every intellect which conceives the terms. Our propositions about God, such as "An infinite Being exists," "A highest Good exists," are not self-evident to us by virtue of the terms. We may well be in possession of the terms and yet it will not be until some time later

---

61. Demonstrata *Ass. MS.* We have chosen here the Vivès version because it seems to fit better into the context.

that either we accept these propositions on faith, or before we arrive at a certain knowledge of them through a demonstrative process of reasoning.[62] No proposition, however, which needs belief or demonstration in order to assume the character of true certitude, is self-evident:

> Secundo sic: propositio per se nota cuilibet intellectui ex terminis cognitis est per se nota, sed haec propositio, ens infinitum est, non est evidens intellectui nostro ex terminis. Probo: terminos enim nos concipimus antequam eam credamus vel per demonstrationem sciamus, et in illo priori non est nobis evidens; non enim certitudinaliter eam tenemus ex terminis nisi per fidem vel demonstrationem *(ibid.* VIII, 405b).

Thirdly, nothing is known self-evidently of a concept which is not irreducibly simple unless it is first self-evident that the component parts of that concept constitute a unity. None of our proper concepts of God are irreducibly simple, at least none of those we apprehend distinctly as proper to God. Consequently, nothing will be self-evident of such concepts unless their component parts are self-evidently associated. This association, however, is not self-evident, because it fails to produce certitude except through demonstration:

> Tertio, quia nihil est per se notum de conceptu non simpliciter simplici, nisi sit per se notum partes illius conceptus uniri. Nullus autem conceptus quem habemus de Deo, proprius sibi et non conveniens creaturae, est simpliciter simplex, vel saltem nullus quem nos distincte percipimus esse proprium Deo est simpliciter simplex; ergo nihil est per se notum de tali conceptu, nisi sit per se notum partes illius conceptus uniri; sed hoc non est per se notum, quia unio illarum partium demonstratur per duas rationes[63] *(ibid.;* VIII, 405b-406a).

Proof of the major premise of this syllogism: It can be shown from a passage of Aristotle that nothing is self-evidently predicated of a non-irreducibly simple concept unless the parts of the latter are known to constitute a true unity. According to the Philosopher,[64] a concept which is false in itself is false of everything else. No concept can be truly predicated of anything unless it is true in itself, nor can it serve as a subject of which something is predicated.

---

62. It seems that Scotus is here referring to the demonstration *a posteriori* which is possible *to us*, contrary to the hypothetical *a priori* demonstration of the preceding text.

63. Ergo nihil.../ om. *Ass. MS.*

64. *Metaphysics* IV, c. 29; 1024b, 27-32.

Consequently, before a proposition is formulated in which a non-irreducibly simple term occurs, we must first ascertain whether the component parts of the concept expressed in such a term constitute a
true unity. No true or self-evident proposition can result if this condition is absent. Thus the proposition, "Homo irrationalis est animal," cannot be self-evident, because the subject includes contradictory elements:

> Major manifesta est per Philosophum 5. *Metaph. cap. de Falso,* quia
> ratio in se falsa est de omni falsa; ergo nulla ratio est de aliquo vera
> nisi sit in se vera; ergo ad hoc quod cognoscatur aliquod esse verum de
> aliqua ratione, vel ipsam esse veram de aliquo, oportet cognoscere
> ipsam in se esse veram. Non est autem ratio in se vera nisi partes
> illius rationis sint unitae...Exemplum, illa (propositio): Homo irrationalis
> est animal, non est per se nota, loquendo de praedicatione quidditativa,
> quia subjectum in se includit falsum, quia propositionem in se includen-
> tem contradictoria *(ibid.* VIII, 406a).

Proof of the minor premise of the syllogism: None of the irreducibly simple concepts which we predicate of God are proper to Him
unless we determine them in such a way as to render them capable
of being applied to God alone. In other words, we must transform
the irreducibly simple concepts into composed concepts. The
concepts of *true* and *good,* for instance, (which, by reason of their
transcendentality and coextension [65] with the concept of being
belong to the order of irreducibly simple notions) cannot be predicated of God in the proper sense unless a qualification is added to
make them composite concepts.

> Probatio minoris. Quemcumque conceptum concipimus sive boni sive
> veri, si non contrahatur per aliquid ut non sit conceptus simpliciter sim-
> plex, ut dicendo: summum bonum, vel infinitum bonum, vel increatum,
> vel immensum, et sic de aliis [66] non est proprius conceptus Deo *(ibid.).*

2. Self-Evidence not in Proportion to Necessity of Terms

Among the arguments in favor of the self-evidence of the existence of an Infinite Being, one is found which tries to base the
self-evidence of the propositions concerning the Highest Being on
the greater necessity of the terms. The reasoning proceeds as
follows. We have propositions which are self-evident although they
are so merely accidentally (*secundum quid*), for their self-evidence

65. Wolter, *op. cit.,* p. 89.
66. Ut dicendo.../ *add. Viv.*

proceeds from terms which exist only in the intellect, and hence have only an accidental entity. A fortiori, the evidence of a proposition which is formulated of absolutely *(simpliciter)* necessary terms must even be superior, as its terms are of greater necessity. Scotus' opponents base their inference on the fact that the existence or non-existence of the terms *in re* is absolutely irrelevant for the necessity and knowability of the first principles. They are knowable and necessary through the mutual relation or connection of the terms as they are conceived in the intellect:

> Propositiones habentes veritatem secundum quid ex terminis habentibus entitatem secundum quid, scilicet ex hoc quod sunt in intellectu, sunt per se notae, sicut prima principia...; ergo multo magis erit per se nota quae habet necessitatem ex terminis simpliciter necessariis vel notis, qualis est illa: Deus est. Assumptum patet, quia necessitas primorum principiorum et noscibilitas eorum non est propter existentiam terminorum in re, sed tantum propter connexionem extremorum, ut est in intellectu concipiente *(Oxon.* I, d. 2, q. 2, f. 14v, a; n. 1, 395 VIII, 395b).

Scotus' answer to this argument makes it clear that the evidence of a proposition is neither dependent on, nor in proportion to, the necessity of its terms. The definition of a self-evident proposition disregards every qualification of the terms; it is not the intrinsic necessity of the terms which is responsible for self-evidence, but only the relationship existing between the terms. Self-evidence consists in the evidence of the conformity between the composition (i.e., the proposition as a whole) and its terms. No proposition which lacks this conformity between composition and terms is to be considered self-evident, however necessary its terms may be. Thus the proposition "Ens infinitum est" is not known as evident by our intellect through the terms, despite the necessity of the Being to which they refer.

Conversely, there are propositions whose terms are less necessary and still are truly self-evident, due to the evident relation between the terms. The proposition, "The whole is greater than any of its parts," is evident to every mind which perceives the terms and their meaning, even though the entities for which they stand may be not necessary at all. The proposition would remain self-evident even if its terms were conceived only in the intellect and independently of every reality. The necessity of the terms or of their correspondents in reality, therefore, has no bearing on the evidence of the proposition:

> Ad ultimum dico quod non dicuntur propositiones per se notae, quia extrema habent majorem necessitatem in se, sive majorem in re extra intellectum, sed quia extrema ut sunt extrema talis propositionis evidenter ostendunt complexionem esse conformem rationibus terminorum et habitudini eorum, et hoc qualecumque esse termini habeant, sive in re sive in intellectu.
>
> Evidentia enim hujus conformitatis est evidentia veritatis in propositione, quod est propositionem esse per se notam. Nunc autem ista: Ens infinitum est in intellectu nostro, non nata est habere evidentiam ex terminis, sed bene ista:[67] Omne totum est majus sua parte...in quocumque intellectu concipiente terminos nata est habere talem evidentiam ex terminis...qualecumque esse termini habeant, et ideo licet sit major necessitas terminorum, non sequitur quod sit minor evidentia propositionum *(loc. cit.,* 15r, b; n. 9, VIII, 409a).

In order that the reader may obtain an overall view of Scotus' concept of a self-evident proposition and of the function of the terms, we shall close the present chapter with a short summary of its main conclusions.

SUMMARY OF CONCLUSIONS

1. By saying that a proposition is known *per se* we do not exclude every causality *(Oxon.* I, d. 2, q. 2, n. 2; VIII, 396a).

2. The expression *per se* does not indicate that the proposition is innate in the intellect *(Metaph.* II, q. 1, n. 2; VII, 97a).

3. *Per se* indicates that the cause of the truth and certitude of a self-evident proposition is nothing else but its own proper terms *(Oxon.* I, d. 2, q. 2, n. 2; VIII, 396a).

4. A proposition is called *per se* evident, in opposition to the conclusion of a syllogism, which is evident *per aliud (Oxon.* I, d. 2, q. 2, n. 2; VIII, 396a-b).

5. A self-evident proposition is composed of either distinct or confused terms *(loc. cit.,* 396b).

6. Confused knowledge precedes distinct knowledge *(ibid.).*

7. Propositions with distinct terms are evident through distinct concepts *(Oxon.* I, d. 2, q. 2, n. 3; 398b).

8. Propositions with confused terms are self-evident in virtue of confused concepts *(ibid.).*

---

67. Ens infinitum.../ *om. Assisi MS.*

9. No proposition is self-evident which is formulated with confused terms which must be defined. *(ibid.)*.

10. Propositions composed of irreducibly simple terms are immediately evident *(loc. cit.,* n. 5; 406a).

11. Propositions composed of non-irreducibly simple concepts are not self-evident unless it is self-evident that the component parts of the concepts constitute a unity *(ibid.)*.

12. The self-evidence of a proposition is neither dependent on, nor in proportion to, the necessity of its terms *(loc. cit.,* n. 9; 409a).

13. Self-evident propositions are either of the first or of the second mode of predication *(Report.* I, d. 3, q. 2, f. 21v).

14. No proposition of the first mode is self-evident unless a metaphysical or essential definition of the terms is first given. In contrast, many propositions of the second mode are truly self-evident in virtue of a confused knowledge of the terms *(loc. cit.,* f. 22r).

15. Principles of subalternate sciences are evident either by derivation from the subalternating science, or through experience *(Report.* prol. q. 3, f. 9v).

16. Many principles of particular sciences are known self-evidently through confused terms taken from experience *(Oxon.* prol. q. 3, n. 29; VIII, 189b; *Rep. Paris.* prol. q. 2, n. 5; XXII, 36a).

17. No proposition is known as self-evident unless the terms are apprehended in their proper meaning. Hence a proposition that is self-evident to the metaphysician may not be so to the geometrician, not because the proposition itself is less self-evident, but because the geometrician is unable to conceive the proper meaning of the terms *(Oxon.* I, d. 3, q. 2, n. 25; IX, 50a). Likewise, although the proposition "Deus est" is self-evident, we cannot conceive it as such, due to our imperfect apprehension of the terms *(Oxon.* I, d. 2, q. 2, n. 4; VIII, 402b-403a).

18. There is no distinction between a *propositio per se nota* and *per se noscibilis,* or between a *propositio per se nota in se* and *in nobis,* or between a *propositio per se nota sapientibus* and *insipientibus.* The apprehension or non-apprehension of the terms (on which these distinctions are based) does not affect the proposition itself, and is, therefore, no reason for the aforementioned subdivisions *(Oxon.* I, d. 2, q. 2, n. 3; VIII, 399a).

CHAPTER II
EPISTEMOLOGICAL ASPECTS OF SELF-EVIDENT
PROPOSITIONS

In his detailed analysis of the self-evident proposition, Scotus does not overlook its significance in the scheme of human knowledge. The conclusion of the question just analyzed points to the *propositio per se nota* as constituting a most sure source of true knowledge. Scotus identifies the self-evidence of propositions with the evidence of truth. It is the self-evidence of truth which causes a proposition to become self-evident:

> Evidentia enim hujus conformitatis (compositionis ad extrema) est evidentia veritatis in propositione, quod est propositionem esse per se notam (*Oxon.* I, d. 2, q. 2, f. 15r, b; n. 9, VIII, 409a).

This is a fitting transition to the important question[1] which contains Scotus' detailed and *ex professo* treatment of the truth-value of the self-evident proposition. It is true that in the present question Scotus speaks mainly of the *prima principia*. But as has been said before,[2] Scotus' conception of a self-evident proposition in general, does not differ from his conception of the first principles. Hence the following considerations are applicable (at least in their essential implications) to all self-evident propositions.

A. OBJECTIVE EVIDENCE AND SUBJECTIVE
CERTITUDE IN FIRST PRINCIPLES

Scotus' intention here is to prove, against the sceptics, that the human intellect is capable of acquiring certain and infallible cognitions. One of these is the cognition of first principles. It is well to recall some of the conditions which Scotus has laid down regarding certitude. Only that knowledge is certain "which excludes every deception and doubt."[3] There is no certitude in the apprehension of truth unless the intellect is aware that what it appre-

1. *Oxon.* I, d. 3, q. 4, nn. 7-8; IX, 173a-174b.
2. *Supra*, p. 124.
3. *Quodl.* q. 17, n. 11; XXVI, 220a; *Oxon.* prol. q. 3, n. 26; VIII, 183b.

hends is true.[4] The intellect must perceive "that from which the act derives its certitude:"

> Et hoc (scil. certitudo excludens deceptionem et dubitationem) non est nisi intellectus percipiat id a quo actus habet quod sit certus (*Quodl.* q. 17, n. 11; XXVI, 220a).

In other words, our knowledge, in order to be truly certain, must be based on objective evidence. As stated in the first part of this dissertation,[5] Scotus identifies objective evidence with the entity of the object itself. All objects are evident in themselves, i.e., they can be known as to their entity by every adequate intellect. This holds true, not only of real objects, but also of logical structures; for these too are objectively true, regardless of any apprehending intellect.

1. *Basis of Certitude: Mutual Inclusion of the Extremes*

Scotus describes the objective character of the evidence of first principles in terms of identity, and in terms of a relation of mutual and necessary inclusion existing between the extremes:

> Quantum ad certitudinem de principiis. dico sic: termini principiorum per se notorum talem habent identitatem ut alter evidenter necessario alterum includat (*Oxon.* I, d. 3, q. 4, f. 31v, a; n. 7, IX, 173b).

The terms of self-evident principles include one another in a necessary and evident manner because they are identical, in the sense that the predicate is essentially contained in the subject. Thus in the principle, "Every whole is greater than any of its parts," the term "part" is contained in the term "whole" so that the latter cannot even be conceived without the former. The principle, therefore, is formulated on the basis of an objective relation between the terms, or, in other words, on the basis of objective evidence. The first principles are no arbitrary constructions of the mind. As logical structures they possess their own intrinsic truth-value, independently of the apprehending intellect. This is why, according to Scotus, "a proposition is not said to be self-evident because it is known as such by some particular intellect. For then,

---

4. *Metaph.* I, q. 4, n. 12; VII, 58a: "Certitudo nunquam est in apprehendendo verum, nisi talis sciat...illud esse verum quod apprehendit." Vide *supra*, pp. 104 ff.
5. *Supra*, pp. 71 ff.

if no intellect were actually perceiving it, there would be no self-evident proposition. A proposition is called self-evident because, through the nature of the terms, it is able to be true (i.e., to be known as true) by reason of the evident truth contained in the terms, and this in any intellect conceiving the terms. If, however, some intellect does not conceive the terms nor consequently the proposition, the latter is herewith not less self-evident in itself." [6]

2. *Subjective Certitude of First Principles*

It has been shown that the mutual relation between the terms of the principles is objectively necessary and evident. As a consequence, as soon as the terms are conceived and compared with each other by the intellect, the same relation becomes subjectively known. This relation is immediately expressed by the intellect in the form of a proposition or "composition." With the terms and their objective relation the intellect is also given the necessary cause of the conformity of the composition with the terms themselves. Since a necessary cause never fails to produce its effect,[7] it follows that the said conformity is necessarily known to the mind. It is not in the power of the intellect to refuse to see the relation between the terms once it has apprehended them in their proper meaning. Scotus compares the conformity between composition and terms to the likeness existing between two white objects. As it is impossible that there is no likeness between the latter so it is impossible not to apprehend the conformity between the former:

> Et ideo intellectus componens illos terminos, ex quo apprehendit eos, habet apud se necessariam causam conformitatis illius actus componendi ad ipsos terminos quorum est compositio, et etiam causam evidentem talis conformitatis; et ideo necessario patet sibi illa conformitas cujus causam necessariam et[8] evidentem apprehendit in terminis; igitur non potest in intellectu apprehensio esse terminorum et compositio eorum, quin stet conformitas illius compositionis ad terminos sicut stare non potest album et album quin stet similitudo *(ibid.)*.

The conformity between terms and composition constitutes the truth of the composition. Since there is a necessary mutual relation

6. For Scotus' original text see *supra*, p. 165.
7. *Supra*, p. 99.
8. Necessariam et *om. Ass. MS.*

between the terms, it follows that the composition by which the
same relation is expressed is also necessarily true. It likewise
follows that it is impossible for the intellect to conceive the terms
and their composition without perceiving simultaneously the conformity of the composition with the terms, or, in other words, without apprehending the truth of the composition. For this truth is
evidently contained in the terms and their composition:

> Haec autem conformitas compositionis ad terminos est veritas compo-
> sitionis; ergo non potest stare compositio talium terminorum quin sit
> vera; et ita non potest stare perceptio illius compositionis et perceptio
> terminorum, quin stet perceptio conformitatis compositionis ad terminos,
> et ita perceptio veritatis, quia prima percepta evidenter includunt per-
> ceptionem istius veritatis *(ibid.)*.

As is implicit in the cited text, the intellect also assents necessarily to the composition thus obtained. Once the composition is
formulated, the intellect is as incapable of refusing its assent to
such a proposition as it is incapable of denying the principle of
contradiction. Aristotle writes[9] that the mind is unable to grasp the
opposite of the principle of contradiction. For this would suppose
the coexistence in the mind of two formally repugnant propositions, one affirming and the other denying the same predicate of
the same subject. This is an intellectual impossibility. A similar
repugnance (although not formally the same) obtains between the
affirmation and the negation of any first principle. Thus the denial
of the proposition, "The whole is greater than its part," is incompatible with the apprehension of the terms "whole" and "part" and
of the relation between them. For in the terms and their composition
the conformity of the composition with the terms is contained as in
a necessary cause. If the intellect were to consider a proposition
thus formulated as false, then two virtually repugnant cognitions
would be present in the mind.[10] In fact, to admit that a self-evident
proposition and its opposite can exist simultaneously in the mind

9. *Metaphysics* III, c. 4; 1005b 35 - 1006a 4.
10. Cf. R. Messner, O.F.M., *Schauendes und begriffliches Erkennen nach Duns
Skotus* (Freiburg, 1942), p. 220: "Es waere widersinnig, einerseits den Inhalt des
Praedikatsbegriffes als Teil des Subjektsinhaltes zu denken und anderseits die
Zusammengehoerigkeit des vom Praedikat Gemeinten zu dem vom Subjekt Gemeinten
zu leugnen."

is equivalent to admitting that two contradictory cognitions 'can be produced, and necessarily produced, by one and the same cause (i.e., the terms and their composition). This, obviously, is impossible. In the same manner as it is impossible for white and black to exist together by reason of their formal contrariety, so it is unthinkable that whiteness be found in association with that which is not only the necessary but also the exclusive cause of blackness. Again, darkness and light are exclusive of each other. Let it be supposed that the sun is the only source of light, and furthermore that it produces light necessarily. Under this presupposition it must be admitted that, as it is impossible for darkness and light to exist together, so it is also impossible for darkness to be found together with that necessary and exclusive cause of light which is the sun. Similar to the relation between light and sun is the relation between the truth of principles and their causes, i.e., the terms and their composition. For the latter, as has already been pointed out, exercise the function of an exclusive and necessary causality with regard to the truth of principles. Hence, as the sun can only produce light and exclude darkness, so the terms and their composition can only engender certain and evident knowledge of truth, and exclude deception and falsity:

> Confirmatur ratio ista per simile per Philosophum IV *Metaph.*, ubi vult quod oppositum primi principii non potest in intellectu alicujus venire, scilicet hujus: impossibile idem esse et non esse, quia tunc essent opiniones contrariae simul in mente... Ita arguam in proposito repugnantiam aliquam intellectionum in mente, licet non formalem; si enim stat in intellectu notitia totius et partis et compositio eorum, cum ista includant sicut causa necessaria conformitatem compositionis ad terminos, si stat in intellectu haec opinio quod ipsa compositio sit falsa, stabunt notitiae repugnantes, non formaliter, sed notitia una stabit cum alia, et tamen una erit causa necessaria oppositae notitiae ad illam, quod est impossibile; sicut enim impossibile est album et nigrum simul stare, quia sunt contraria formaliter, ita impossibile est simul stare album et illud quod est praecise causa nigri, ita necessario quod non potest esse sine eo, absque contradictione (*Oxon.* I, d. 3, q. 4, f. 31v, a; n. 8, IX, 173b-174a).

The Scotistic doctrine on the first principles is faced with a peculiar problem inasmuch as their evidence is placed in the sole apprehension and comparison of the terms. It is well known that for Aristotle and his followers there is no intellectual cognition without a preceding sense perception. Now, what will be the function of sense perception with regard to the truth-value and evidence of the principles?

B. THE FUNCTION OF THE SENSES
IN FIRST PRINCIPLES

Scotus, as we have seen, speaks not only of an evident knowledge, but even of a *necessarily* evident knowledge of self-evident propositions and first principles. And this, despite the fact that the terms of these propositions are taken from sensible contingent things. How, it may be asked, can terms obtained from contingent things produce a necessary relation in the mind, as the terms of principles do? It would seem that the inescapable evidence of first principles cannot be sufficiently accounted for through sense perception. For an effect cannot be more perfect than its cause. Only two ways can lead us out of this empasse. Either we admit that the intellect has an inborn knowledge of the principles, or we must deny to sense perception the function of true causality and lay a correspondingly stronger stress on the activity of the intellect.

1. *First Principles are not Innate*

Scotus does not admit an inborn knowledge flowing from the very nature of the intellect. Against Plato [11] he defends the need of experience for all knowledge, including first principles. In fact, if we knew them by nature, they could not remain hidden to us. But actually we do not become aware of the principles before we have acquired them through study. Hence they cannot be inborn:

> Contra opinionem Platonis arguit Aristoteles [12] II *Post.*, cap. ult., sic: Inconveniens est cognitiones certissimas demonstrantem latere: sed antequam addiscantur, non percipimus eas in nobis; ergo non insunt (*Metaph.* I, q. 4, n. 9; VII, 56a).

As Aristotle [13] puts it, the soul is of itself like a blank page, on which as yet nothing is written. Scotus' application of the Aris-

---

11. For a detailed refutation of Plato's doctrine on reminiscence vide *Metaph.* I, q. 4; nn. 8-10; VII, 55b-57a.
12. *Posterior Analytics* II, c. 19; 99b 24-27.
13. *De anima* III, c. 4; 429b 32-430a 2.

totelian formula to the first principles is even more emphatic. He remarks that the fact that our intellect cannot err concerning first principles is no reason for saying that they are given with the intellect, or identical with it, as it were:

> Intellectus noster non est sua prima principia intelligibilia, quia ante omnia intelligere est sicut tabula rasa, in qua nihil depictum est, et tamen intellectus noster circa prima principia non potest errare *(Oxon.* II, d. 23, q. un., n. 5; XIII, 160b).[14]

If it is said, at times, that first principles are innate, this must be taken in the sense that they are grasped by the intellect's own power or "light:"

> Non enim sic sunt principia intellectui innata, quod sint sibi concreata, sed pro tanto dicuntur innata, quia sunt sicut januae...quia statim ex sensu occurrunt notis terminis ex lumine ipsius intellectus *(Rep. Paris.* II, d. 23, q. un., n. 3; XXIII, 107b).

Although the intellect apprehends the principles by its own intrinsic power, this does not mean that it needs no help whatsoever from othér faculties. It can never dispense with the help of the senses. For it is through the senses that the *simplicia* or *incomplexa,* i.e., the subject and predicate, are apprehended. Hence even in the formulation of first principles the usual process of knowledge takes place, at least in the first three of the four steps which Scotus distinguishes in the genesis of knowledge: First, the senses are stimulated by a simple object; secondly, the sense-datum is transmitted to the intellect whose first act is the intellection of the same simple datum; thirdly, the intellect composes one simple datum with another, i.e., it formulates a proposition by either affirming or denying the one of the other; fourthly, in the case of first principles, the intellect gives immediate assent to the truth of the proposition, and that in virtue of its own "natural light:"

> Omnis nostra cognitio ortum habet ex sensu. Primo enim movetur sensus ab aliquo simplici, non complexo, et a sensu moto movetur intellectus, et intelligit simplicia, quod est primus actus intellectus; deinde post apprehensionem simplicium sequitur alius actus, qui est componere simplicia ad invicem; post illam autem compositionem habet intellectus ex lumine naturali quod assentiat veritati complexorum, si illud complexum sit principium primum *(Metaph.* II, q. 1, n. 2; VII, 96b).[15]

14. Cf. *Rep. Paris.* II, d. 23, q. un., n. 3; XXIII, 107b.
15. Cf. also *Metaph.* VI, q. 3, n. 7; VII, 339a.

First principles have this in common with every other process of knowledge, that they start from sense perception. However, they differ from them inasmuch as they are always true, and knowable as such, independently of true or false sense perception. This brings us to our second point.

2. Sense Perception, Occasional Cause of Evidence in First Principles

Scotus grants that the intellect cannot act unless it is stimulated by sense perception. However, he does not exaggerate the dependence of intellectual activity on sense perception to the point of making the trustworthiness of every mental judgment dependent on the trustworthiness of the senses. This is plain from his definition of a *propositio per se nota*. A self-evident proposition is not defined on the basis of sense apprehension but on the basis of the terms. It follows that the evidence of such a proposition can be apprehended by the intellect even though the senses should deceive us.[16] For the senses play here the role of a merely occasional cause, or of a *conditio sine qua non*. If the intellect apprehends the simple concepts "whole" and "greater than" by experience, it has all it needs' to formulate the principle, "The whole is greater than any of its parts," and this, regardless of whether the terms are obtained through erring senses. The intellect also assents to this proposition by its own power and in virtue of the terms as they stand in the proposition, and not only because it has seen the relation between the terms *in re*, as is the case with contingent propositions:

> Sed numquid in ista notitia principiorum et conclusionum non errabit intellectus, si sensus omnes decipiantur circa terminos? - Respondeo quantum ad istam notitiam quod intellectus non habet sensus pro causa, sed tantum pro occasione, quia intellectus non potest habere notitiam simplicium nisi acceptam a sensibus; illa tamen accepta, virtute sua potest simul componere simplicia; et si ex ratione talium simplicium sit complexio evidenter vera, intellectus virtute propria et terminorum

16. This seems to be one of the reasons why Scotus gives the axiom "Nihil est in intellectu quod non prius fuerit in sensu" the less exclusive formulation: "Omnis nostra cognitio ortum habet in sensu" (*Metaph.* II, q. 1, n. 2; VII, 96b). Cf. S. Belmond, O.F.M., "Le mécanisme de la connaissance d'après Jean Duns Scot" in *La France Franciscaine*, XIII (1930), p. 309.

assentiet illi complexioni, non virtute sensus a quo accipit terminos exterius. - Exemplum: Si ratio totius et ratio maioritatis accipiantur a sensu, et intellectus componat istam, omne totum est majus sua parte, intellectus virtute sui et istorum terminorum assentiet indubitanter isti complexioni, et non tantum quia vidit terminos conjunctos in re, sicut assentit isti, Sortes est albus, quia vidit terminos in re uniri *(Oxon.* I, d. 3, q. 4, f. 31v, a; n. 8, IX, 174a-174b).

Scotus goes further. He maintains that the intellect is never deceived with regard to first principles, not even on the assumption that all our senses erred, or what would be even worse, that some senses were wrong and some right. Since the terms are the exclusive cause of truth in such propositions, the intellect can apprehend their truth as soon and as long as it is in possession of the terms:

> Imo dico quod si omnes sensus essent falsi, a quibus accipiuntur tales termini, vel quod plus est ad deceptionem, aliqui sensus falsi, et aliqui sensus veri, intellectus circa talia principia non deciperetur, quia semper haberet apud se terminos qui essent causa veritatis *(ibid).*

In his commentary on metaphysics, Scotus explains the reason why first principles produce infallible certainty in the intellect even though the terms are apprehended through deceptive sense perception. With regard to first principles, the intellect depends on sense perception for its first operation only, i.e., for the simple apprehension of the terms. The composition of the terms is effected independently of the senses:

> Intellectus judicat...per notitiam ab actu sensus acceptam occasionaliter, vel quoad apprehensionem simplicium, non quoad compositionem principiorum *(Metaph.* I, q. 4, n. 13; VII, 58b).

The first operation of the intellect is always true[17] even when it follows upon an erroneous sense perception. Thus the simple concept of whiteness obtained by falsely apprehending a black object as white is exactly identical with the concept of whiteness obtained from a white object. For a true concept of whiteness it is sufficient that a species or image truly representing whiteness be transmitted to the intellect:

> Prima operatio intellectus semper vera est, licet sequens sensum errantem; ita enim concipitur albedo, si visus apprehendit illud esse

---

17. For an explanation of how simple concepts may be considered as true cf. *supra,* pp. 56 ff.

album quod est nigrum, sicut si albedo conciperetur a sensu vere vi-
dente album, quia sufficit quod species vere repraesentativa albi ve-
niat ad intellectum, ad hoc ut simplici apprehensione album vere appre-
hendatur *(loc. cit.,* n. 14; 59a).

3. *Experience Helpful in Acquisition of First*
Principles

The above considerations concerning the role of sense perception in first principles may give rise to the impression that
Scotus underrates the importance of experience in his theory of
knowledge. This, however, is not the case. We must bear in mind
that in the present question the Franciscan Doctor is opposing
absolute scepticism which denies every kind of knowledge and
certainty based on sense perception. [18] In order to convince these
thinkers of at least one certain cognition, Scotus was obliged, if
not to disregard sense perception altogether, at least to avoid
basing his argumentation on it as on a trustworthy source of information. All he wants his opponents to acknowledge is that we do
have some sense perceptions which furnish us certain notions or
terms, as, for instance, the notion of "whole" and of "part," or of
"being" and "not-being." It makes no difference whether or not
these terms have any objective validity. Scotus shows that, as
soon as this is admitted, the intellect is in possession of the
elements with which to formulate first evident principles, and
this independently of any outward reality, and in spite of any illusion in the senses.

On the other hand, Scotus realizes that the number of absolute
sceptics is rather limited. Furthermore, nobody is more firmly convinced of the reliability of sense perception than Scotus, provided
the senses are controlled and checked by the intellect. Far from
underrating experience, he considers it a valuable ally of the intellect, even for the acquisition of first principles. He actually asserts
that the truth of certain principles can be known through frequent
sensible, memorative and experimental cognition which shows the
association in actually existing things of the terms of the principles. Thus the principle, "Every whole is greater than any of its

---

18. Cf. Scotus' introductory remark: *Oxon.* I, d. 3, q. 4, n. 7; IX, 173a: "Ut in
nullis cognoscibilibus locum habeat error Academicorum..."

parts," can be arrived at through repeated observation of the relation between a concrete whole and its parts:

> Conceptus autem complexi, si sint primorum principiorum...etiam cog-
> nosci possunt quia veri sunt ex frequenti cognitione sensitiva, memora-
> tiva, et experimentali, per quas cognoscimus terminos talis principii, in
> suis singularibus in re esse conjunctos, sicut sensus frequenter vidit
> hanc totalitatem et hanc minoritatem conjungi (*Metaph.* I, q. 4, n. 4; VII,
> 53b).

Needless to say that Scotus' admission of experimental knowledge
as conducive to evident principles does not militate against his
definition which places evidence in the terms. On the one hand,
Scotus' definition of the self-evident proposition does not exclude
sense perception but only the need of a *trustworthy* sense perception; on the other hand, knowledge of principles through experience does not dispense with the terms. Experience leads up to the
principle precisely because it sees the association *of the terms in
re*.

Scotus repeatedly states that experimental knowledge[19] is helpful
in moving the intellect to give a readier assent to affirmative and
negative principles, if the composition or division of the extremes
is apprehended by the senses. Sensible apprehension of the composition or division, however, is not necessarily required to produce
assent to the truth, although experience cannot be dispensed with
for the apprehension of the terms. The intellect gives immediate
assent to the principle of contradiction, even though the senses
never apprehend a formal affirmation or negation in reality.[20] And
supposing that the senses do actually apprehend the association or
dissociation of terms in reality, yet the certitude produced by the

---

19. "Experientia," in the scholastic sense, means a "frequens acceptio sensibilium" (*Metaph.* I, q. 4, n. 5; VII, 53b).

20. Cf. E. Gilson, "Avicenne et le point de départ de Duns Scot" in *Archives
d'histoire doctrinale et littéraire du moyen âge*, II (1927), p. 122: "Personne n'a
jamais vu de ses yeux une *affirmation* ni une *négation;* cependant, une fois que
l'intellect a formé ces deux concepts à partir du sensible, il est capable de con-
clure: *de omni est affirmatio vera, vel negatio vera.* Prétendra-t-on que l'intellect
ait été renseigné par les sens sur la vérité de cette proposition? Evidamment non;
jamais nous n'avons perçu le rapport d'une chose à son affirmation ou à sa négation,
pas plus qu'une affirmation ou une négation en elle-même; la position de ce rapport
est donc l'oeuvre du seul intellect.

natural light of the intellect is still greater than that proceeding from sense experience. Even if a sense perception is false and known as such, the intellect nevertheless is able to formulate a true principle by means of the simple notions thus obtained:

> Juvat cognitio experimentalis ut citius assentiatur principio affir-mativo, si per sensum cognoscatur conjunctio extremorum in singulo, negativo si disjunctio, sed non est necessaria nec ipsa, nec aliqua apprehensio sensitiva. Licet enim nunquam per aliquem sensum videatur haec separatio in re, si tamen ex sensibilibus apprehenditur affirmatio vel negatio, et intellectus componat hanc propositionem: De omni est affirmatio, vel negatio vera, assentitur isti. Et etiam ubi sensus per-cipit conjunctionem singularium terminorum in re, adhuc certius adhae-retur principio complexo per naturale lumen intellectus quam propter aliquam apprehensionem sensus. Si enim in apprehensione sensus esset error, et intellectus judicaret sensum errare in hoc et tamen a sensu errare acciperet notitiam simplicium, et illa componeret ex sua virtute, adhuc intellectus circa illud principium non erraret, quantum ad veri-tatem compositionis (Metaph. I, q. 4, n. 5; VII, 54a).

It may be asked how Scotus' statement that the truth of princi-ples can be known independently of true sense perceptions is to be reconciled with Aristotle's saying that all intellectual knowledge is had either through syllogisms or through induction.[21] According to the Stagirite, even first principles are known through induction. This would seem to imply that singulars are better known than universal principles, otherwise these could not be derived from them. Scotus replies that induction is here taken in the sense that at least *some* singular must be known before a universal principle is formulated. For the terms of the principles come to us from the senses:

> Contra praedicta arguitur: Dicit Aristoteles I. *Post.*, omnia cognos-cuntur per syllogismum, vel per inductionem; conclusiones per syllogis-mum, principia per inductionem. Sed hoc tu negas, quia principia no-tiora sunt secundum te singularibus inducentibus. - Potest responderi ad intellectum ejus ibi, quod sensus est necessarius propter notitiam terminorum. Unde universalia non cognoscuntur sine inductione, id est, sine cognitione alicujus singularis (Metaph. I, q. 4, n. 16; VII, 60a).

"Induction" must not be taken in this connection as a proof of the principles, but rather as a *manuductio*, inasmuch as it gives the intellect the material to work with. It stops, so to speak, at the door of the intellect which dispenses with its further assistance:

21. *Posterior Analytics* I, c. 1; 71a 1-9.

> Inductio est hic non simpliciter...nec forte probatio dicitur, sed manu-
> ductio, quia quandocumque iste (intellectus) intelligit principium,
> magis adhaeret illi quam singulari inducenti *(loc. cit.,* 60b).

We shall see later that Scotus does not deny the validity of induction as a means of acquiring certain knowledge; on the contrary,
he develops it to a remarkable degree of perfection. However, since
induction starts from contingent singulars, it never yields the grade
of evidence found in the first universal principles. For the same
reason the knowledge deduced from self-evident principles is more
scientific (i.e., more certain, because more evident) than that obtained through induction. Thus the conclusion, "Every whole is
greater than its part; therefore, this particular whole and that particular whole is greater than its part," is more scientific than the
following induction: 'This particular whole, and that particular
whole is greater than its part; therefore, every whole is greater than
its part:"

> Inductio non sufficit ad scientiam, nec ideo scitur universale quia ex
> particularibus deducitur. Unde magis sequitur scientia quia si omne
> totum est majus vel magis sua parte, ergo hoc totum et illud, quam e
> converso, hoc et illud, ergo omne *(Oxon.* III, d. 24, q. un., f. 167v, b; n.
> 19, XV, 49a).

Intimately related with self-evident propositions are the conclusions deduced from them through syllogistic reasoning. Scotus'
treatment of the evidence of conclusions is rather cursory. For
this reason we must content ourselves with a brief analysis of the
nature of the syllogism and the evidence proper to it. This will be
the subject matter of our next chapter.

CHAPTER III
EVIDENCE IN SYLLOGISTIC REASONING

After explaining the evidence and resulting certitude of the first principles, Scotus briefly alludes to the evidence of syllogistic reasoning as another source of certain knowledge:

> Habita certitudine de principiis primis, patet quomodo habebitur de conclusionibus illatis ex eis, propter evidentiam formae[1] syllogismi perfecti, cum certitudo conclusionis tantummodo dependeat ex certitudine principiorum et ex evidentia illationis (*Oxon.* I, d. 3, q. 4, f. 31v, a; n. 8, IX, 174a).

Since in the present question the Franciscan Doctor intends to prove the possibility and actual existence in the mind of true and infallible knowledge, he confines his considerations to the order of strictest evidence. He refers only to evident and necessary conclusions drawn from evident and necessary premises (matter) through evident syllogistic reasoning (form). These two conditions are fulfilled, on the one hand, if the premises are first principles, and, on the other, if the form of the syllogism[2] is a perfect one. In order to understand this second condition we must first consider the nature of syllogistic reasoning.

A. THE NATURE OF SYLLOGISTIC REASONING

"A syllogism," writes Aristotle,[3] "is discourse in which, certain things being stated, something other than what is stated follows of necessity from their being so." A syllogism is made up of two premises and a conclusion following from the premises. Any argumentation containing less or more than two premises is not considered a syllogism in the strict sense. Moreover, the syllogism must con-

---

1. Formae *add. Viv.*
2. For a critical evaluation of the various forms of syllogisms vide R. Messner, O.F.M., *Schauendes und begriffliches Erkennen nach D. Skotus* (Freiburg, 1942), pp. 280-292.
3. *Prior Analytics* I, c. 1; 24b 18-20.

tain no more and no less than three terms. These terms must be thus
disposed in the premises that the conclusion follows in virtue of
this distribution of the terms. One of the terms occurs twice in the
premises, viz., once in the first or major premise, and once in the
second or minor premise. This term is called the middle term, because it is placed somehow between the major extreme and the
minor extreme, and because it is with the help of this term that the
relation or connection between the two other terms is brought out.
"In the first premise," writes Mastrius,[4] "one of the extremes is
connected with the middle term, and in the other premise the second
extreme is connected with the same middle term; in the conclusion
the two extremes are connected with each other." Scotus himself
gives essentially the same interpretation of the nature of syllogistic reasoning. "In the same degree as two things are identical
with a third," he writes, "they are also identical with each other.
For we cannot conclude to the identity of two extremes unless
they are both identical with a middle term in that same respect, and
unless the middle term remains identical with itself. Every syllogistic figure holds true in virtue of this principle. If either one of
these conditions is lacking, i.e., if either the identity of the middle
term with itself, or that of the extremes with the middle term is
absent, then we have no longer a syllogism but a fallacy of the
accident:"

> Quaecumque aliqua identitate sunt eadem alicui, tali identitate inter
> se sic sunt eadem; quia non potest concludi aliqua identitas extremorum
> inter se nisi secundum illam identitatem sint eadem medio et medium
> sin se sit sic idem. Et per hanc propositionem sic intellectam tenet
> omnis forma syllogistica; omissa enim altera conditione, vel unitatis
> medii in se, vel extremorum ad medium, non est syllogismus, sed para-
> logismus accidentis (*Oxon.* I, d. 2, q. 3, f. 24r, b; Viv. q. 7, n. 47, VIII,
> 630a).

Hence the validity and evidence of syllogistic reasoning, too,
is reduced in the last analysis, to a self-evident principle, viz.,
"Quae sunt eadem uni tertio sunt eadem inter se," or in a negative
formulation: "Quorum unum non est idem cum uno tertio, cum quo
alterum non est idem, non possunt esse eadem inter se."

4. *Cursus philosophicus*, tom. I, Logica (Pars Prima Institutionum), tract. III,
c. 5, n. 99.

B. THE PERFECT SYLLOGISM AND ITS EVIDENCE

Now we are able to understand what a perfect syllogism is.[5]
According to the distribution of the terms in the premises, the
Scholastics commonly distinguish three figures of syllogistic
reasoning. The figures vary according as the middle term appears
(1) as subject in the major and as predicate in the minor, (2) as
subject both in the major and the minor, or (3) as predicate in the
major and in the minor. Again, within these figures various modes
are distinguished, according to the quantity and quality of the
propositions. Every mode, in turn, is said to conclude either directly or indirectly. In a direct conclusion the major extreme is
predicated of the minor; in an indirect conclusion the minor is
predicated of the major.

When speaking of the "evidence of the form of a perfect syllogism," Scotus obviously refers to the first figure, and among the
various modes of this figure, to those which conclude directly. For
it is only in the first four modes of the first figure (viz., in Barbara,
Celarent, Darii, Ferio) that the mutual identity or inclusion of the
extremes in the middle term appears evidently, i.e., in virtue of the
syllogistic structure itself, and without further proof or explanation.
In no other figure does the relation appear more clearly. In point of
fact, the other figures must be reduced to one of these four perfect
modes of the first figure if we wish them to become perfectly evident.[6]

1. Evident and True Conclusions from Evident
and True Principles

The preceding considerations on the nature of the syllogism
apply to every syllogism formulated according to the rules of deductive reasoning, irrespective of whether the syllogism is true or
false. From the point of view of the form even false premises yield
valid conclusions, and this in an evident manner. The validity of
the conclusion is independent of the content of the syllogism.[7]

---

5. Cf. Aristotle, *Prior Analytics* I, c. 4; 25b 27-26b 33.

6. Aristotle, *loc. cit.*, c. 6; 29a 30-31: "It is clear that all the imperfect syllogisms are made perfect by means of the first figure."

7. Cf. *Metaph.* IV, q. 4, n. 6; VII, 180a.

In order to obtain a true conclusion it must first be ascertained that the premises are true. Likewise, in order to arrive at an evidently true conclusion we must make sure that the premises are evidently true. Scotus, as we have seen, wants to prove against the sceptics and illuminationists that true and certain knowledge is possible to natural reason. He refrains, therefore, from considering here the less evident forms of syllogistic reasoning, and is satisfied with pointing out those conclusions which are unquestionably evident both in regard to the inference *(consequentia)* and to the truth of the conclusion *(consequens)*. Such are all the conclusions drawn from evident principles. A syllogism which is evident both as to form (or logical structure) and to matter (of content of the premises) cannot but yield an evident conclusion. [8]

2. *Effects of Syllogistic Evidence: Necessary Assent and Absolute Certitude*

Two acts of assent can be distinguished in the intellect, according to the nature of evidence proper to a proposition. One is given to a proposition for its own sake, and the other for the sake of something other than itself. The first act of assent is produced by the principles which are evident *per se,* and the second by the conclusions which are evident *per aliud.* The latter differs from the former inasmuch as its truth is received from the principles:

> In intellectu sunt duo actus assentiendi alicui complexo: unus quo assentitur alicui vero propter se, sicut principio; alius quo assentitur alicui vero complexo non propter se, sed propter aliud verum, sicut conclusioni...; conclusioni assentitur propter principium quia conclusio veritatem suam habet a principio...Sunt enim alteri propter alteram evidentiam hujus et illius veri *(Oxon.* I, d. 1, q. 3, f. 11v, a; n. 2, VIII, 344a-b).

In like manner there is a difference between the certitude of the two acts of assent. While a principle is certain of itself due to its evident truth, a conclusion becomes certain only through the causality of principles:

> Cognitio principii seipsa est certa vel ab objecto, scilicet a principio quod est a se verum manifestum...Conclusio autem est certa per principium tamquam per causam suae certitudinis *(Quodl.* q. 17, n. 11; XXVI, 220a). [9]

8. Cf. *Metaph.* VI, q. 1, n. 4; VII, 305.
9. Cf. *Metaph.* VI, q. 3, n. 11; VII, 342b.

Since an effect cannot be equal to its cause in perfection, it follows that the certitude of conclusions is necessarily inferior to that of principles:

> Conclusio est minus certa quam principium, ex quo tota certitudo illius est a certitudine principii (*Oxon.* III, d. 23, q. un., f. 165v, a; n. 8, XV, 12a). [10]

Despite this lesser grade of certitude a conclusion derived from first principles compels the assent of the intellect, once the latter apprehends the terms and the syllogistic arrangement of the premises. The intellect cannot but give its unrestricted assent to an inference formulated on the basis of the evidence of syllogistic discourse. Not even the will is able to prevent this assent or to induce the intellect into error concerning these conclusions:

> Forma syllogistica est evidens ex se omni intellectui, patet ex definitione syllogismi perfecti, I. *Priorum;* ergo terminis apprehensis et compositis, et facta deductione syllogistica, necesse est intellectum acquiescere conclusioni, cujus notitia dependet praecise ex notitia terminorum principii et notitia deductionis syllogisticae; igitur impossibile est voluntatem facere intellectum considerantem principia per deductionem syllogisticam errare circa conclusionem...; et ideo nullo modo excaecabitur intellectus ita ut erret (*Oxon.* III, d. 36, q. un., f. 178r, b; n. 12, XV, 631a). [11]

This compulsion exercised by the evident syllogistic reasoning process, however, must not be confused with the *evidence itself* of the process. Objective evidence does not depend on, or consist in, the easiness or readiness with which a conclusion is apprehended. Scotus realizes that there are those who contend that a proposition is not demonstrated because it fails to compel the assent of every intellect. "This objection is worthless," he replies, "because if it did hold, then it would follow that there is no demonstration in geometry. For not a single geometrical proof compels (the assent of) every intellect." Scotus, of course, is far from implying that such demonstrations are not capable of producing evident and certain knowledge. If they fail, at times, to effect such

10. Cf. *Report. Paris,* III, d. 23, q. un., n. 10; XXIII, 437b.
11. Cf. *Oxon.* IV, d. 43, q. 2, n. 10; XX, 40b: "Experimur quod cognoscimus ignotum ex noto per discursum, ita quod non possumus dissentire evidentiae discursus nec cognitionis illatae."

knowledge, this is due to the absence of certain indispensable prerequisites, such as an adequate concept of the terms:

> (Objection:) Illa non est demonstratio, quia non cogit omnem intellectum, et demonstratio debet omnem intellectum cogere.
>
> (Answer:) Sed illud nihil valet, quia tunc sequitur quod nulla esset demonstratio in Geometria; nulla enim est quae cogit omnem intellectum. Unde potest esse demonstratio specialis et potissima, licet non statim assentiat intellectus notis terminis confuse (Report. Par. II, d. 1, q. 4, n. 12; XXII, 544a).

We must, therefore, distinguish between the epistemological and the psychological evidence of conclusions. As Messner[12] points out, a conclusion does not become evident and critically certain because it is actually apprehended as caused by the premises. It is sufficient that the relation between premises and conclusion be *such as to be capable* of conveying the truth of the conclusion to any intellect.

12. *Op. cit.*, pp. 283 f.

PART THREE
FUNCTION OF EVIDENCE
FOR
OTHER KINDS OF CERTITUDE

PRELIMINARIES: SCOTUS EXTENDS THE CONCEPT
OF SCIENTIFIC KNOWLEDGE

Every student of classical Scholasticism knows the strict conditions a discipline had to fulfill to deserve the name of *scientia* or scientific knowledge. As Wolter[1] points out, scientific knowledge "is understood primarily of a single proposition which forms the conclusion of a demonstrative syllogism. Only secondarily it is understood of a body of such conclusions generically or specifically related in the sense that they deal more or less with the same subject matter." To be strictly scientific, a proposition has to fulfill the following requirements: First, it must be certain, i.e., exclusive of deception and doubt; secondly, it must be of a necessary object; thirdly, it must be produced by a cause that is evident to the intellect; fourthly, it must be applied to the object by a syllogistic reasoning process:

> Scientia stricte sumpta quatuor includit, videlicet quod sit cognitio certa absque deceptione et dubitatione; secundo quod sit de cognito necessario; tertio quod sit causata a causa evidente intellectui; quarto quod sit applicata ad cognitum per syllogismum vel per discursum syllogisticum *(Oxon.* prol. q. 7, f. 6r, a; Viv. qq. 3 et 4 lateralis, n. 26; VIII, 183b).[2]

Scotus insists on these conditions wherever there is a question of scientific knowledge in the strictest sense. But the Franciscan Doctor does in no wise confine certain knowledge to the demonstrative *scientiae.* An unconditional insistence on the aforementioned conditions would reduce the sphere of certain knowledge to an ex-

---

1. "The 'Theologism' of Duns Scotus" in *Franciscan Studies,* VII (1947), p. 264. Fr. Wolter refers here to *Metaph.* VI, q. 1, n. 2; VII, 303a.
2. Cf. *Oxon.* III, d. 24, q. 1, n. 13; XV, 44b; *Report. Par.* III, d. 24, q. un., n. 16; XXXIII, 454a-b.

tremely limited area. Especially the condition of necessity on the
part of the object is not always fulfilled, as in all disciplines concerned with contingent objects. Contrary to what takes place in
demonstrative or *a priori* sciences, there is no necessary relation
between a contingent object and its predicates. The knowledge of
a contingent object is not sufficient to convey by itself the
knowledge of its properties or qualities, because these are merely
accidental:

> Contingentia non habent subjectum secundum quod ponitur subjectum
> in scientia, quia nulla scientia continet illud quod est sibi accidentale
> (*Report. Exam.* prol. q. 2, f. 7r).[3]

Would it be right to question the reliability of knowledge on the
grounds that it is concerned with contingent objects? Or to deny
every scientific character to contingent knowledge? Scotus does not
think so. "The perfection of scientific knowledge," he says, "consists in its being certain and evident." He does not hesitate in
dispensing with objective necessity as long as knowledge is based
on objective evidence:

> In scientia illud perfectionis est quod sit cognitio certa et evidens.
> Quod autem sit de necessario objecto, haec est conditio objecti, non
> cognitionis (*Oxon.* prol. q. 7, f. 6r, b; Viv. qq. 3 et 4 later., n. 28, VIII,
> 187a-b).[4]

Accordingly, far from restricting certain knowledge to necessary
or demonstrated conclusions, Scotus defends the reliability and
sufficiency of sense perceptions as a source of evident certitude:

> Visio extremorum veritatis contingentis et unionis eorum necessario
> causat certitudinem de tali veritate evidente (*loc. cit.*; 187b).[5]

Scotus, therefore, has full confidence that under the influence of
objective evidence the powers of the human mind are perfectly suf-

---

3. Cf. *Oxon.* prol. q. 3, f. 5r, a; Viv. q. 2 later., n. 13, VIII, 156a: "Nullum
subjectum continet nisi veritates necessarias de ipso; quia ad contingentes de
ipso aequaliter se habet ex se et ad oppositas." See also: *Quodl.*, q. 7, n. 10;
XXV, 291a.

4. Cf. *Oxon.* II, d. 5, q. 2, n. 7; XII, 317b; *Metaph.* VI, q. 2, n. 4; VII, 327a.

5. Cf. Efrem Bettoni, O.F.M., *L'ascesa a Dio in Duns Scoto* (Milan, 1943),
p. 36: "Duns Scoto...evita l'esagerazione di considerare valevole solo ciò che si
può dimostrare con metodo matematico...Infatti l'esperienza ci mette sott'occhio
fatti di cui non possiamo negare la verità..."

ficient to arrive at a certain, and in many cases, infallible knowledge of contingent things and truths.

This broad conception of scientific knowledge must be understood in connection with Scotus' teachings on intuitive cognition. It is intuitive cognition which "gives us knowledge of an existent as existing."[6] As Day[7] remarks, "Scotus fully appreciated the epistemological significance of intuitive cognition, especially in view of his assertion that without intuitive cognition our intellects could not be certain of the existence of *any* objects:

> Cognitio quae dicitur intuitiva potest esse intellectiva, alioquin intellectus non esset certus de aliqua existentia alicujus objecti *(Oxon.* IV, d. 45, q. 2, f. 267v, b; n. 12, XX, 305b)."

To this text another important passage may be added where Scotus states that the truth of contingent propositions cannot be known from the nature of the terms (i.e., *a priori*), but solely by an intellectual *visio* or intuition of the terms as actually united or separated *in re:*[8]

> Quandoque (complexionem cognosco esse veram) nullo modo ex natura terminorum vel includentium ipsos, sed a causa extrinseca conjungente ipsa vel disjungente... Quando (intellectus) componit terminos propositionis contingentis, non videt actum esse conformem nisi videndo habitudinem terminorum in re, quia causa extrinseca si facit eam, facit circa terminos ut in re, non ut in conceptu, et tunc oportet *videre intellectualiter terminos in re conjungi vel dividi* (Metaph. VI, q. 3, n. 10; VII, 341b-342a).

Scotus' insistence on intuitive cognition, however, must not be interpreted as if he considered intuition a completely sufficient source of certitude for all contingent knowledge. We shall see in the subsequent chapters that the intellect is frequently faced with apparently conflicting evidences in the contingent world. In such

6. Sebastian J. Day, O.F.M., *Intuitive Cognition a Key to the Significance of the Later Scholastics* (St. Bonaventure, 1947), p. 82

7. *Ibid.,* pp. 82 f.

8. The historic importance of Scotus' teaching on the evident certitude of intuitive cognition cannot be sufficiently emphasized. See: Messner (*op. cit.,* p. 364): "Skotus hat durch seine Lehre von der Intuition und ihrer einwandfreien Sicherheit, sowie durch seine Lehre, dass Existenz grundsaetzlich nur durch Intuition sicherzustellen sei und auch nicht aus apriorischen Urteilen sich ableiten lasse, eine Ueberwindung des einseitigen Aristotelischen Intellektualismus vorbereitet." Cf. also Bettoni, *op. cit.,* pp. 32 ff.

cases, we are unable to decide on the basis of intuition alone how these evidences may be reconciled with one another, or which of two or more "conflicting" evidences the intellect should trust. Intuition is incompetent for this task, because it remains on the level of simple apprehension.[9] Intuition establishes no comparisons between simple concepts, nor does it present one concept more emphatically than another. Conflicting evidences, therefore, must be reconciled or corrected by means of some higher evidence. This higher evidence is present in propositions which are evident of themselves, irrespective of whether their simple concepts are received from true or false sense perceptions. These propositions play a particularly important role in establishing the truth-value of induction and sense knowledge. The only kind of contingent knowledge which dispenses with an intervention of higher evidence is introspection. Introspective knowledge constitutes, so to speak, a class of its own in the sphere of contingent knowledge. Its certitude is given with the intrinsic evidence of internal acts and states.

Thus, Scotus, while avoiding an exaggerated rationalism on the one hand, does not commit the error of falling into a materialistic sensualism on the other. He succeeds in blending the various forms of knowledge into a harmonious whole in which inferior and superior faculties assist and complement one another, thus cooperating toward the acquisition of full certitude.

9. Day, *op. cit.*, p. 49.

CHAPTER I
EVIDENCE OF INTERNAL ACTS AND STATES

Throughout the works of Scotus we find allusions to introspection as a source of certain knowledge. Although he does not use the word "evidence" in his description of internal experience, there is no doubt that Scotus considers it as truly evident,[1] as will be shown in this chapter.

A. INTERNAL EXPERIENCE A SOURCE OF EVIDENCE

Introspective cognition fulfills to the letter all the conditions laid down for evident contingent knowledge. We have seen that evident knowledge of contingents presupposes intuition, i.e., a direct contact with an existing and present object. There is no doubt that introspective knowledge meets with this requirement, since nothing can be more closely present to the mind than its own acts.

While describing our consciousness of internal acts and states, Scotus makes repeated use of the expression "experimur." Day[2] has proved that this expression, too, implies a true intuition, i.e., an immediate interior perception of the acts and states of our soul.

This intuitive and evident experience is present, first of all, in the intellective faculty. Not only do we have direct intellectual cognitions of many things and facts, but we also know the act by which we apprehend them. This is done through a reflection on the direct act of knowledge. Furthermore, we know by experience that we give infallible assent to certain propositions, viz., to the first

1. This is clear from the adjective "manifest" which Scotus employs as an e-quivalent of "evident," when referring to acts of the will and intellect: "Primo videndum est de illis quae manifesta sunt inesse in mente...Quantum ad primum, experimur in nobis esse actum intellectionis et actum volitionis" (*Oxon.* I, d. 3, q. 9, n. 3; IX, 406a). Cf. also: *Oxon.* IV, d. 45, q. 4, n. 2; XX, 376a; *ibid.*, n. 7, 384a-b; *Quodl.* q. 15, n. 2; XXVI, 119b.

2. *Op. cit.*, pp. 125 f. Cf. also: Ephrem Longpré, O.F.M., "The Psychology of Duns Scotus and its Modernity" in *Franciscan Educational Conference*, XIII (1931), pp. 19-77; P.C. Albanese, "La teoria delle idee senza immagini nella psicologia di Scoto" in *Studi Francescani*, I (1914), p. 39, note 2.

principles, so as to exclude the possibility of contradiction or
deception. In like manner we experience the evidence of syllogistic
reasoning processes:

> Experimur quod cognoscimus actum illum quo cognoscimus ista et
> illud, secundum quod inest nobis iste actus, quod est per actum reflex-
> um super actum rectum...Experimur etiam quod assentimus complexioni-
> bus quibusdam sine possibilitate contradicendi vel errandi, utpote
> primis principiis. Experimur etiam quod cognoscimus ignotum ex noto
> per discursum, ita quod non possumus dissentire evidentiae discursus,
> nec cognitionis illatae (Oxon. IV, d. 43, q. 2, f. 250r, b; n. 10, XX, 40a-
> b).

The immediate and evident character of these intellectual acts
is forcefully brought out by Scotus. It is useless, he says, to argue
with those who obstinately refuse to admit these internal experiences. It is impossible to convince them of anything whatsoever,
just as it is an idle task to dispute about colors with a person
whose experiences, either allegedly or really, run counter to those
of the normal run of man:

> Si quis proterve neget illos actus inesse homini, nec se experimi
> istos actus in se, non est ulterius cum eo disputandum, sed dicendum
> est sibi quod est brutum; sicut cum dicente, non video colorem ibi non
> est disputandum, sed dicendum sibi, tu indiges sensu, quia caecus es
> (loc. cit., n. 11; 40b).

This confidence in the cognitive powers of man is also the deeper
reason for Scotus' rejection of Plato's innate ideas and principles.
In this he follows Aristotle[3] who calls it incongruous that a most
certain knowledge, as that of the first principles, should be veiled
to the demonstrator. And yet, Aristotle adds, we do not experience
this knowledge before we acquire it through learning. Hence, it
cannot be innate in the soul. Scotus confirms Aristotle's argument
by remarking that not even the inferior degrees of knowledge are
present in the intellect without the latter being conscious of their
presence. Thus we are perfectly aware of our opinions, doubts,
beliefs, although they yield only a limited grade of certitude, or
none at all. As St. Augustine[4] points out, everyone perceives or
sees the faith within himself:

3. *Posterior Analytics* II, c. 19; 99b 18-27.
4. *De Trinitate* XIII, c. 2; PL 42, col. 1016.

Contra opinionem Platonis arguit Aristoteles II *Post.*, c. ult., sic: Inconveniens est cognitiones certissimas demonstrantem latere, sed antequam addiscamus non percipimus eas in nobis; ergo non insunt. Confirmatur major, quia habitus intellectualis etiam debilissimus non est in nobis, quando certi sumus de illo quod nobis inest, nec latet; omnis enim opinans, dubitans, et credens certus est se opinari, dubitare et credere. Unde Augustinus 13. *De Trinitate*, c. 1 et 3: Fidem unusquisque in se videt, etc. *(Metaph.* I, q. 4, n. 9; VII, 56a).[5]

A great number of similar statements can be read in Scotus' works. In the present chapter, however, we shall limit ourselves to quotations and comments on the significant texts found in the discussion about the possibility of natural knowledge.[6] Against the negative opinion of the Illuminationists, who appeal to the authority of St. Augustine, Scotus adduces, first of all, a series of quotations from the same Christian Doctor. He thus shows that St. Augustine, far from denying natural certitude, defends it on the basis of internal experience. From these texts it appears that there are many states and operations, in both the intellectual and emotional spheres, of which man is immediately and absolutely certain. Thus, we are always sure of our being alive as of a fundamental state in all our activities:[7]

Patet...quod Augustinus concedit certitudinem de actibus nostris ibidem *(De Trinitate)*, 15 lib., c. eodem, vel 32: Sive dormiat, sive vigilet, vivit; quia et dormire, et in somniis videre, viventis est *(Oxon.* I, d. 3, q. 4, f. 31v, b; n. 6, IX, 109a).[8]

The objection that *to live* is not a second but a first act, and that we cannot therefore be aware of it, just as we are not directly aware e.g., of the potencies of our soul, is obviated by St. Augustine who adds that at least upon reflection we are infallibly certain of this fact:

Quod si dicas: vivere non esse actum secundum, sed primum; sequitur ibidem: Si aliquis dicat, scio me scire, me vivere, falli non potest,

5. Cf. *Oxon.* IV, d. 49, q. 10, n. 2; XXI, 318b; *Report. Par.* prol. q. 2, n. 7; XXII, 37a.

6. *Oxon.* I, d. 3, q. 4; IX, 162-207.

7. *De Trinitate* XV, c. 12; PL 42, col. 1073s.

8. Cf. *Report. Par.* II, d. 3, q. 3, n. 11; XXII, 593a: "Anima nostra certa est quod vivit, vel quod est quo totum vivit." See also: *Oxon.* IV, d. 49, q. 8, n. 5; XXI, 306b; *Metaph.* VII, q. 18, n. 8; VII, 458a; *Quodl.* q. 8, n. 12; XXV, 350b; q. 14, n. 25, XXVI, 106a-b.

etiam quotiescumque reflectendo super primum scitum *(ibid.)*.

Likewise everyone is conscious of the operations of his intellect and will.[9] Nobody doubts the personal character of these acts, or their existence in the soul. Again, this first awareness of internal acts can also be the object of a reflection. The resulting "double" consciousness, a consciousness of consciousness, can further be known through a new reflection, and so forth *usque in infinitum:*

> Et ibidem si quis dicat, scio me hoc velle, et hoc me scire scio, jam his duobus et tertium potest addere, quod haec duo sciat, et quartum, quod haec duo scire se sciat, et similiter in infinitum numerum pergere *(ibid.)*.[10]

Even granted that the mind should actually err, it still has the unshakeable certitude of its desire not to err. Indeed, it is this attitude of mind alone which urges man to persevere in the quest for truth, despite the many errors to which he is exposed:

> Ibidem,[11] se quispiam dicat, errare nolo, nonne eum errare nolle verum est? *(Ibid.,* 169b).

Another fundamental certitude is brought out in the consideration of St. Augustine that the soul can never be in error concerning its desire for happiness. This consciousness is so certain that St. Augustine considers it altogether out of order to question the truthfulness and certainty of a person who tells me that he wants to be happy:

> Et ibidem,[12] si quis dicat, volo esse beatus, quomodo non impudenter respondetur, forte falleris *(ibid.,* 169a).

So much for St. Augustine's teaching on the natural certitude of internal acts and states in general. From here, Scotus proceeds to examine the peculiar evidence of certain internal phenomena and their function in the realm of knowledge.

9. Cf. L. de Sesma, "La volonté dans la philosophie de J. Duns Scot" in *Estudis Franciscans,* XXXIX (1927), pp. 248-249: "Nous voyons qu'il est en notre pouvoir de poser un acte de vouloir ou de l'arrêter quand et comme il nous plait, de nous décider pour un bien ou son contraire, de nous abstenir de l'un et de l'autre."

10. *De Trinitate* XV, c. 12, PL 42, cols. 1073-1074.

11. *De Trinitate* XV, c. 12; PL 42, col. 1074.

12. *Loc. cit.*

B. INTERNAL ACTS AND STATES ARE SELF-EVIDENT

Many of our acts, Scotus maintains, are known with a certitude comparable to that of the first self-evident principles. In other words, they are known of themselves. In his *Metaphysics,* [13] speaking of those who "puzzle over the question whether we are now asleep or awake," Aristotle says that all such questions are meaningless. And he goes on to say: "These people demand that a reason shall be given for everything," and to reproach them "for seeking a reason for things for which no reason can be given; for the starting point of demonstration is not demonstration." Therefore, according to the same Stagirite, the fact that we are awake is known of itself as much as is a principle of demonstration:

> De tertiis cognoscibilibus, scilicet de actibus nostris, dico quod est certitudo de multis eorum sicut de primis et per se notis, [14] quod patet IV *Metaph.*, ubi dicit Philosophus de rationibus dicentium omnia apparentia esse vera, quod isti rationes quaerunt utrum nunc vigilemus an dormiamus. Ponunt autem idem omnes dubitationes tales, omnium enim rationem hi significant esse. Et subdit: Rationem quaerunt quorum non est ratio; demonstrationis enim principii non est demonstratio. Ergo per ipsum ibidem, nos vigilare est per se notum, sicut principium demonstrationis *(Oxon.* I, d. 3, q. 4, f. 31v, b; n. 10, IX, 179a).

Scotus terms the awareness of internal acts not simply evident but *self-evident.* What justification does he have in ascribing this highest degree of certitude and evidence to purely contingent acts? In Scotus' mind the fact that we are treating here of contingent states of affairs does not obviate our speaking of self-evidence. For in the contingent sphere, too, a certain order is to be observed. Indeed, unless we admit some first and immediate propositions in the contingent order, we must fall back either on an infinite regress or on some necessary propositions from which contingent propositions proceed. Both of these hypotheses, however, are impossible and absurd:

> Nec obstat quod est contingens, quia...ordo est in contingentibus, quod aliqua est prima et immediata, vel esset processus in infinitum in

---

13. B. IV, c. 6; 1011a 4-13.
14. Sicut de principiis per se notis *Viv.* There is obviously no essential difference between the two readings, for a few lines later in the *Ass. MS.* Scotus refers to the same acts as being known "sicut principium demonstrationis."

contingentibus, vel aliquod contingens sequeretur ex causa necessaria: quorum utrumque est impossibile *(ibid.).*

Aristotle's remark on the indemonstrability of the principles of demonstration can be applied to the contingent order as well. In a series of necessary propositions we arrive at a primary proposition or first principle which is immediately evident. Likewise in contingent propositions we must finally stop at some first contingent proposition which admits of no further reason or cause than itself:

Indisciplinati est quaerere omnium demonstrationes...principiorum enim non est demonstratio; et eodem modo in contingentibus; alioquin foret processus in infinitum in contingentibus, quia contingentia non sequuntur ex necessariis *(Oxon.* II, d. 1, q. 2, f. 98v, b; n. 9, XI, 65a).[15]

In order to understand Scotus' expositions on the immediate evidence of contingent propositions, we must briefly recall the notion of contingency. Contingency implies indifference to existence and non-existence. "I call that contingent whose opposite could have come about when this came about," writes Scotus. [16] To say that something is contingent is equivalent to saying that it "can pass from non-existence to existence." [17] - For Scotus, the whole world bears the mark of radical contingency. Its origin, therefore, cannot be necessary. For if it were, then all things would be necessary. It is clear, then, that in our inquiry of the causes, we must finally arrive at a first cause whose activity is contingent, and yet cannot be accounted for by any other cause. In other words, we must arrive at a first, immediate, and contingent cause which has the whole reason of its activity in itself alone. In this free creative activity of the Divine Will, Scotus locates the root of all contingency. [18] With reference to God, therefore, the contingent order is indemonstrable and irretraceable to a higher cause. To ask why God

15. Cf. *Report. Mag.* I, d. 8, q. 7, f. 37v: "Sicut in necessariis est invenire propositiones immediatas quarum non quaeruntur causae, sic et in contingentibus."
16. "Dico hic contingens...cujus oppositum posset fieri quando istud fit" *(De Primo Principio,* c. 4; ed. by Evan Roche, O.F.M., St. Bonaventure, N.Y., 1949, p. 84).
17. "Quia aliqua est contingens, igitur possibilis esse post non esse" *(ibid.,* c. 3, p. 37). Cf. A. Wolter, O.F.M., *The Transcendentals and Their Function,* pp. 150 ff.
18. Cf. E. Longpré, O.F.M., "St. Augustin et la pensée franciscaine" in *La France Franciscaine* XV (1932), p. 68; Wolter, "The 'Theologism' of Duns Scotus" in *Franciscan Studies* VII (1947), p. 370.

has willed to create these objects in preference to others, or why
He created the world at this time rather than at another, would
prove just as useless as to ask for the reason why God has given
this human nature to this individual rather than to another, or why
human nature is possible and contingent. The only reason why it is
better for these things to be thus rather than otherwise is because
God willed to act in this manner and not in another. [19] To inquire
further is to search for reasons where there are no reasons:

> Et ideo ista voluntas Dei, qua vult hoc et pro nunc, est immediata
> et prima causa, cujus non est aliqua alia causa quaerenda; sicut enim
> non est ratio quare voluit naturam humanam esse in hoc individuo, et
> esse possibile et contingens, ita non est ratio quare hoc voluit nunc et
> non tunc; sed tantum quia voluit hoc esse, ideo bonum fuit illud esse;
> et quaerere hujus propositionis, licet contingentis, immediate aliam
> rationem, est quaerere rationem cujus non est ratio quaerenda *(Oxon.* II,
> d. 1, q, 2, f. 98v, b; n. 9, XI, 65a). [20]

Just as it is impossible to establish a cause for the creative
activity of the First Cause, so it is often impossible to find causes
for certain activities of caused causes. Here as there we meet with
immediate and indemonstrable causalities. Thus the proposition,
"Heat produces heat," is an immediate proposition for which there
is no demonstration or proof. Just as the question, "Why is heat
capable of producing heat?" is equivalent to asking why heat is
heat, so the question, "Why does heat produce heat?" admits of
only one answer: "Because it is heat:"

> Sicut in necessariis est invenire propositiones immediatas quarum non
> quaeruntur causae, sic et in contingentibus. Unde haec est immediata:
> calor est calefactivus, et necessaria; et haec similiter immediata: calor
> calefacit, sed contingens. Quaerere igitur causam quare calor est cale-
> factivus non est aliud nisi quaerere quare calor est calor. [21] Si quaeras

---

19. Cf. E. Gilson, *La philosophie au moyen âge,* 3rd ed. (Paris, 1947), pp. 598f.
While insisting on the important role assigned to Divine liberty in the system of
Scotus, Gilson does not make the mistake to identify Scotus' liberty with the
absolute indifferentism of Descartes, as so many "historians" have done in the
past.

20. "Quando quaeritur quare voluntas divina est volitiva producere creaturas...
certe non est alia causa nisi quia voluntas est voluntas" *(Rep. Exam.* I, d. 8, q.
7, f. 37v).

21. Et haec est causa quare est calefactivus, quia calor est calor *add. Merton
College MS.* 59, 58v.

de ista: quare calor calefacit, dico similiter quod nihil est quare, quia calefacit eo quod calor est *(Rep. Exam.* I, d. 8, q. 2; f. 37v).[22]

The Commentary on Metaphysics places the ultimate reason for immediate contingent propositions in the fact that a non-contingent effect follows from a necessary cause. This can be seen in the following reasoning. A contingent proposition is either immediate or mediate. If it is immediate, then our contention that there is a first contingent proposition is established. If it is mediate, then we must look for a middle term by which the proposition is inferred from a premise which must also be contingent, for a contingent effect cannot follow from a necessary cause. Again, the premise is either mediate or immediate. If it is immediate our point is proved. If it is mediate, then it must have been derived from another contingent premise, which in turn is either immediate or mediate. And so on *in infinitum,* unless we stop at some first, immediate, and contingent proposition:

> Ex necessariis non sequitur contingens. Patet: accipiatur aliqua contingens; si est immediata habetur propositum; si non, detur medium; altera praemissa ad ipsam est contingens, alias ex necessariis infertur contingens; ista praemissa contingens si est mediata, altera praemissa ad ipsam erit contingens, et sic in infinitum, nisi stetur in aliqua contingente immediata *(Metaph.* IX, q. 15, n. 4; VII, 609b).

Scotus' intention in referring to the "orde in contingentibus" when speaking of self-evident psychological states seems to be no other than this. Just as there is no further reason for the fact that the will wills or that heat heats, etc., than that they are will or heat, so there is no reason for the fact that I am awake, or hearing, or seeing, than the actual existence in my soul or body of these acts or dispositions. As in external contingent experience the intellect must often content itself with simply ascertaining the facts as they present themselves, so in the sphere of inner experience we must be satisfied with ascertaining the dispositions as they are present in us. We cannot account for their being there, or for their being what they are.

Here it may be asked, Why does Scotus call these propositions self-evident, although they are essentially dependent on experience?

22. Cf. *Oxon.* I, d. 2, q. 7, n. 26; VIII, 562a-b.

Thus the proposition, "Ego vigilo," is obviously not self-evident in virtue of its terms. It can be known to a person who is actually in the state of waking; in other words, its evidence is essentially a result of actual experience.

It must be noted here that the expression, "per se," indicates a double function of the terms in a self-evident proposition. First, it refers to the self-evidence through the terms; a proposition is called "per se nota" inasmuch as it is knowable through the mutual relation of the terms as they stand in the proposition. Secondly, "per se" expresses the logical immediacy of a self-evident proposition; it indicates that no middle term is needed to make the proposition evident or knowable. This is obviously the case with the contingent propositions under consideration. Indeed, the only reason Scotus adduces *expressis verbis* for calling contingent propositions self-evident is their immediacy:

> Nos vigilare est per se notum...quia...aliqua est prima et immediata (*Oxon.* I, d. 3, q. 4, f. 31v, b; n. 10, IX, 179a).

Therefore, it is in the sense of immediacy that the expression, "per se," is applied to these propositions. Their evidence, therefore, cannot be placed on the same level with that of self-evident propositions in the strict sense. This would be incompatible with the very nature of contingent propositions. Known, as they are, by experience, they cannot be self-evident in virtue of the terms. [23] If Scotus nevertheless calls them self-evident it is because the intellect grasps them in the same immediate way as it grasps self-evident propositions.

From a subjective standpoint, the self-evidence of inner states and operations, such as to be awake, to be aware, to be thinking, etc., is even more basic than the self-evident principles themselves. [24] Not that the latter are in any way dependent on the knowing subject for their validity or trustworthiness; but their objective self-evidence would never become known unless it were

23. Cf. Aniceto de Mandonedo, O.F.M., "Abstraccion y realismo según el B.J.D. Escoto" in *Collectanea Franciscana,* VI (1936), pp. 548f.

24. Cf. Déodat de Basly, O.F.M., *Scotus docens* (Paris, 1934), p. 9: "Dans l'ordre de nos moyens de connaître, l'expérimentation *interne* occupe la toute première place."

first self-evidently known that we are subjectively disposed
to apprehend them. The relation between the evidence of psychological states and first principles is further developed in Scotus'
discussion of certain objections raised against the certitude of
natural knowledge.

C. INTROSPECTIVE EVIDENCE IS AT THE BASIS
OF ALL EVIDENCE

Henry of Ghent, impressed by the illusions to which man is
exposed in dreams and hallucinations, had come to the conviction
that no true knowledge whatsoever is possible without a special
light from on high. No one, argues Henry, has a certain and infallible knowledge of truth unless he has the means by which to
distinguish what is true from what is apparently true. Both in
dreaming and waking, however, we make use of the same instru-
ments of knowledge, viz., of images or species. In the former state
these species appear to us as real objects, whereas in the latter
we apprehend them as mere images or similitudes of objects. These
two representations, as is obvious, cannot be true at the same
time. Yet it is impossible to decide which is true and which false,
since nothing seems to justify one to ascribe truth to what we
perceive in one state in preference to what we perceive in another. [25]

Scotus is aware of the serious and far-reaching nature of the
problem posed by Henry. For he, too, admits the activity of phantasy as indispensable for true knowledge. But contrary to Henry, he
maintains that the intellect has at its disposal a reliable criterion
of correctly evaluating the activity of phantasy. First, there is the
following truth which "rests in the intellect" *(quiescens in intellectu):* "A disposed faculty does not err concerning the objects
proportionate to it." Secondly, while actually understanding, the
intellect knows self-evidently that it is awake; [26] hence, it also
knows that the phantasy is not indisposed in waking as it is in
dreaming:

> Quomodo sciet vel erit tunc intellectus certus, quando non errat
> virtus phantastica, quam tamen non errare requiritur ad hoc quod intel-

25. *Supra,* pp. 23 ff.
26. Cf. *Oxon.* IV, d. 45, q. 2, n. 11; XX, 303b: "Naturale est quod in vigilia
homo habeat usum rationis, in somno autem non."

lectus non erret? - Respondeo, ista veritas quiescit in intellectu, quod potentia non errat circa objectum proportionatum, nisi indisposita; et notum est intellectui virtutem phantasticam non esse indispositam in vigilia tali indispositione quae facit phantasma repraesentare se tamquam objectum, quia per se notum est intellectui quod intelligens vigilat *(Oxon.* I, d. 3, q. 4, f. 32r, b; n. 14, IX, 182b-183a).

In the state of waking, therefore, the phantasy does not function at random or haphazardly, but is under the control of the intellect. Moreover, in this state we are conscious not only of the control exercised by the intellect here and now, but also of the fact that it had no control over the phantasy in the state of sleep. Hence, man is not necessarily led into error, for there is a state in which he can both judge the actual operations of his phantasy and intellect, and exclude as not trustworthy the representations and operations of unconscious and abnormal states.

As for those who stubbornly refuse to admit any immediate certitude in the domain of introspection and sense perceptions, there is no hope of convincing them of anything whatsoever. Aristotle [27] takes recourse to arguments *ad hominem* against those who deny the principle of contradiction, by showing the inconsistencies into which they have fallen. Likewise, we have only one means to discard the objections of those who deny introspective evidence: to show them how inconsistently they act. On the one hand, they do not admit that any disposition or operation of the soul is known with certainty. On the other hand, they do not act accordingly. For waking from a dream in which they imagined that they were about to possess something, they do not pursue it, as they would do in waking if a thing were thus close by. [28] By acting in this manner they implicitly admit that it can be known whether a faculty is disposed or not; otherwise there would be no reason for not pursuing the thing seen in dreams.

It is useless to argue with those who demand further extrinsic or intrinsic criteria to decide whether we are now awake or asleep.

27. *Metaphysics* III (*alias* IV), chaps. 4 ff.
28. *Loc. cit.*, chap. 5; 1010b 3-10: "It is fair to express surprise at our opponents' raising the question..whether...those things (are) true which appear to the sleeping or to the waking. For obviously they do not think these to be open questions; no one, at least, if when he is in Libya he has fancied one night that he is in Athens, starts for the concert hall. "

To these we shall say: "You cannot be convinced of anything, because you do not want to be convinced." There are no reasons against bad will. "To doubt the value of this intuitive evidence" (of introspection), comments Bettoni,[29] is to render impossible all affirmation and all reasoning. It is a doubt from which there is no escape. And it is precisely this impossibility of escape which reveals the absolute gratuitousness of such a doubt."

> Contra negantem primum principium...Philosophus...inducit alia inconvenientia manifestiora...Ita hic, si contendis nullam propositionem esse per se notam, nolo disputare tecum, quia constat quod protervis et non es persuasus, sicut patet in actibus tuis, quomodo objicit Philosophus IV *Metaph.* Somnians enim de aliquo quasi in proximo consequendo sive obtinendo, et postea evigilans, non persequeris illud, sicut prosequeris vel prosequereris si ita esses proximus in vigilando ad illud consequendum *(loc. cit.,* 183a-b).[30]

Entirely different is Aristotle's procedure with those who admit the first principles. True, he does not pretend to prove the principles, because they are indemonstrable. But he makes it clear that they are known in such evident manner that their opposites are simply inconceivable.[31] Likewise, there is no cogent proof for a *per se notum* in the sphere of human operations. Yet we are in a position to verify how such knowledge comes about, and how the denial of its self-evidence implies contradictions and incongruities. Thus, if you reject introspective evidence, you must logically reject all self-evident propositions. And conversely, if you grant that there is a self-evident proposition you must also concede that we can know with certainty when the faculties are disposed and when they are not. An indisposed faculty can err with regard to anything, not excepting the first principles themselves, as we know from dreams. Therefore, in order that a proposition be known *per se* or self-evidently, it is first necessary that we be able to know immediately and evidently when our intellectual faculty works

29. *Duns Scoto* (Brescia, 1945), p. 171.

30. Cf. *Oxon.* IV, d. 43, q. 2, n. 6; XX, 37b ss.; *Rep. Par.* IV, d. 43, q. 2, n. 7; XXIV, 490b ss.

31. Aristotle admits that someone may affirm and deny the same thing *in words*, but no one in his right mind can *think* contradictory statements true, "for what a man says, he does not necessarily believe." *Loc. cit.,* chap. 3, 1005b 23-26. - Cf. also: *Oxon.* I, d. 2, q. 2, n. 31; VIII, 478b.

normally and when not.[32] In other words, you must admit that it can be known through our own internal operations that the faculty is actually disposed. Otherwise it would be impossible to ascertain whether a proposition which appears to us as self-evident is in fact self-evident:

> Recipientibus primum principium (Aristoteles) ostendit quomodo sit notum, ita quod oppositum ejus non possit evenire in mentem...Si admittis aliquam propositionem esse per se notam[33] et circa quamcumque potest potentia indisposita errare, sicut patet in somniis; ergo ad hoc ut aliqua cognoscatur per se esse nota, oportet quod possit cognosci quando potentia est disposita et quando non. Et per consequens potest haberi notitia de actibus nostris, quod potentia est ita disposita quod illa est per se nota quae apparet sibi per se nota (*loc. cit.*, 183b).

Similar is Scotus' solution of the difficulty raised against the possibility of distinguishing between real and imaginary sense perceptions. It is said that in dreams it often seems to us that we are having real sense perceptions. Hence, no certainty is possible concerning the reliability of any sense perception. For if we cannot distinguish between the value of the perceptions of the states of waking and dreaming, then no sense perception can be trusted.

In answering this objection, Scotus again concedes, at least implicitly, that there is no proof for such an immediate and primary activity as is sense perception. As before, he takes recourse to an argument *ad hominem,* by pointing out the absurdities which result from the sceptical attitude of his opponent. No illusions occurring in dreams can render a principle less self-evident. Likewise, no illusion in the senses can prevent a hearing or seeing person from knowing evidently that he is actually hearing or seeing. Although an indisposed intellectual faculty may err with regard to either first principles or sense perceptions, a disposed faculty does not. But when it is disposed, and when not, this is known of itself. Otherwise it could not be determined that any other proposition is self-evident. For it would be impossible to decide which proposition should be considered self-evident, whether that to which the

32. "And when not" does not indicate that we can know the indisposition of the faculty at the time of its indisposition. But we become aware of the error as soon as we are restored to the normal use of the faculty.

33. Oportet quod possit cognosci *add. Viv.*

intellect assents in the state of waking or in the state of dreaming:[34]

> Dico ad formam illius cavillationis, quodsi sicut apparet somnianti se videre, ita posset sibi apparere oppositum unius principii per se noti speculabilis; et tamen non sequitur quin illud principium sit per se notum. Et ita non sequitur quin sit per se notum audienti quod audiat, quia circa utrumque potest potentia indisposita errare, non autem disposita. Et quando sit disposita, et quando non, hoc est per se notum. Alias non posset cognosci aliam aliquam esse per se notam, quia non posset cognosci quae foret per se nota, utrum illa cui intellectus sic dispositus, vel cui sic, assentiret (ibid.).

Nothing could express more poignantly the great importance Scotus attaches to introspective evidence than the concluding sentence of this text. It may be said that the immediate evidence of the disposition of our cognitive faculties is so basic that its rejection implies the downfall of all knowledge. This primary evidence cannot be denied without at the same time rendering impossible any meaningful statement. As Mandonedo[35] remarks, even those who doubt the speculative principles presuppose, at least implicitly, the certainty of the act by which this doubt is known. To be consequent with themselves, those who reject introspective evidence should refrain from stating anything, not excluding their doubts. Scotus' argumentation may be summed up in the following alternative: Either you do not admit of self-evident principles, and then it is useless to argue with you; or you admit that we can and do know self-evident principles, and then you cannot help granting that we can also know whether our faculties are disposed or not.

Having carefully followed our Doctor's expositions on introspective evidence, we are now in a position to comprehend his reasons for stressing so strongly the fact of self-consciousness. It is because the knowledge of our own acts is "the most certain knowledge of all and the foundation of all certitude."[36] While

34. Cf. Bettoni, op. cit., p. 170: "Non c'è altra garanzia (della validità oggetiva de'miei ragionamenti) che quella della mia coscienza, coscienza che non è altro che l'intuizione dei miei atti. Sebbene io, in sogno, possa fare gli stessi ragionamenti di quando sono sveglio, tuttavia distinguo benissimo fra ciò che ho pensato in sogno e ciò che penso da sveglio. Insomma i miei atti e la bona disposizione o meno della mia facoltà intelletiva mi è nota intuitivamente, e contro questa evidenza e certezza intuitiva non c'è cavillo che valga."

35. Loc. cit., p. 17.

36. C.R.S. Harris, Duns Scotus (Oxford, 1927), vol. II, p. 26.

rejecting Augustinian illuminationism, Scotus is broad-minded enough to adopt St. Augustine's views on introspection and thus to supply the Aristotelian doctrine on natural certitude with a firm foundation in the eminent sense of reality proper to the great bishop of Hippo. With Bettoni [37] we must recognize that "it was certainly not from Aristotle that Duns Scotus has learned to appreciate intuitive cognition in general, and to attribute to the intuition of our acts in particular the great importance which we have just given consideration. All this is Augustinian heritage, emerging victoriously from under Aristotelian problematics and formulas. While adopting the latter, Duns Scotus has reserved for himself the liberty to integrate and melt them with the teachings of St. Augustine."

37. *Op. cit.*, p. 172.

CHAPTER II
THE FUNCTION OF EVIDENCE IN INDUCTION

A. NATURE OF INDUCTIVE REASONING

Induction[1] is an intellectual procedure which attempts to solve the acute question of universally valid conclusions in the sphere of experimental sciences. The problem underlying the inductive process may be formulated thus. It is possible to conclude to a uniformity of operations in natural agents on the basis of a limited number of particular observations or experiments?

This problem was by no means unfamiliar to the Scholastics. Aristotle himself had given considerable thought to the validity of inductive reasoning and to the conditions which regulate it.

Although Scotus does not mention Aristotle's theory of induction, it is not without interest to establish a brief comparison between Scotus' and Aristotle's conception of this method of knowledge.

1. *Aristotelian and Scotistic Induction*

For Aristotle the only legitimate way of concluding to universal propositions by means of experience is that which proceeds through the enumeration of all particular cases. Thus we can conclude to the longevity of certain animals by the fact that they are bileless, in the following manner: Man, the horse, etc., are long-lived; man, the horse, etc., are bileless; therefore, animals which are bileless are long-lived.

This procedure, however, as Zeller[2] points out, applies only when the minor concept ("animals which are bileless") has an

---

1. Let it be noted at once that Scotus does not use the term "induction" in the modern sense of the word. Instead he uses the terms "experientia," "cognitio experimentalis," and the like. G.H. Joyce, S.J., in his *Principles of Logic* (London, 1908), pp. 232 f. remarks that the reason why modern textbooks generally state that Scholastic philosophers knew of no inductive process lies "in the fact that the most famous of the Scholastics do not employ the term Induction as the distinctive name of the inference by which we establish universal laws of nature." For the different usages of the term in the Scholastics vide: Hans Meyer, *Thomas von Aquin* (Bonn, 1938), pp. 47f.

2. *Aristotle and the Earlier Peripatetics* (London, 1897), vol. I, pp. 242 ff.

equal extension with the middle concept ("man, horse, etc."), and when the minor proposition ("Man, the horse, etc., are bileless") can be simply transposed, so that in its place this proposition, "The animals which are bileless are man, the horse, etc.," can be put. In other words, the middle term must comprise all the particulars, "for Induction proceeds through an enumeration of all the cases."[3]

This procedure, it is generally admitted,[4] shows serious defects and omissions and can therefore be considered as being practically useless as an instrument of new knowledge. If all particular cases have to be ascertained before we can conclude to all cases in general, it follows that induction for the most part adds only to the intensity of knowledge, but never to its extension. Zeller[5] indicates the main weakness of this "perfect induction" by calling attention to the fact that it is never permissible to conclude to a universal proposition from all the cases *known to us*. For who can ever be sure of having exhausted all the particular cases in matters of experience? Hence, if we were to accept Aristotle's rule of induction, we would never be justified in drawing an inference reaching further than the cases actually known to us. In order to really advance the extension of knowledge, the problem of induction must be approached from a different angle. As a first step we must examine whether from all the cases known to us we may establish a law which will apply to all similar cases.[6] That is how Scotus formulates the problem of the validity of induction. We shall see that his solution is not unlike that which is generally considered as one of the achievements of modern science. First, let us quote Scotus' text:

3. *Prior Analytics* II, c. 23; 68b 11-36.

4. P. Raymond, O.F.M. Cap., "La Théorie de l'Induction - Duns Scot précurseur de Bacon" in *Etudes Franciscaines* XXI (1909), p. 121: "C'est donc à sa nature même: *locus a partibus totius in quantitate ad suum totum,* que tient l'impuissance scientifique de cette forme de raisonnement." According to Raymond, the complete induction of Aristotle has but a provisional value, since new cases must be constantly reckoned with.

5. *Op. cit.,* p. 258.

6. Cf. A. de Mandonnedo, O.F.M. Cap., "Abstracción y realismo según el B.J.D. Escoto" in *Collectanea Franciscana,* VI (1936), pp. 548 f.

De cognitis per experientiam dico quod licet experientia non habeatur de omnibus singularibus, sed de pluribus, neque quod semper, sed quod pluries, tamen expertus infallibiliter novit quod ita est et semper et in omnibus, et hoc per istam propositionem quiescentem in anima: quidquid evenit ut in pluribus ab aliqua causa non libera est effectus naturalis illius causae, quae propositio nota est intellectui, licet accepisset terminos ejus a sensu errante *(Oxon.* I, d. 3, q. 4, f. 31v, a-b; n. 9, IX, 176a-b).

In modern terminology the gist of this text might be worded thus: Does the scientist who has observed a certain phenomenon in a limited number of cases have the right to conclude that the same phenomenon will always occur in connection with the same cause? Scotus answers: If repeated experience reveals a constant reaction on the part of a natural agent, then we can conclude with infallible certitude, first, that the observed effect is proper to that particular agent here and now *(quod ita est),* and secondly, that the same agent will always and everywhere *(semper et in omnibus)* produce the same effect. These conclusions are justified through the following proposition "which rests in the mind:" The effect which frequently follows a non-free cause is a natural effect of that cause. This proposition is self-evident in the sense of the first principles. Its validity and truth do not depend on the trustworthiness of any sense perception. All the mind needs in order to be absolutely certain of this proposition is to consider the relation of a non-free cause on the one hand, to the concept of a constant effect on the other.

As Raymond[7] observes, "it would be unreasonable to assume that a non-free cause should produce ordinarily a phenomenon which is strictly specified, and in conditions which are not less strictly specified, unless it be irresistibly compelled to such an effect in virtue of an inner final principle." We may find external final causes which account for the uniform activity of free agents. But we cannot discover any external causes which would account satisfactorily for the uniformity of reactions in natural agents. A uniform and constant effect in a non-free agent must be ascribed to the natural constitution itself of the agent.

7. *Loc. cit.,* p. 274.

2. *Exclusion of Chance-Causality*

It is sometimes suggested that the effects observed in nature are to be attributed to a casual concurrence of a greater or lesser number of agents, and not to any particular and unchangeable agent. Although not ordered to each other in virtue of their natures, the said agents happen to produce certain effects through an accidental association of their particular activities.[8]

According to Scotus, such fortuitous concurrences of non-ordered agents cannot explain the uniformity of effects in nature. For the agents which here and now are said to act as chance-causes are normally ordered to the very opposite of the effect they now produce accidentally; or at least to some other effect, different from the one they produce here and now. Chance-causality, in fact, always implies the concept of the unusual and extraordinary. It is obviously absurd that a series of non-free agents as these chance-causes are, should produce *in pluribus,* i.e., frequently and under varying circumstances, a constant and uniform effect:

> Causa non libera non potest producere ut in pluribus effectum non liberae ad cujus oppositum ordinatur, vel ad quam ex sua forma non ordinatur. Sed causa casualis ordinatur ad producendum oppositum effectus casualis, vel non ad istum producendum; ergo nihil est causa casualis respectu[9] effectus frequenter producti ab eo, et ita si non sit libera, erit causa naturalis. Iste autem effectus evenit a tali causa etc.; ergo illud est causa naturalis effectus frequenter producti ab eo, quia non est casualis; iste enim effectus evenit a tali causa ut in pluribus[10] *(loc. cit.,* 176b).

It is clear, then, that no effect frequently found in connection with a particular agent is attributable to chance. Scotus, of course, does not deny the possibility of exceptions in nature.[11] Exceptional occurrences, however, do not invalidate the method of induction. For they cannot shake our certitude of the principle of induction which remains self-evident and true. Exceptions, however, serve to show the occasional inapplicability of the method, and to render the observer more cautious in attributing a particular effect to a

---

8. For an exhaustive description of chance-causality see: *Metaph.* VI, q. 2; VII, pp. 323b ss.: "Utrum de ente per accidens possit esse scientia?"

9. Respectu *add. Viv.*

10. Iste autem.../ *om. Viv.*

11. *Metaph.* VI, q. 2, *passim;* VII, 323b ss.

particular cause. We shall elaborate upon this point in a later paragraph of this chapter.

3. *Application of the Inductive Method*

We have seen that the principle of induction is evident through its terms. The occurrence of a frequent effect in natural agents, however, must be learned from experience. By observing a natural agent we often discover that at one time it is accompanied by this accident, at another by that other accident. If the agent, despite the varying accidents, produces constantly and invariably the same effect, then we must conclude that this effect is not the result of the changing accidents but of the underlying permanent nature of the agent:

> Effectus evenit a tali causa ut in pluribus, hoc acceptum est per experientiam; quia inveniendo nunc talem naturam cum tali accidente, nunc cum tali, inventum est quod quantacumque esset diversitas accidentium talium, semper istam naturam sequebatur talis effectus; ergo non per aliquod accidens istius naturae, sed per naturam ipsam in se sequitur talis effectus *(ibid.)*.

It is not without interest to point out the similarity of Scotus' position and solution of the problem of induction, with that adopted in our day. It has often been said that scientific induction was entirely unknown to the Scholastics. Even among Catholic authors this view still prevails to a great extent. In one of Brunner's recent works[12] we read that "scientific induction was unknown to the Scholastics," and that "with the discovery of the inductive scientific methods the problem of the value of their results was raised for the first time." The Scholastics are said to have confused the evident principles "with the abstract and hypothetically necessary formulas of the general laws of nature." "It is commonly stated in English textbooks of Logic," writes Joyce,[13] "that the Scholastic philosophers knew of no inductive process save Perfect and Imperfect Induction, and that they believed that our certainty as to the laws of nature was based on mere enumeration...." And he goes on to criticize this erroneous opinion: "It may indeed be owned that the subject of Induction received far less attention from the

---

12. Auguste Brunner, S.J., *La connaissance humaine* (Paris, 1943), pp. 289f.
13. G.H. Joyce, S.J., *Principles of Logic* (London, 1908), pp. 232f.

medieval writers than it merits. Yet to say that they believed our knowledge as to the laws of nature, to rest on a process of Imperfect Induction by mere enumeration, argues a remarkable want of acquaintance with their writings.... The more prominent amongst them base our certainty in regard to natural laws on the principle, that when the operation of some natural agent produces regularly and habitually some particular result, this result is not due to an accidental circumstance, but is an effect having for its cause the specific nature of the agent." Coffey [14] shows that already St. Thomas made use of the method of agreement, although he "does not explicitly state the principle (od induction), or examine the process by which the ascent is made." Both Joyce and Coffey give full credit to Scotus for having analyzed "with a good deal of precision the procedure by which the generalization is effected." [15] The principle by which Scotus proceeds from particular effects to a universal law is essentially identical to the so-called *law of concatenation (Verknuepfungsgesetz)* which, according to modern logicians, lies at the basis of the inductive method of agreement. [16]

Yet, as we shall presently see, Scotus carefully avoids attributing an exaggerated grade of certitude to the inductive method. He constantly keeps in mind that inductive reasoning is made up of two elements or essentially different values, viz., of a necessary element on the one hand, and a contingent element on the other. The necessary factor is the self-evident principle of induction. The contingent element is the actual instance or series of instances in which a specific effect is observed. Instead of hastily concluding to an absolute degree of certitude from repeated experience, Scotus constantly distinguishes between the absolute truth and certainty of the self-evident principle and the relative value of the laws of nature. He knows well that from two premises, one of which is absolutely certain, and the other only relatively so, no absolutely

---

14. *The Science of Logic* (London, 1912), vol. II, pp. 34f.

15. Professor J. Maritain, in his *Formal Logic* (New York, 1946), pp. 282 f., states that among the Scholastics the theory of incomplete induction was treated particularly by Albert the Great and John of St. Thomas. Curiously enough, the illustrious author does not even mention the name of Scotus.

16. Messner, *op. cit.*, pp. 294 f.; Bettoni, *op. cit.*, pp. 168f.

certain conclusion follows. Hence his painstaking efforts to determine the true grade of certitude proper to the inductive process.

B. CERTITUDE OF INDUCTION

1. *The Basis of Inductive Certitude*

As is implicit in the above expositions, the validity and applicability of the inductive process presuppose the uniformity of nature and its operations. This is an assumption which lies at the basis of natural science as a whole. To reject it is tantamount to renouncing all certitude in this realm. [17] The Schoolmen used to express this postulate in the formula, "Natura determinatur ad unum." This expression, Scotus tells us, is not to be understood in the sense that nature is limited to the production of only one singular effect, but in the sense that nature is directed to one determined manner or pattern of production. By this mode of activity natural agents differ from free agents which determine themselves freely to one or the other of two opposite objects or actions:

> Est intellectus hujus propositionis: natura determinatur ad unum, non quidem ad unum producibile, unum inquam numero sive singulare; sed determinatur ad unum determinatum modum producendi, quia non est ibi principium indeterminatum respectu oppositorum sicut est voluntas. (*Quodl.* q. 2, n. 10; XXV, 71a).

It is from this uniformity of nature that induction, which concludes from several past effects to the repetition of the same effects in the future, draws its certitude. As Raymond[18] observes, the principle of induction itself, i.e., "quidquid evenit ut in pluribus ab aliqua causa non libera, est effectus naturalis illius causae," presupposes this belief in the uniformity of nature. This concept of nature is part of the Aristotelian heritage. Since nature is the ultimate source of being and the first principle of all its operations, it is only logical to see in the immutability of its causal determination the reason for the constancy and invariability *(fixité)* ob-

---

17. Messner, *op. cit.*, p. 298 f.: "Voraussetzung aller Induktion und aller Wirklichkeitswissenschaft bleibt immer, dass man an eine objektive *Weltordnung* glaube. Wo das Vertrauen auf diese verloren geht, dort muss auch das Vertrauen erliegen, allgemeine Gesetze aufzufinden; der Gedanke der allgemeinen Weltordnung muss der Leitstern jeder Wissenschaft bilden."

18. *Loc. cit.*, p. 274.

served in the production of a phenomenon and its accompanying modalities. Yet, contrary to certain modern philosophers, Scotus does not base inductive certitude on a blind or instinctive belief in the constancy of physical laws (Scotch School), or in some *a priori* forms of causality and finality (Lachelier); rather he traces it back to repeated observation of the operations of nature.[19] It is the evidence of experience which tells us that nature acts uniformly and orderly:

> Expertus...certitudinaliter sine demonstratione cognosceret quia... *videt* et certus est naturam ut in pluribus uniformiter agere et ordinate (*Metaph.* I, q. 4, n. 19; VII, 62a).[20]

It might be asked, Is the constancy of nature so firmly established as not to admit of any exception whatever? Does the fact that hitherto nature has acted in this manner give the scientist a guarantee that it will invariably, and infallibly, and always act in the same way? Will no interference of any kind be able to cause it to deflect from its regular course? No Christian thinker can give an affirmative answer to these questions. The radical contingency or, in other words, the essential dependence of the world on its Creator and Conserver prevents him from ascribing an absolute invariability to the laws of nature. This is also Scotus' position. He maintains that those agents which produce their effects in virtue of their form or essence do this in a necessary manner. Yet he adds that this necessity is conditional (*secundum quid*), i.e., the effect occurs only if the natural agent in question is left to itself. In other words, he leaves room for exceptions through the intervention of the First Cause which acts contingently or freely, and may therefore prevent the natural agent from producing its normal effect:

> Licet aliqua connexio (effectus ad causam) sit secundum quid necessaria, nulla tamen simpliciter est necessaria, quia quaelibet dependet

---

19. Idem, *ibid.*, p. 274.

20. In this Scotus employs the same criterion used by Stuart Mill and his followers. "D'autres," writes Raymond (*ibid.*), "à la suite de Stuart Mill, expliquent l'origine de cette croyance (à la constance des lois physiques) par la répétition des constatations expérimentales." Cf. also: *Metaph.* I, q. 4, n. 17; VII, 60b-61a: "Ex multis singularibus cum hac propositione, natura agit ut in pluribus, nisi impediatur, sequitur universalis; et si non sit causa impedibilis, sequitur simpliciter quod in omnibus."

a prima causa quae contingenter causat...similiter communiter secundae causae sunt impedibiles, et causa impedibilis quantumcumque non impediatur non est necessaria *(Metaph.* V, q. 3, n. 5; VII, 206a).

Physical laws, therefore, are not absolutely but conditionally necessary.[21] The course of nature is predictable only on the condition that it be left to itself, and not interfered with by Divine Omnipotence:

> Ad intentionem Aristotelis[22]...an scilicet sicut scibile est pluviam fore sub Capricorno, per causam naturalem ordinatam ad ejus eventum, tamen impedibilem, ita etiam scibile sit pluviam fore sub Cane; *et hoc supposito, quod causae naturales sibi dimittantur,* scilicet quod *per virtutem divinam non impediantur,* quam suppositionem Aristoteles putavit necessariam *(Metaph.* VI, q. 2, n. 7; VII, 329a).

As Longpré[23] points out, the Divine Legislator is not bound by the laws He has freely established, which means that the laws of nature are always liable to be suspended.

Apart from the possibility of direct intervention on the part of the Creator, the scientist must also reckon with the so-called chance causes[24] or *causae per accidens,* as Scotus calls them.[25] Natural causes which normally produce their effects in a necessary manner *(per se)* may sometimes be impeded in their normal operations by the interference of certain extrinsic factors:

> Causa naturalis, licet ex se terminetur ad effectum, potest tamen impediri...si ab extrinseco ponatur impedimentum *(Metaph.* IX, q. 14, n. 10; VII, 589a).[26]

21. Cf. William of Ockham's clear formulation of this hypothetical necessity: "De contingentibus formantur propositiones necessariae hypotheticae, scilicet conditionales vel temporales." *Sent.* prol., q. 4, K; we are quoting from E. Hochstetter, *Studien zur Metaphysik u. Erkenntnislehre W. v. Ockham* (Berlin, 1927), p. 168, note 1.

22. *Metaphysics,* V, c. 2; 1026b 33-36.

23. *La philosophie du Bienheureux Duns Scot* (Paris, 1924), p. 64. Vide also: E. Gilson, *L'esprit de la philosophie médiévale* (Paris, 1944), p. 359.

24. We say "so-called chance causes" because Scotus admits of no chance effects in the strict sense. True, an effect *per accidens* is not knowable through the cause to which it is related accidentally. Absolutely speaking, however, any accidental effect can be traced back to a cause *per se (Metaph.* VI, q. 2, n. 7; VII, 329b). We usually try to conceal our inability to perform the mentioned operation by speaking of "chance causes."

25. *Metaph.* VI, q. 2, *passim;* VII, 323b ss.

26. Cf. *Oxon.* II, d. 7, q. un., n. 26; XII, 407a; *Metaph.* VI, q. 2, n. 7; VII, 330a.

Yet, despite the occasional occurrence of such impediments, Scotus does not doubt the value of the inductive process. Although the possibility of exceptions in nature should caution the observer against placing an exaggerated confidence in the method, it can be stated that induction is a sure way of arriving at certain knowledge. As is implied in the texts, the mentioned interference of extrinsic factors always remains the exception. As a rule, nature acts in a necessary and uniform manner. "A natural cause," writes Scotus, "produces its effect to the utmost of its power as often as it is not prevented from doing so:"

> Causa naturalis agit ad effectum suum secundum ultimum potentiae suae quando non est impedita (Oxon. I, d. 3, q. 2, f. 27r, b; n. 23, IX, 48b). [27]

Every natural cause, if left to itself, produces its proper effect:

> Omnis causa sibi dimissa...producit effectum cujus est per se (Metaph. VI, q. 2, n. 7; VII, 329a).

In other words, natural causes produce necessarily all that they are capable of producing, due to their strict determinism. [28] Therefore it is legitimate to infer: If fire is given, then light is also given. For the inference is based on a natural, non impeded causality:

> Dico quod sequitur: ignis est in hoc nunc et non impeditus, ergo lux est: locus est a causa naturaliter causante et non impedita; et non solum hoc, sed etiam a ratione quadam communiore in antecedente potest ista consequentia tenere, scilicet a ratione producentis naturaliter, et non impediti (Oxon. II, d. 1, q. 3, f. 99v, a; n. 11, XI, 76a).

Thus, to the principle already mentioned that "the effect which proceeds for the most part from a non-free cause is a natural effect of this cause" another self-evident principle may be added: "Every natural cause, if not impeded, produces its effect necessarily." The latter principle contains the formal reason which justifies a universal conclusion from a limited number of observations.

---

27. Cf. Oxon. II, d. 2, q. 8, n. 13; XII, 195a; IV, d. 43, d. 3, n. 5; XX, 68a; Metaph. I, q. 7, n. 2; VII, 79b; IX, q. 14, n. 10, VII, 589a.

28. S. Belmond, O.F.M., "L'idée de création d'après S. Bonaventure et Duns Scot" in Etudes Franciscaines, XXXI (1914), pp. 10 ff.

2. *Grades of Inductive Certitude*

Having established the basic principles of induction and their certitude, we must now try to ascertain the various grades of certitude which may be had in the actual application of the method.

Induction concerns itself for the most part, if not exclusively, with reactions, effects, and properties, which are by their nature accidental to the agents in which they occur. Every accident, however, is absolutely speaking, separable from its subject. For the definition of an accident implies that it is not necessarily connected with the substance of the subject in which it inheres. Hence, from the presence of the subject we cannot conclude with absolute certainty to the presence of the accident. According to Scotus, it is never contradictory to say that the prior can be without the posterior: [29] "The prior according to nature and essence," he writes, "is that which is able to exist without the posterior, but not conversely. I take this in the following sense: Even if the prior necessarily causes the posterior and therefore cannot exist without it, still this is not because it needs the posterior for its own being, but conversely. For if it be assumed that the posterior does not exist, the prior will nevertheless exist without the inclusion of a contradiction." [30] In this sense all accidents are posterior to the substance, for they depend on substance for their existence, while substance does not depend on anyone of its accidents.

Moreover, "to be able to produce an absolutely necessary effect does not pertain to the perfection of a created cause; in fact, there is no such thing (as a necessary effect) in a created cause...for (the concept of) an absolutely necessary causation includes a contradiction." [31]   Hence, while the self-evident principle, "A

29. Cf. Messner, *op.cit.*, p. 251.

30. *De Primo Principio*, c. 1, prima divisio; ed. by Evan Roche, O.F.M. (St. Bonaventure, 1949), p. 4 f.: "Prius secundum naturam et essentiam est, quod contingit esse sine posteriori, non econverso. Quod ita intelligo, quod, licet prius necessario causet posterius et ideo sine ipso esse non possit, hoc tamen non est quia ad esse suum egeat posteriori, sed econverso; quia si ponatur posterius non esse, nihilominus prius erit sine inclusione contradictionis."

31. *Oxon.* II, d. 1, q. 3, n. 12; XI, 77b-78a: "Posse habere causatum simpliciter necessarium non est perfectionis in causa secunda; immo et hoc nulli causae secundae convenit...Simpliciter enim necessario causare includit contradictionem et ideo hoc nulli causae secundae convenit." Cf. *Oxon.* I, d. 8, q. 5, n. 25; IX,

frequent effect of a non-free cause must be ascribed to the nature of the cause," has an absolute and unshakeable validity, the same cannot be said of the reverse of that principle, viz., of this proposition: "As often as this cause is posited, its proper effect must also be posited." The contingency of secondary causes and of their effects does not allow this conclusion. No contingent thing, therefore, can enable the observer to conclude demonstratively to the existence of another contingent thing or to an accidental modification of it.

True, repeated observation may lead the scientist to the knowledge that a certain herb is "warm." But he will never discover a self-evident principle or a middle term by which the mentioned quality could be demonstrated in a necessary manner *(propter quid)* of the herb. This is equivalent to saying that no infallible knowledge can be had of the *actual presence* of warmth in a given herb. For it is not incompatible with the nature of an accidental quality to be separated from its subject. The only infallible knowledge the inductive process conveys is that the herb is *capable* of producing warmth. It is for this reason that the knowledge resulting from the application of the inductive process is termed by Scotus the lowest degree of scientific knowledge:

> Quandoque est experientia de principio, ita quod non contingit per viam divisionis invenire ulterius principium ex terminis, sed statur in aliquo vero ut in pluribus, cujus extrema per experientiam scitum est frequenter uniri, puta quod haec herba talis speciei est calida, nec invenitur medium aliud prius per quod demonstretur passio de subjecto propter quid, sed statur in isto sicut primo noto propter experientiam. Licet tunc incertitudo et fallibilitas removeantur per istam propositionem, effectus ut in pluribus alicujus causae non liberae est naturalis effectus ejus, tamen iste est ultimus gradus cognitionis scientificae, et forte ibi non habetur cognitio actualis unionis extremorum, sed aptitudinalis; si enim passio est alia res absoluta a subjecto, posset sine contradictione separari a subjecto, et expertus non haberet cognitionem quia ita est, sed quia ita aptum natum est esse *(Oxon.* I, d. 3, q. 4, f. 31v, b; n. 9, IX, 177a).

In the commentary on *Metaphysics* we find a more detailed description of the grade of certitude proper to the various steps of

---

765a: "Necessitas repugnat omni respectui ad posterius, quia ex quo omne posterius est non necessarium, primum non potest habere necessariam habitudinem ad aliquod eorum."

the inductive process. Scotus again points out that demonstrative cognition is denied the *expertus* or scientist. Yet by means of experience *(sciens quia est)*, the natural scientist can know *with certainty* the cause of an observed effect, for he sees that nature, as a rule, acts uniformly and orderly:

> Expertus demonstratione carens, sciens quia est, certitudinaliter, sine demonstratione cognosceret, quia videt et certus est naturam, ut in pluribus, uniformiter agere et ordinate *(Metaph.* I, q. 4, n. 19; VII, 62a).

There is no doubt that this first step of inductive reasoning produces certitude. For it is based on a twofold evidence, viz., on the evidence of the experienced effects (quia *videt)*, and on the self-evidence of the principle formulated at the occasion of this experience *(natura ut in pluribus...).*

A lesser degree of certitude is ascribed to the second step of the process which concludes from one or more particular effects of a natural agent to a similar effect in all the agents of the same kind. Experimental knowledge, however frequent, does not justify the inference that the observed effect will be necessarily the same in all cases. Experience yields only *probable* knowledge:

> Experimentalis cognitio quantumcumque frequens, non infert necessario ita esse in omnibus, sed tantum probabiliter *(loc. cit.,* n. 6; 55a).

This need not be in contradiction with the *infallible* knowledge of the *Oxoniense.* For, as we have already remarked, the infallibility in that passage refers only to the *aptitude* of a given agent to produce the same effect in all cases, and not to the actual production of the effect.

Scotus' statement that induction produces only probable knowledge does not imply a positive denial of certitude. This is made clear in the following paragraph. The observation of many singular facts enables the observer to conclude, *per simile,* that the effect which was produced in many particular instances by a certain agent will also be produced in all similar cases. This inference is not based on a merely external or superficial likeness, such as are the elements which change with every case, but on the very essence or common nature of the agents in question:

Expertus per singularia arguit per simile, quod sicut est de uno singulari, et de pluribus, sicut est in multis singularibus, sic est in omnibus. Quod autem simile sit de uno singulari et de aliis, idem accipitur, quod subjectum comparatur ad praedicatum, non secundum accidens, nec secundum illud in quo differt ab alio singulari, sed per se et secundum naturam sui communis (*Metaph.* I, q. 4, n. 6; VII, 55a).

The observer, therefore, concludes to absent and future cases, not simply on the evidence of sense perception, but on the evidence of an intellectual principle that is always true, viz., on the evidence of the proposition, "Nature, for the most part, acts uniformly and orderly." [32] On the basis of these considerations we may safely conclude that Scotus' *probability* is the equivalent of what we would term *physical certitude* which is based on exactly the same uniformity and constancy of the ordinary course of nature.

It might be asked why a twofold evidence as is present in the inductive process is not capable of producing a strictly scientific conclusion. We answer that in order to obtain such a conclusion the conclusion would have to be both evident and necessary. These conditions, however, are not fulfilled. First, the conclusion from a limited number of cases to all similar cases is not truly evident. For induction always deals with contingent facts, i.e., with conclusions from one contingent fact or series of facts to another contingent fact or series of facts. Contingent facts, however, cannot be evidently known unless they are actually existent and present to the knower. It lies in the very nature of induction that the facts to which it concludes are either absent or not yet in existence. An inductive conclusion, therefore, cannot be evident.

Secondly, it is clear that a conclusion known in this manner is never necessary. For induction is essentially a mixed method of cognition. Besides an analytical, self-evident factor, it always contains a purely synthetical factor, viz., the fact or series of facts to which the self-evident principle is applied. The experimental factor, although evident, is always of a contingent nature. From two premises, however, one of which is contingent and the other necessary, only a contingent conclusion can follow:

32. *Metaph.* I, q. 4, n. 19; VII, 62a: "Expertus...certus est naturam, ut in pluribus, uniformiter agere et ordinate."

Ex duabus praemissis, quorum una est necessaria et alia contingens, non sequitur conclusio necessaria. Et ratio est, quia quod dependet ex pluribus, non potest esse perfectioris conditionis quocumque illorum *(Quodl.* q. 15, n. 7; XXVI, 12a).

Scotus, therefore, does not ascribe the same degree of certitude to inductive and deductive knowledge. Although the conclusions obtained by induction are truly certain, they cannot be placed on the same level with strictly scientific conclusions in the Aristotelian sense. [33] In some cases, however, experimental knowledge serves as a starting point toward scientific knowledge, insofar as it offers the intellect an opportunity of arriving at the cognition of the causes of the observed phenomena. Once in possession of the causes, the intellect may be able to know, by way of demonstrative reasoning, one or more conclusions which at first were known by experience alone.

3. A Case of Demonstrative Certitude from Experience

Scotus, who is always in search of the best possible basis for intellectual knowledge, maintains that in certain instances experimental knowledge may lead up to an absolute or demonstrative certitude. Scotus distinguishes two steps in the process. First, the scientist must find the precise cause of the phenomenon he is observing, i.e., he must make sure that there is no alternative cause by which the phenomenon in question may be explained. This is done through the method of division or elimination *(per viam divisionis)*. Secondly, the scientist must find a self-evident proposition which, when used as a major premise together with the proposition resulting from the previous operation as minor premise, enables him to know by demonstration the effect which he had known at first by experience alone. For instance, the observer knows through frequent experience that the moon is frequently eclipsed. This is as yet a conclusion *quia est,* i.e., a synthetical judgment based on empirical cognition. Once in possession of this experimental knowledge, the scientist sets out to inquire the cause of the phe-

33. *Oxon.* III, d. 24, q. un., n. 19; XV, 49a: "Inductio non sufficit ad scientiam, nec ideo scitur universale quia ex particularibus educitur. Unde magis sequitur scientifice: omne totum est majus sua parte, igitur hoc totum, quam econverso, scilicet hoc et illud totum, igitur omne."

nomenon. He does this by discarding all the possible factors which might constitute the cause of the darkening of the moon. By this process of elimination he finally arrives at the certain conclusion that the only cause preventing the light of the sun from reaching the moon is the interposition of the earth.

Now there is a principle which goes as follows: "An opaque body which interposes itself between a luminous body and an illumined object impedes the transmission of light from the former to the latter." This principle is self-evident and true in virtue of its terms, and therefore absolutely certain. It suffices to have a distinct idea of the nature of an opaque body and the manner of the transmission of light to make it clear and evident to the mind that an opaque body is always an obstacle to the transmission of light. As soon, therefore, as the observer comes to the cognition that the earth is the only opaque body interposed between sun and moon, he concludes with absolute certainty that the actual eclipse of the moon is caused by this interposition. His knowledge of the phenomenon is no longer merely empirical or a *conclusio quia est,* but it has become a strictly scientific or *propter quid* cognition which is obtained through an evident and necessary syllogistic reasoning in this manner: An opaque body which interposes itself between a luminous body and the object illumined by it impedes the transmission of light to the latter. The earth is such an opaque body between sun and moon. Hence it impedes the transmission of light from the sun to the moon:

> Sed ulterius notandum quod quandoque accipitur experientia de conclusione, puta quod luna frequenter eclipsatur; et tunc supposita conclusione quod ita est, inquiritur causa talis conclusionis per viam divisionis, et quandoque devenitur ex conclusione experta ad principia nota ex terminis, et tunc ex tali principio noto ex terminis potest conclusio prius tantum secundum experientiam nota, certius cognosci, scilicet primo genere cognitionis, quia ut deducta ex principio per se noto: sicut istud est per se notum, quod opacum interpositum inter perspicuum et lumen impedit multiplicationem luminis ad tale perspicuum; et si inventum fuerit per divisionem quod terra tale est corpus interpositum inter solem et lunam, scietur certissime demonstratione propter quid, quia per causam, et non tantum per experientiam, sicut sciebatur ista conclusio ante inventionem principii *(Oxon.* I, d. 3, q. 4, f. 31v, b; n. 9, IX, 176b-177a).[34]

34. Raymond *(loc. cit.,* p. 277) observes that modern sciences use a great number of general principles comparable to the self-evident major premise employed

A similar description of demonstrative knowledge on the basis of experience is found in the *Commentary on Metaphysics*. Scotus shows that a perfect *propter quid* cognition (as opposed to mere belief) is had only if the scientist is able to ascertain, by elimination, that the effect under consideration is produced by this particular cause, and by no other. Only after this has been ascertained can the observer conclude, through application of a self-evident principle, that the same effect will follow uniformly from the same cause. For the method of elimination enables him to know the effect not only through experience or mere observation, but through an immediate or *a priori* knowledge of the cause:

> Primus...quantumcumque inquirat per viam divisionis...in fine non sciet, sed tantum credet...Secundus vero per viam divisionis sciet conclusionem propter quid, sciunt enim ita esse, et per viam divisionis scit quod propter aliud nihil ita est nisi propter hoc; sciet ergo propter hoc ita esse. Tertius vero applicando principium sciet propter quid; ergo secundus est dispositus ad sciendum propter quid dispositione propinqua, sed tertius propinquiori. Secundus enim quasi immediate demonstrabit causam per effectum quem novit, et ex hoc ultra cognoscet effectum per causam; sed tertius jam immediate per causam notam cognoscet effectum (*Metaph.* I, q. 4, n. 19; VII, 62a-b).[35]

Hence it is the ability of the scientist to trace his particular conclusions to general self-evident principles or laws which impart his conclusions the highest possible degree of certitude.

All inductive certitude, therefore, rests in the final analysis on self-evidence. "Imperfect" induction which proceeds mainly on observation derives its scientific value from the general principle, "A frequent effect of a non-free cause proceeds from the nature of that cause." "Demonstrative" induction which is based on the knowledge of the causes owes its exceptional grade of certitude to other, more specific self-evident principles.

---

by Scotus: "On distingue en effet deux sortes de lois induites, des *lois empiriques* et des *lois explicatives*. Les premières indiquent les modalités constantes de l'activité d'une substance spécifiquement déterminée; les secondes en donnent une raison beaucoup plus générale."

35. Cf. also: *Oxon.* prol. q. 1, n. 27; VIII, 62a.

CHAPTER III
THE ROLE OF EVIDENCE FOR SENSE KNOWLEDGE

The insistence with which Scotus has endeavored to establish the independence on true sense knowledge of first principles and other self-evident propositions may have given rise to the impression that he doubts the objective value of sense knowledge as such.

Scotus is well aware of the insufficiencies of many of our sense perceptions, especially if they are taken uncritically. For the senses lie open to numerous illusions which are due either to subjective factors, such as indispositions of the sense organs, or to objective conditions, such as an unfavorable medium, a disproportionate distance or size of the object. But far from despairing of the possibility to arrive at true knowledge of sensible things, Scotus thinks that such knowledge can be had as long as sense activity is checked and controlled by the intellect. The Franciscan Doctor is continually on the outlook for ways and means of correcting the senses, and for supplementing the deficiencies of their information. His search has not been in vain, as the present chapter is about to show.

A. LIMITATIONS OF SENSE KNOWLEDGE
1. *Imperfection of Sense Knowledge*

Certain knowledge through the senses has often been denied on the authority of St. Augustine. Time and again we meet with the time-honored formula of the bishop of Hippo: "A sensibilibus non est expectanda sincera veritas."[1] Henry of Ghent who shares this distrust toward sense knowledge tries to justify his position by an appeal to the mutability of all sensible things. He maintains that there is no certain knowledge of truth unless it is had under the aspect of immutability. But sensible things are subject to continual change. Therefore, the unassisted human reason cannot obtain certain knowledge of contingent things. Any "sincere" or perfect knowledge about sensible things presupposes the assistance of

---

1. *Liber LXXXIII Quaestionum* q. 9; PL 40, col. 13.

the Uncreated Light which makes these things known under at least some aspect of immutability. [2]

Scotus rejects both the assumption and the conclusion of Henry's argumentation. Even if we granted the assumption that all things are mutable, there would still be a possibility of certain knowledge, viz., of the fact that all things are continually changing. Even here an element of constancy is present, viz., the unceasing process of coming-to-be and passing-away. Moreover, it is clear that Henry is mistaken when he states that all things are absolutely changeable. Not everything in nature changes; in fact, many objects, though changing under one aspect, remain constant under another:

> Ad illud de mutatione objecti, antecedens est falsum; non enim sensibilia sunt in continuo moto, imo permanent eadem in aliena duratione. ...Et consequentia non valet, dato quod antecedens esset verum; quia adhuc secundum Aristotelem[3] posset haberi certa cognitio de hoc, dato quod omnia continue moventur (*Oxon.* I, d. 3, q. 4, f. 32r, a; n. 13, IX, 181a-b). [4]

Yet Scotus is well aware that even though a certain degree of constancy is found in the sensible world, the senses are of themselves incapable of apprehending it. "Sincere truth," he writes, "is not grasped by the senses in such wise as to enable them to perceive the immutability of the truth they apprehend, or for this matter, the immutability itself of the object. For the senses perceive present objects only as long as these are present." Since sensible objects are not always present to the senses, these cannot perceive whether or not the aforementioned objects remain in the same state. Even supposing that I should have the object A uninterruptedly in my presence, and that I should gaze upon it without intermission, so that my vision would retain the same grade of sharpness throughout the whole process, I would still be unable to perceive the immutability of A, for at each moment of my vision I would perceive the object precisely as it is constituted at that same moment:

> Ad auctoritatem Augustini salvandam, dici potest, quod sincera veritas non cognoscitur a sensu, ita quod sensus percipiat immutabilitatem veritatis quam apprehendit, nec objectum inquantum immobile; sensus

2. *Summa,* art. I, quaest. II, fol. 3v ss.
3. *Metaphysics* IV, c. 5; 1010a 6-20.
4. Cf. *Metaph.* I, q. 4, n. 23; VII, 64b.

enim non percipit nisi praesens, et dum est praesens, et ideo non cognoscit ex se aliquid se habere, nisi dum praesens est, et non semper
praesens est sensui corporali... Posito etiam quod semper continuare-
tur visio mea circa A objectum, sicut in primo instanti, non percipio
immutabilitatem A quia pro tunc non percipio nisi ipsum ut tunc est
praesens; ita etiam in tota visione quantumcumque continuata, nunquam
percipiam immutabilitatem A, sed pro omni nunc percipiam quomodo se
habet pro tunc *(Metaph.* I, q. 4, n. 23; VII, 65a).

Scotus, therefore, grants to the objector that the senses are
unable to convey truth formally; yet he refuses to acknowledge that
it was St. Augustine's intention to reject simply and unconditionally
all true knowledge through the channel of the senses. All that St.
Augustine wanted to say is that the senses are unable to apprehend
the truth of their own perceptions and to distinguish true perceptions
from false ones. Since the senses probably do not reflect upon
their species, they cannot discern whether they are informed by a
mere species or image, or whether the species is produced in the
phantasy by a real and present object:

Quoad secundam probationem Augustini dicendum quod forte sensus
non reflectitur supra speciem, et ideo non discernit utrum tantum specie
informetur, vel utrum objectum sit praesens specialiter de phantasia
(loc. cit., n. 24; VII, 65b). Bene concludunt quod non sit impossibile
esse aliquam veritatem sinceram de sensibilibus,..sed illam veritatem
sinceram esse, sive ejus sinceritatem sive immutabilitatem, et a falso
distinctam non percipit sensus, sicut dicit Augustinus *(ibid.).*

From these considerations it follows that the senses are neither
to be trusted nor to be distrusted *a priori.* They only furnish the
material of information to the intellect, without passing judgment
on the value or reliability of their data. This is the task of the
intellectual faculty as we shall see presently.

2. *Intellectual Knowledge Superior to Sense Knowledge.*

Intellectual knowledge, Scotus maintains, is absolutely superior
to sense knowledge. In proof of his point, the Franciscan Doctor
points out that the intellect can judge the value of every sense
perception, by deciding upon the good or bad disposition of the
senses. Furthermore, intellectual knowledge alone conveys true
certitude. Certitude cannot be had by simply apprehending what is
true *(verum);* it is also required that the truth *(veritas)* of what is

apprehended be known. In other words, the knower must be able to render account to himself that what he apprehends is true. Only the intellect, however, can reflect upon its acts and thus judge that it apprehends the *verum:*

> Videtur concedendum quod in nobis cognitio intellectiva sit certior simpliciter quam sensitiva, quod probatur: tum quia de omni sensitiva potest intellectus judicare qualis ipsa est;[5] tum quia certitudo nunquam est in apprehendendo verum, nisi talis sciat veritatem apprehensam, vel sciat illud esse verum quod apprehendit...solus autem intellectus reflectitur judicando se apprehendere verum *(Metaph.* I, q. 4, n. 12; VII, 58a).

It may be objected that the intellect cannot judge the truth or falsity of any sense knowledge except through another sense perception. It would seem, therefore, that the aforementioned judgment of the intellect is possible only on the condition that this new sense perception be obtained through a truer and more reliable sense. But what will happen if all the senses should err in their perceptions? On what basis will the intellect judge, in this case, whether a given sense is now deceived or not?

> Sed contra hoc arguitur sic: Primo quia nullus intellectus judicat de actu sensus nisi per notitiam aliquam acceptam a sensu, forte veriori, et tunc judicat hunc sensum nunc non errare; sed si in omni actu sensus erraret, intellectus non haberet per quid judicaret sensum nunc errare *(loc. cit.,* n. 13; 58b).

Scotus replies that the knowledge by which the intellect evaluates a sense perception is dependent on the senses as on an occasional cause only. There are certain principles the truth of which can be known regardless of true or false sense perceptions. The task of the latter is limited to the apprehension and transmission to the intellect of the *simplicia,* i.e., of the subject and predicate of the principle:[6]

> Respondeo ad hoc, quod intellectus judicat de actu sensus per notitiam ab actu sensus acceptam occasionaliter, vel quoad apprehensionem simplicium, non quoad compositionem principiorum *(ibid.).*

It is irrelevant whether the simple terms are obtained through a correct or erroneous sense perception. For, according to Scotus,

5. Cf. *Metaph.* I, q. 4, n. 24; VII, 65b: "Est alia virtus superior ipsa sensitiva, quae semper judicat de bona et de mala dispositione sensus."
6. Cf. *supra,* pp. 125 ff.

first intellectual apprehensions are always true. A black object which by some reason or other is erroneously taken for white by the sense of sight produces exactly the same concept of whiteness in the mind as would an object which is white in reality. In order that whiteness be apprehended it is sufficient that a species which truly represents whiteness be transmitted to the intellect:

> Prima operatio intellectus semper vera est, licet sequens sensum errantem; ita enim concipitur albedo, si visus apprehendat illud esse album quod est nigrum, sicut si albedo conciperetur a sensu vere vidente album, quia sufficit quod species vere repraesentativa albi veniat ad intellectum ad hoc ut simplici apprehensione album vere apprehendat (*ibid.*, 59a).

Scotus concedes that the intellect falls into error as often as it relies on the testimony of an erring sense for the formulation of a contingent proposition. This happens, we may add, not as a result of any intrinsic weakness or defect of the intellect, but as it were by accident, i.e., insofar as the intellect accepts the sense data without duly probing them as to their value. With regard to first principles, however, the intellect never errs, notwithstanding false sense information:

> In compositione autem et divisione...errat intellectus sequens sensum errantem. Sed non circa prima principia, nec circa conclusiones quas ex primis principiis deduxit, sed circa alias conclusiones quarum notitiam non habet nisi ex sensu errante (*ibid.*).

It is by means of this superior certainty that the intellect can correct the mistakes of the senses. Whatever illusions may occur in the senses, the intellect is not necessarily led into error, for it is never forced to follow the erring sense. Rather, it should embrace the very opposite of what is conveyed by the sense, as soon as it becomes aware of the error:

> Sed adhuc circa tales, licet aliquis sensus erret, tamen non oportet intellectum sequi, sed oppositum tenere, si judicat hunc sensum errare (*loc. cit.*, 59b).

The main question, however, still remains to be answered, namely, How can the intellect decide which sense is true and which false? Henry of Ghent[7] thinks that a sense is true if it is

---

7. *Summa*, art. I, quaest. I, fol. 2v: "Semper oportet credere sensui particulari non impedito, nisi alius sensus dignior in eodem alio tempore, vel in alio eodem tempore contradicat, vel virtus aliqua superior percipiens sensus impedimentum."

not contradicted by the testimony of another sense which is truer,
or by its own perceptions in a more favorable disposition. Likewise,
the reliability of a sense perception may also be ascertained by an
intellectual cognition obtained either through a truer sense, or
through the same sense in a better disposition:

> Sed quomodo (intellectus) judicabit quis sensus est verus, et quis
> errat? Responsio, Gandensis in *Summa* dicit quod omnis sensus est
> verus cui non contradicit alius sensus verior; vel ipsemet alias melius
> dispositus; vel notitia aliqua intellectualis accepta ab alio sensu veri-
> ori, vel eodem alias melius disposito *(loc. cit.,* n. 15, 59b).

Scotus seems to subscribe to these criteria, but he proposes a
further question. Henry no doubt does rightly in contending that the
perceptions of well disposed senses are more reliable than those
of indisposed senses. But how, asks Scotus, can the intellect be
sure that a particular sense is actually well disposed? This brings
us to our next point.

<h3 style="text-align:center">B. CORRECTION OF SENSES THROUGH
SELF-EVIDENT PRINCIPLES</h3>

In both the *Commentary on Metaphysics* and the *Oxoniense,* Scotus
uses the self-evident principle of induction as a means of correcting
the senses. "It seems to be self-evident," he writes in the *Metaphysics,* "that since nature (i.e., any natural agent) is a necessary
(per se) or non free cause, it will for the most part act rightly. If
errors occur, they will be in the smaller number." Belonging as they
do to the category of natural agents, which do not determine themselves freely, the senses react naturally or necessarily to external
stimuli. Hence the representation which an object produces in the
greater number of cases or habitually, will be the true representation
of it:

> Quomodo judicatur quis sensus est bene dispositus? Responsio, per
> se notum videtur quod natura, ex quo est causa per se et non libera,
> ut in pluribus recte agit, et error si contingat, in minori parte accidet;
> quod ergo sensus ut in pluribus dicit, hoc est verum *(Metaph.* I, q. 4, n.
> 15; VII, 59b).[8]

8. Cf. E. Gilson, "Avicenne et le point de départ de Duns Scot" in *Archives
d'hist. doctr. et litt. du M.A.* II (1927), p. 125. Gilson attributes the solution
presented in the text to Henry of Ghent. However, there is no evidence for this in
the *Summa.* True, Henry seeks a solution in repeated experience ("habet iudicare
intellectus ex pluribus experimentationibus" art. I, quaest. I, f 3r G); but the
application of the principle of induction is original with Scotus.

It may be objected that judgments based merely on the majority of cases are often misleading. If the trustworthiness of a sense is to be decided on the greater number of identical perceptions, we would have to conclude that, if there were only three sane or normal persons among all mankind, we would have to reject the judgment of the three sane persons in favor of that of the majority. This is obviously absurd.

Scotus answers that the criterion of truth is not the convergency of many simultaneous sense perceptions, but the convergency of a great number of successive sense perceptions. In other words, if one and the same sense experiences repeatedly and habitually the same quality in a thing, it can and should be trusted:

> Contra, unum non oportet pluralitate judicare, quia tunc si tantum tres essent sani, et omnes alii infirmi, judicium sanorum refutandum esset....Ad primum, non pluralitate sensuum simul, sed pluralitate sensationum, hoc est, quia sensus frequenter ita sentit (oportet judicare) *(ibid.,* 60a).

A similar, but more extensive, solution is presented in the *Oxoniense.* Scotus starts his expositions by introducing an important distinction. In our various sense perceptions we are confronted either with convergent or with divergent sense data. Accordingly, the evaluation and correction of the senses must also differ from case to case.

1. *Evaluation of Convergent Sense Perceptions*

"How is certitude had," asks Scotus, "about the objects which fall under sense perception, as for example, that something which appears as white or hot is really so?"

> Sed quomodo habetur certitudo eorum quae subsunt actibus sensus, puta quod aliquod extra est album vel calidum, quale apparet? *(Oxon.* I, d. 3, q. 4, f. 32r, a; n. 11, IX, 179b).

Scotus replies that either various senses have opposite perceptions of the object in question, or else not, but all senses have identical perceptions of it. If the second alternative is realized, i.e., if an object produces convergent or uniform impressions on two or more senses, then we are certain of the truth of what is thus known. In fact, if the same effect is produced on two or more senses by one and the same object, this effect must be ascribed to the very nature of the object. For that which proceeds frequently from a non-free cause is its natural effect.[9] Nature, because of the determinateness of its activity, cannot deceive. Hence, the species or impression produced successively in the same sense, or simultaneously in two or more senses, truly represents the external reality of the object. "Thus a thing outside will be white or hot or such as is naturally represented by the species it generates in several cases:"

> Respondeo, aut circa tale cognitum eadem opposita apparent diversis sensibus, aut non, sed omnes sensus cognoscentes illud habent idem judicium de eo. Si secundo modo, tunc certitudo habetur de veritate talis cogniti per sensus, et per istam propositionem praecedentem, quod evenit in pluribus ab aliquo illud est causa[10] naturalis ejus, si non sit causa libera; ergo cum ab ipso praesente ut in pluribus evenit talis immutatio sensus, sequitur quod immutatio vel species genita sit effectus naturalis talis causae, et ita tale extra erit album vel calidum, vel tale aliquid quale natum est repraesentari per speciem genitam ab ipso ut in pluribus *(ibid.)*.

If applied to the convergency of several senses, the present rule is of course applicable only to those objects which can be apprehended by more than one sense; these are the so-called *sensibilia communia* or common sense objects, such as size, number, motion, rest, and configuration, all of which can be apprehended by at least two senses. Thus the quadrangular configuration of a brick can be perceived by both sight and touch; an explosion can be perceived by the senses of hearing, sight, touch, and smell.

It is easily seen that this application of the inductive method goes beyond that of the commentary on *Metaphysics*. Scotus confirms and completes the latter in at least one important aspect. While in the *Metaphysics* certitude is based on a uniform testimony of the *same* sense in a great many successive instances,[11] the *Oxoniense* sees the best foundation for certitude in a convergent and simultaneous perception of the same object by *several* senses. Moreover, while the principle of induction was introduced somewhat hesitatingly in the mentioned Commentary ("per se notum videtur"),[12] it is applied here with full confidence as to its self-evidence.

9. Cf. *supra*, p. 254.
10. Effectus *Viv*.
11. *Supra*, p. 291.
12. *Metaph.* I, q. 4, n. 15; VII, 59b.

2. Correction of Divergent Sense Perceptions

It frequently happens that one and the same thing produces conflicting impressions in two or more senses. Thus a staff partly dipped into water appears to the sense of sight as broken or bent. The sense of touch, however, tells us that the staff is and remains straight. Which of the two senses is to be trusted? Likewise, the sun appears to the sense of sight as being smaller than it is in reality. And in general, the further an object is removed from the observer, the smaller it appears. Does this indicate that the sense of sight is necessarily exposed to error? And if not, how is it to be rectified?

> Si autem diversi sensus habeant diversa judicia de aliquo viso extra, puta visus dicit baculum esse fractum cujus pars est in aqua et pars est in aere;[13] visus semper dicit solem esse minoris quantitatis quam est, et omne visum a remotis esse minus quam sit? (Ibid.).[14]

Here again Scotus offers a solution which is indeed worthy of his subtle mind. Mandoñedo [15] rightly remarks that in the paragraph we are about to quote the problem of the existence and reality of the external world is exposed with the clarity and exactness of a philosopher of our own day. [16] For instance, the theory of inference or illationism, which has been so widely propounded in Modern Scholasticism by the School of Louvain, can be found in its basic points in Scotus' doctrine as presented in the Oxoniense. Illationism maintains that once the possibility of illusion is admitted in both the internal and external senses, one must search for an absolutely reliable point of departure in some higher faculty, by which the senses can be corrected. This is precisely the way in which Scotus solves the problem. He, too, demands a higher type of certitude by which the value of divergent sense perceptions may be estimated.

13. Et tactus potest experiri contrarium add. Viv.

14. Cf. Metaph. I, q. 4, n. 15; VII, 60a.

15. "Abstracción y realismo según el B.J.D. Escoto" in Collectanea Franciscana, VII (1937), pp. 18 ff. Concerning Scotus' influence on Card. Mercier, the founder of the mentioned School, see: J.M. Martinez, O.F.M., "Criteriologia Escotista" in Verdad Y Vida, III (1945), p. 652, note 2, and p. 671, note 38. - Cf. also: Fr. Raymond, O.F.M. Cap., "La Philosophie de l'Intuition et la Philosophie du Concept" in Etudes Franciscaines, XXI (1909), p. 693.

16. Cf., for instance, Georges van Riet, L'Epistémologie Thomiste (Louvain, 1946, pp. 174f.)

According to the Franciscan Doctor, man is not in want of a higher court of appeal of this sort. The human intellect is provided with propositions known through their terms and dependent on sense perception as on an occasional cause only. Scotus goes as far as to state that for every case of conflicting sense testimony some self-evident proposition is provided. Since these propositions "which rest in the soul" are more certain than any sense perception, they can always advise the intellect whether a given sense datum is true or false:

> In talibus est certitudo quid verum sit, et quis sensus erret per propo-sitionem quiescentem in anima certiorem omni judicio sensus, et per actus plurium sensuum concurrentes, ita quod semper aliqua propositio rectificat mentem vel intellectum de actibus sensus, quis sit verus et quis fallat, in qua propositione intellectus non dependet a sensu sicut a causa sed sicut ab occasione *(loc. cit.,* IX, 180a).

The reader will have noticed that Scotus also mentions the convergency of several senses ("per actus plurium sensuum con-currentes") as a criterion. The following example makes it clear that this criterion is not out of place, as would appear at first sight. There is of course no convergency of sight and touch in the actual apprehension of a staff partly dipped into water. Yet there is convergency in the sense that both sight and touch attest to the fact that water recedes from a hard or solid object. These two convergent perceptions give occasion to the formulation of a self-evident proposition by means of which the illusion produced by the staff can be corrected. Every intellect that apprehends the meaning of the terms "solid" and "soft" is in a position to formu-late this proposition: "No solid object can be broken by contact with a soft body which recedes from it." This proposition fulfills the requirements of a self-evident principle. It is not only evident in virtue of its terms, but even if these resulted from erring senses, the intellect still could not doubt its truth. No intellect can deny the proposition without incurring contradiction. It follows, therefore, that the staff is not bent as it appears to the sense of sight. "And thus," Scotus concludes, "the intellect judges through something more certain than any act of sense, which sense errs and which does not err with respect to the breaking of the staff:"

Exemplum: intellectus habet istam propositionem quiescentem: Nullum durius frangitur tactu alicujus mollis sibi cedentis; haec est ita per se nota ex terminis, quod etiamsi essent accepti a sensibus errantibus, non potest intellectus dubitare de illa, imo oppositum includit contradictionem; sed quod baculus sit durior aqua, et aqua sibi cedat, hoc dicit uterque sensus, tam visus quam tactus; sequitur ergo: Baculus non est fractus sicut sensus visus[17] judicat ipsum fractum; et ita quis sensus erret et quis non circa fractionem baculi, intellectus judicat per certius omni actu sensus *(loc. cit.,* 180a).

A similar self-evident proposition enables the intellect to correct the illusions of the sense of sight concerning distant things:

Similiter ex alia parte, quod idem quantum applicatum quanto omnino est aequale sibi, hoc est notum intellectui, quantumcumque notitia terminorum accipiatur a sensu errante. Sed quod idem quantum possit applicari viso propinquo et remoto, hoc dicit tam visus quam tactus; ergo quantum visum sive prope sive a remotis est aequale; igitur visus dicens hoc esse minus errat *(loc. cit.,* 180b).

The principle, "Idem quantum applicatum quanto omnino est aequale sibi," seems to be understood in this sense: A *quantum* or body of which we know that it remains unchanged or identical with itself can also be known to remain equal in size. That a body remains unchanged or identical can be ascertained thus. By closely observing a present object through the senses of touch and sight I can determine its exact size. Then, after the object has been removed to a certain distance, I notice that it appears smaller to the sense of sight. In order to assure myself I approach the object again, and verify through the same two senses that the thing has not changed in size. On the basis of the identity of these repeated experiences I conclude that a body remains equal in size or quantity whether it is seen nearby or at a distance.[18] Hence the sense of sight errs in presenting a distant object with a smaller size. The ultimate reason for the illusions produced by distant things is that *size* belongs to the *sensibilia communia.* A *sensibile commune* does not, as such, stimulate any particular sense. It is only accidentally related to one or more faculties of sensation. Hence it happens that when a *sensibile commune* is considered in relation

17. Visus *add. Viv.*
18. Cf. Martinez, *loc. cit.,* p. 673.

to one sense only, it is not apprehended as it is in reality. [19] The truth can therefore be known only with the assistance of infallible intellectual cognitions and through the convergency of two or more sense perceptions:

> Haec conclusio concluditur ex principiis per se notis et ex actibus duorum sensuum cognoscentium ut in pluribus ita esse *(ibid.)*.

In the *Commentary on Metaphysics* Scotus adduces another principle for the correction of erroneous sense information regarding distant things. The sense of sight, he explains, would make us believe that distant things are smaller than they are in reality. Natural reason, however, tells us that remote agents act more feebly, because of their limited energy. In other words, it is self-evident that the degree of fidelity with which a sense object is apprehended is always conditioned by the proportion between object and sense:

> Ad secundum[20] per idem, quia sensus dicit distans minus apparere, et ratio naturalis dicit quia remotius agens debilius agit, cum sit finitae virtutis *(Metaph.* I, q. 4, n. 15; VII, 60a).

It is not without good reasons that proportion is so frequently mentioned among the prerequisites for trustworthy sense perception. The sense faculties, whose constitution is not purely spiritual but physical as well, are also subject in their operations to the conditions which govern physical reactions in general. Proportion in the present instance is equivalent to an adequate degree of nearness or proximity, without which a material agent cannot produce its adequate effect on the senses.

We may conclude from the preceding texts and comments that although we are not in a position to determine the exact size or configuration of many objects through the senses alone, one thing, however, is clear: we are not necessarily led into error by the

---

19. P. F. Cherubini, *Cursus philosophicus ad mentem Doctoris Subtilis* (Rome, 1905) II, pp. 247 f.: "Sensile commune non afficit *primo* sensus, potest accidere ut relatum tantum ad unum sensum, non plene percipiatur sicut est in se; v.g., statuae magnitudo in distanti: tunc autem homo ne decipiatur in parte (nam in visione statuae in genere non accidit deceptio) debet aliis sensibus et praecipue ratione uti...;v.g. in casu statuae debet accedere ad eam, manibusque contrectare."
20. Scotus is here replying to this objection: "Semper visus errat de quantitate solis et lunae, et fractione baculi in aqua, etc." *(ibid.)*.

senses. Moreover, even concerning such distant things as are the heavenly bodies, our condition is not such as to make us despair of attaining at least a proximate, it not exact, knowledge of their size and shape. Once we realize that our unassisted senses cannot give reliable information, we start searching for means and ways to make up for this inadequacy. This, for example, is what the science of astronomy has accomplished with the assistance of other exact sciences.

Scotus sums up his inquiry by stating that in all cases where the intellect judges and corrects the erring sense, this is done by a twofold superior kind of knowledge. First, it is done by a cognition which is not dependent on the senses as its cause, but is merely occasioned by them. With regard to this knowledge the intellect never errs, although all the senses should err. Secondly, this correction by the intellect is effected by a cognition produced in one or more senses in the greater number of cases. This sense knowledge is true in virtue of the principle of induction. For an identical effect produced in several senses, or in the same sense successively, must be attributed to the nature itself of the agent:

> Et ita ubicumque ratio judicat sensum errare, hoc judicat non per aliquam notitiam praecise acquisitam a sensibus ut causa, sed per aliquam notitiam occasionatam a sensu, in qua non fallitur, etiamsi omnes sensus fallantur, et per aliquam aliam notitiam acquisitam a sensu vel a sensibus ut in pluribus, quae sciuntur esse vera per propositionem saepe allegatam, scilicet quod in pluribus, etc. *(Oxon.* I, d. 3, q. 4, f. 32v, a; n. 12, IX, 180b).

CONCLUSION

In conclusion, we may confidently state that Scotus' teaching on evidence constitutes both an innovation in, and a major contribution to, the Scholastic theory of knowledge. It is an innovation inasmuch as evidence is considered a sufficient foundation of true and certain knowledge, regardless of whether the latter is of a necessary or contingent nature. By shifting the stress from objective necessity to objective evidence, Scotus has opened the road to a new concept of scientific knowledge which is both more realistic and more comprehensive than the aprioristic *scientia* of Aristotle and his followers.

Scotus' doctrine is a major contribution to epistemology insofar as it offers a satisfactory solution to the problems concerned with certain knowledge of contingents. Not only does he offer a keen analysis of introspective evidence, he also sets forth its basic function for all subjective certitude, not excepting that of first principles.

The originality of Scotus' teaching on induction, in which he complements the limitations of sense knowledge by infallible self-evident principles, should be apparent to anyone acquainted with medieval thought.

Finally, by his ingenious application of self-evident principles to sensible knowledge, the Franciscan Doctor succeeds in solving the crucial and ever reverting problem posed by really or apparently conflicting evidences in sensible knowledge.

BIBLIOGRAPHY

PRIMARY SOURCES AND MANUSCRIPTS

Joannis Duns Scoti Opera Omnia, 26 vols. Vivès edition, 1891-1895.

Commentaria Oxoniensia, 2 vols. Fernandez Garcia edition, Collegium S. Bonaventurae, Quaracchi, 1912-1914.

The De Primo Principio of John Duns Scotus, A Revised Text and a Translation, by Evan Roche, The Franciscan Institute, St. Bonaventure, 1949.

Selections from Medieval Philosophers, vol. II, *From Roger Bacon to William of Ockham*, edited and translated by Richard Mckeon, Charles Scribner's Sons, New York, 1930.

Assisi Manuscript, cod. 137.

Reportatio Examinata, cod. Vienn. 1453.

————, MS. Merton College 59.

BOOKS AND ARTICLES

Albanese, Cornelio, "Intorno alla nozione della verità ontologica," *Studi Francescani*, I (1914-1915), 274-287.

————, "La teoria delle idee senza immagini nella psicologia di Scoto," *Studi Francescani*, I (1914-1915), 39-65.

Aristotle, *Opera Omnia*, ed. I. Bekker, Berlin 1831-1870.

————, *The Basic Works of Aristotle*, ed. by Richard McKeon, Random House, New York, 1941.

Arnou, R., art. *"Platonisme des Pères"* in *Dictionnaire de Théologie Catholique* t. XII, Librairie Letouzey et ané, Paris, 1935, cols. 2338-2392.

Auer, J., *Die menschliche Willensfreiheit im Lehrsystem des Thomas von Aquin und Johannes Duns Scotus*, Max Hueber Verl., Munich, 1938.

Augustine, St. *De beata vita. Florilegium Patristicum*, fasc. XXVII, P. Hanstein, Bonn, 1931.

————, *De liber arbitrio*, Migne edition, *Patrologiae Cursus Completus*, Series Latina (PL) v. 32, cols. 1221-1310.

————, *De vera religione*, PL 34, 121-172.

————, *De diversis quaestionibus* LXXXIII, PL 40, 11-148.

————, *De Trinitate libri quindecim*, PL 42, 819-1098.

Avicenna, *Opera*, transl. Dominicus Gundissalinus, Venice, 1508.

Balić, Carolus, *Relatio a Commissione Scotistica exhibita Capitulo Generali Fratrum Minorum Assisii A. D. 1939*, Rome, 1939.

————, *Annua Relatio Commissionis Scotisticae*, vols. I-II, Rome, 1939-1940.

Basly, Déodat de, *Scotus docens*, La France Franciscaine, Paris, 1936.

Belmond, Séraphin, *Dieu, existence et cognoscibilité*, Beauchesne, Paris, 1913.

————, "L'idée de création d'après S. Bonaventure et Duns Scot," *Etudes Franciscaines*, XXXI (1914), 5-17.

————, "Le mécanisme de la connaissance d'après Jean Duns Scot," *La France Franciscaine*, XIII (1930), 485-323.

————, "Le fondement de la certitude," *Etudes Franciscaines*, LI (1939), 415-422.

Bettoni, Efrem, *L'ascesa a Dio in Duns Scoto*, Società Editrice "Vita e Pensiero," Milan, 1943.

————, *Duns Scoto*, Tip. Società "La Scuola," Brescia, 1945.

Boehner, Philotheus, and Etienne Gilson, *Die Geschichte der christlichen Philosophie*, Ferdinand Schoeningh, Paderborn, 1937.

————, "Ockham's Theory of Truth," *Franciscan Studies*, V (1945), 138-161.

————, *History of Franciscan Philosophy* (manuscript).

Boethius, *Quomodo Substantiae in eo quod sint, bonae sint*, PL 64, 1311-1314.

Brunner, Auguste, *La connaissance humaine*, Aubier, Paris, 1943.

Cherubini, P. F., *Cursus philosophicus ad mentem Doctoris Subtilis*, Rome, 1905.

Claverie, A.-Fr., "L'existence de Dieu d'après Duns Scot," *Revue Thomiste*, XVII (1909), 87-94.

Coffey, *The Science of Logic*, Longmans, Green and Comp., London, 1912.

Day, Sebastian J., *Intuitive Cognition a Key to the Significance of the Later Scholastics*, The Franciscan Institute, St. Bonaventure, 1947.

Fernandez-Garcia, Maria, *Lexicon Scholasticum Philosophico-Theologicum*, Coll. S. Bonaventurae, Quaracchi, 1910.

Geyser, Joseph, *"Zur Einfuehrung in das Problem der Evidenz in der Scholastik,"* *Beitraege zur Geschichte der Philosophie des Mittelalters*, Supplementband, 161-182, Muenster, 1923.

Gilson, Etienne, "Avicenne et le point de départ de Duns Scot," *Archives d'histoire doctrinale et littéraire du Moyen Age*, II (1927), 89-149.

————, "Sur quelques difficultés de l'illumination augustinienne," *Revue néoscolastique de philosophie*, XXXVI (1934), 321-331.

————, and Philotheus Boehner, *Geschichte der christlichen Philosophie*, Ferdinand Schoening, Paderborn, 1937.

————, *Introduction a l'étude de saint Augustin*, Vrin, Paris, 1943.

————, *La philosophie au moyen âge*, Payot, Paris, 1947.

Grabmann, Martin, *Die theologische Erkenntnis-und Einleitungslehre des heiligen Thomas von Aquin*, Paulusverlag, Freiburg i. d. Schweiz, 1948.

Harris, C. R. S., *Duns Scotus*, Clarendon Press, Oxford, 1927.

Heiser, Basil, "The Primum Cognitum According to Scotus," *Franciscan Studies*, II (1942), 193-216.

Henry of Ghent, *Summa*, Iodocus Badius Ascensius, Paris, 1620.

Hochstetter, Erich, *Studien zur Metaphysik und Erkenntnislehre Wilhelms von Ockham*, Berlin, 1927.

Joyce, G. H., *Principles of Logic*, Longmans, Green and Comp., London, 1908.

Klein, Joseph, "Der Glaube nach der Lehre des Johannes Duns Skotus," *Franziskanische Studien*, XII (1925), 184-212.

Klug, Hubert, "Das Objekt unseres Verstandes und die okkulte Erkenntniskraft unserer Seele nach dem sel. Johannes Duns Skotus," *Franziskanische Studien*, XIV (1927), 68-90.

————, "L'activité intellectuelle selon le B. Duns Scot," *Etudes Franciscaines*, XLI (1929), 5-23; 113-139; 244-209; 381-391; 517-538; XLII (1930), 129-142.

Krebs, Engelbert, "Theologie und Wissenschaft nach der Lehre der Hochscholastik," *Beitraege z. Geschichte d. Phil. d. Mittelalters*, XI, Munich, 1912.

Longpré, Ephraem, *La philosophie du Bienheureux Duns Scot*, Paris, 1924.

————, "The Psychology of Duns Scotus and its Modernity," *Franciscan Educational Conference*, XIII (1931), 19-77.

————, "St. Augustin et la pensée franciscaine," *La France Franciscaine*, XV (1932), 49-76.

Lychetus, Franciscus, *Commentaria*, in *Opera Omnia Scoti*, Vivès ed., passim.

Mandoñedo, Aniceto de, "Abstracción y realismo según el B. J. D. Escoto," *Collectanea Franciscana*, VI (1936), 529-551; VII (1937), 5-22.

Maritain, Jacques, *Formal Logic*, Sheed and Ward, New York, 1946.

Martinez, J. M., "Criteriologia Escotista," *Verdad Y Vida*, III (1945), 651-681; IV (1946), 61-86.

Mastrius, Bartholomaeus, *Cursus Philosophicus*, apud Nicolaum Pezzana, Venice, 1708.

Messner, Reinhold, *Schauendes und begriffliches Erkennen nach Duns Skotus*, Herder, Freiburg i. Breisgau, 1942.

Meyer, Hans, *Thomas von Aquin*, P. Hanstein, Bonn, 1938.

Migne, J. P., *Patrologiae Cursus Completus*, Series Latina, 222 vols., Paris, 1844-1855, (PL).

Minges, Parthenius, *I. D. Scoti doctrina philosophica et theologica*, Quaracchi, Collegium S. Bonaventurae, 1930.

————, "Zur Erkenntnislehre des Duns Scotus," *Philosophisches Jahrbuch*, XXX (1918), 52-74.

Paulus, Jean, "Henri de Gand et l'argument ontologique," *Archives d'histoire doctrinale et littéraire du Moyen Age*, X (1936), 265-323.

————, *Henri de Gand* (Etudes de Philosophie Médiévale), Paris, Vrin, 1938.

Pelzer, A., "La grande Réportation examinée avec Jean Duns Scot," *Annales de l'Institut Supérieur de Philosophie*, V (1923), 447-491.

Raymond, "La philosophie de l'Intuition et la Philosophie du Concept," *Etudes Franciscaines*, XXI (1909), 669-687.

————, "La théorie de l'Induction - Duns Scot précurseur de Bacon," *Etudes Franciscaines*, XXI (1909), 113-126; 270-279.

————, "La philosophie critique de Duns Scot et le criticisme de Kant," *Etudes Franciscaines*, XXII (1909), 117-127; 253-265; 535-547; 659-675.

Ridolfi, Ambrogio, "L'induzione scientifica nel pensiero di Scoto," *Studi Francescani*, I (1914), 103-114.

Schmuecker, Rainulf, *Propositio per se nota, Gottesbeweis und ihr Verbaeltnis nach Petrus Aureoli*, Franziskusdruckerei, Werl i. Westfalen, 1941.

Sesma, L. de., "La volonté dans la philosophie de J. Duns Scot," *Estudis Franciscans*, XXXIX (1927), 220-249.

Shircel, C., "The Case for Intuitive Knowledge," *The Modern Schoolman*, XXII (1945), 222-229.

Stoeckl, A., *Geschichte der christlichen Philosophie zur Zeit der Kirchenvaeter*, Kirchheim, Mainz, 1891.

Straubinger, H., "Evidenz und Kausalitaetsgesetz," *Philosophisches Jahrbuch*, XLIII (1930), 1-17.

Thomas of Aquin, St., *Summa theologica*, Institute of Medieval Studies, Ottawa, 1941-1944.

Van Riet, Georges, *Epistémologie Thomiste*, Institut Supérieur de Philosophie, Louvain, 1946.

Van Steenberghen, Ferdinand, *Epistémologie*, Institut Supérieur de Philosophie, Louvain, 1947.

Veuthey, P.L., "Das moderne Erkenntnisproblem und seine Loesung im Lichte einer franziskanischen konkreten Ontologie," *Wissenschaft und Weisheit*, V (1938), 145-166.

Wolter, Allan, "The 'Theologism' of Duns Scotus," *Franciscan Studies*, VII (1947), 257-273; 367-398.

————, *The Transcendentals and their Function in the Metaphysics of Duns Scotus*, The Franciscan Institute, St. Bonaventure, 1946.

————, "Duns Scotus on the Natural Desire for the Supernatural," *The New Scholasticism*, XXIII (1949), 281-317.

Zeller, Eduard, *Outlines of the History of Greek Philosophy*, transl. by L. R. Palmer, Routledge & Kegan Paul Limited, London, 1948.

————, *Die Philosophie der Griechen*, L. R. Fues, Tuebingen, 1859.

————, *Aristotle and the Earlier Peripatetics*, Longmans, Green and Comp., London, 1897.

Zuccherelli, Donato, "Il pensiero del B. Giovanni Duns Scoto sulla contingenza dell 'ordine etico," *Studi Francescani* I (1915), 385-401.

INDEX

171

---

material, 32; of a proposition, 62; ontological, 39; Scotus' conception of, 31-38; vs. axiom, 65; ways of knowing, 62

Van Riet, G., 161, 170
Van Steenberghen, 33, 170
Veuthy, P.L., 170

Vision, intellectual, 63-64

Walter of Bruges, 10
Will, 55-56
Wolter, A., 41, 54, 72, 82, 84, 94, 117, 126, 170

Zeller, E., 2, 4, 136, 137, 170
Zuccherelli, D., 38, 170